W9-BNY-814

TO BE A FRIEND
IS FATAL

The Fight to Save the Iraqis
America Left Behind

Kirk W. Johnson

SCRIBNER

New York   London   Toronto   Sydney   New Delhi

SCRIBNER

A Division of Simon & Schuster, Inc.

1230 Avenue of the Americas

New York, NY 10020

Copyright © 2013 by Kirk W. Johnson

All rights reserved, including the right to reproduce this book or
portions thereof in any form whatsoever. For information, address
Scribner Subsidiary Rights Department, 1230 Avenue of
the Americas, New York, NY 10020.

First Scribner hardcover edition September 2013

SCRIBNER and design are registered trademarks of The Gale Group, Inc.,
used under license by Simon & Schuster, Inc., the publisher of this work.

For information about special discounts for bulk purchases,
please contact Simon & Schuster Special Sales at 1-866-506-1949 or
business@simonandschuster.com.

The Simon & Schuster Speakers Bureau can bring authors to your live event.
For more information or to book an event, contact the Simon & Schuster
Speakers Bureau at 1-866-248-3049 or visit our website at
www.simonspeakers.com.

Manufactured in the United States of America

1   3   5   7   9   10   8   6   4   2

Library of Congress Cataloging-in-Publication Data is available.

ISBN 978-1-4767-1048-8
ISBN 978-1-4767-1050-1 (ebook)

When men fight,
there is a continuum of war, rubble, and human flight.
Sometimes the flight comes before the war.
Sometimes the war persists even after all is made rubble.
Sometimes the flight lasts longer than both the war
and its rubble.
But these immutable three come together,
reliable as gravity.

I made no war.
I went to Iraq to turn rubble back into
schools and power plants, and failed.

But the third element is flight. I did help some flee.
This is their story, and this book is dedicated to them.

Contents

Part Three   163

TO BE A FRIEND
IS FATAL

Prologue

Two fingers pressed firmly against my forehead. The hand they belonged to wore a pale blue surgical glove the color of oceans on maps, except for the spatter of wine-dark blood. I was lying on a table, writhing but unable to free myself. Other blue gloves pressed against my chest, waist, legs, ankles, arms. My eyes stung. I thrashed again and freed one arm. I heard shouting. More hands appeared, forcing down my bucking knees.

"*Mother*fucker, *how much longer?!*"

A needle entered my blurred frame of vision and burrowed itself into a laceration running between my eyes. My forehead numbed for a moment before the anesthetic seeped back out with the blood, useless.

"*Viente por ciento!*" Loudly. Slowly.

My face was splayed open, and my lunatic flesh needed tying down. A gash ran from my right eyebrow into my left eyebrow and stopped above the eyelid. A piece of my nose was missing from its bridge, leaving behind a divot. My front teeth, dangling from a shattered jaw, had trifurcated my upper lip. Drained of blood, it looked like a worm baking on the sidewalk. My chin appeared as though it were falling off.

My brain was a captured wasp, thudding furiously against the glass walls of a jar, striking everywhere and nowhere. A suturing needle punctured through the cliff of flesh along my brow, ran a thread across the seeping ravine, before reversing course and knotting off where it started.

1

A millimeter to the right, and repeat. After each suture, the surgeon pressed his thumb against the slowly forming rail of stitches, nudging the tracks in line, refashioning the putty of my face.

They ignored my English cries for painkillers, so I pleaded in Arabic, "*Dawa, biddy dawa!*"

Disconnected thoughts erupted with maniacal force: *Twenty percent . . . teeth missing . . . Sheikh Kamal . . . blue gloves . . . beach . . . Fallujah . . . Mom . . . jaw . . . painkillers . . . Who are these people? . . . twenty percent.*

Adrenaline coursed through each limb and muscle until my mind, exhausted, finally relaxed. My legs followed; the flailing subsided. I no longer felt the slow-moving needle, my broken wrists, my crushed nose, my jaw, my bleeding toes. The lava stilled and cooled.

The rubbery hands eased cautiously from my body. The room went quiet, save for an occasional instruction to an attending nurse and the sound of suturing needles clanking upon a steel tray.

Ninety minutes later, my face was stitched shut.

I was wheeled down the hallway on a gurney, bright ceiling lamps sweeping swiftly into my field of vision like rising and setting suns, one after another, lingering eclipse-like when I closed my eyes. The din of the waiting room hushed as orderlies pushed me through. In the operating room, the next team of doctors and assistants was preparing its tools. My jaw would need wiring, my arms would need fiberglass, my face would need masking. At last, they dosed me with general anesthesia, and I fell into a deep sleep.

October 13, 2006

The war was in its fourth autumn when Yaghdan's future was swallowed up.

Late on a Friday afternoon, Yaghdan checked the clock on his computer screen and sighed. A few cubicles away, an American grazed on a microwaved bag of popcorn, and the scent of butter and salt tugged at Yaghdan's hunger. The Muslim holy month of Ramadan was in its final week, and the required fast, made brutal by the long hours and his proximity to nonfasting Americans, was almost over. Yaghdan consoled himself with the thought that his wife, Haifa, was at that moment preparing an *iftar* feast far more sumptuous than American junk food.

The walkie-talkie on his desk squelched, and a young male American voice warbled through the handset, "Dispatch, we need a pickup from the white house, please!"

A few seconds passed, and an Iraqi driver in the motor pool replied flatly, "Okay, ten minutes." The driver had probably only just returned from dropping off the American, Yaghdan thought. "White house" was their radio code word for the liquor store in the Green Zone. Through the thin blue walls of his cubicle in the massive bomb- and mortar-proof office building of the US Agency for International Development, Yaghdan sometimes overheard stories about the Americans' parties. He had seen bottles strewn in the yards of the mortar-proof houses in the compound and recognized how a hangover sat on a face. He had no chance of seeing a party for himself, since Iraqis working for USAID were not allowed to stay overnight in the Green Zone.

At five o'clock, Yaghdan powered down his computer. He nodded at the Nepalese security guards as he exited through the building's doors, reinforced to repel bullets and improvised explosive devices, or IEDs. He climbed into the Chevy Suburban idling out front, alongside other Iraqis who worked for the agency. The van snaked past demolished palaces and the sixteen-foot blast walls of the secretive compounds clotting the Green Zone. Yaghdan's colleagues quietly removed their USAID badges and stuffed them into socks, brassieres, hidden pockets. His went into his shoe.

This daily ritual made Yaghdan nervous, but nervousness had become a function as natural as breathing or eating. It had a use, keeping them vigilant. The women wrapped *hijabs* around their hair and donned sunglasses. The men removed their ties and donned *shemaghs*.

The Suburban pulled up to the checkpoint known as the Assassins' Gate and emptied its passengers. They stood on the edge of the Green Zone. Yaghdan smiled at a listless marine manning the US side of the checkpoint as he walked toward what Americans called the Red Zone, his country. The marine nodded slightly, his face expressionless.

Yaghdan's gait was unsteady. Shortly after the fall of Baghdad, a 7.62 millimeter Kalashnikov round tore through his left leg, but that story belonged to a more hopeful era of his life that he didn't like to think about anymore. He had spent six feverish months on his back, while tens of thousands of soldiers, marines, aid workers, diplomats, mercenaries, and contractors poured into his country and snarled barbed wire atop blast walls. When he could walk again, he took a job with the Americans to help rebuild Iraq.

As he filed around the chicanes rimmed with menacing spindles of concertina wire, Yaghdan's pace quickened. From this point forward, the Iraqi employees of America did not speak to one another. The 14th of July Bridge connected the Green and Red Zones, and the Iraqis trained their eyes on the ground as they crossed.

Yaghdan felt the USAID badge shift uncomfortably under his sock. He saw a handful of men gathered on the other side of the bridge, and lowered his head. These were called *alassas*, slang deriving from the Arabic verb "to chew": militiamen who hunted Iraqis like him by studying the faces of those who emerged from the gates of the Green Zone.

For three years, Yaghdan had avoided the chewers by varying the entry and exit points he used to enter the Green Zone each day, never falling into a pattern. Most days, he switched taxis more than once, wore disguises, and was never dropped off directly in front of his home.

This day, exhausted and hungry, he slipped up.

As he crossed the bridge, he heard a hoarse voice call out his name. "Yaghdan!" Before he could suppress the instinct, he looked up, and in that split second confirmed his identity. Realizing his mistake, he tried to avoid eye contact, but not before his eyes fell upon the familiar face of a neighbor from Street Number 2.

His eyes locked with the menacing glower of his neighbor, and the adrenaline felt cold as it drained into Yaghdan's gut. In any other country, in any other neighborhood, in any other decade, this would have been an unimportant event. He would have smiled and waved, said hello, shared a smoke, asked about work.

But here, just after five o'clock on the twenty-first day of Ramadan in October 2006—1426 *hijri* on the Islamic calendar—the *alassa* opened his jaws wide and chewed him up.

Yaghdan woke early the next morning to the frantic drone of flies; the sound of a feeding frenzy. He opened his front door slowly. At his feet he found a sheet of paper, the kind used in the school workbooks that had been supplied through one of his education initiatives at USAID. He crouched down and picked up the note. Written in blue ink, just below the Date and Subject lines, he read:

"We will cut off your heads, and throw them in the trash . . ."

The buzzing of the flies seemed incomprehensibly loud. He looked up from the letter and settled his gaze on the delicate eye of a small dog. A fly was buzzing around its clouded cornea. Past the upturned ear, he saw the thick cake of blood around the creature's severed neck.

He walked back inside and set the letter on the table. Haifa was still sleeping. He called to wake her and sat down before the letter. She came in with a groggy smile, read the concern on his face, and then saw the letter. She started to cry. He told her not to open the door for anyone, not to call anyone, not to walk by the windows even once. He wrapped his arms around her, but there was no more comfort to be found in this home.

Yaghdan took the letter and slipped out the front door. The air was foul from the scent of rotting flesh. He picked up the severed dog's head and dropped it in a pale green trash can in the corner of the courtyard.

He made his way back to the Green Zone. He would ask his American bosses for help. Surely after three years of distinguished service with the US government, they would do something.

Weeks later, in the Al-Mahata neighborhood of Sharjah in the United Arab Emirates, Yaghdan slinked into an Internet café crowded with other Iraqi refugees and drafted a desperate email to me.

PART ONE

The Johnson brothers, fall 1984.

1.

Jesus and Basketball

The Apology

Every son writes the myth of his father's greatness and weakness, revising and eliding according to the depth of his own generosity, insecurities, and pride. Mine begins not long after my fifth birthday, when my dad traded a chance at fulfilling his dream of becoming a United States congressman for an apology. My mom once called the apology, which came from the leaders of the Illinois Republican Party, his magic beans.

My father is a man of stubborn principle, useful for nurturing a healthy pride but detrimental to a career in politics. He was not born with the thirst for power, and avoided the grease of Illinois machine politics. But when he was thirty-six, he and my mother sold a small, fallow plot of farmland in the nearby town of Addison to seed an upstart campaign for the Fourteenth Congressional District in the far western suburbs of Chicago. The land was my mom's inheritance, and its soil carried the sadness of her father's premature passing, felled at the age of fifty-six by a heart attack after a hard life in the garbage hauling business.

Dad launched the campaign without the blessing of his Republican Party, which barely knew him. The party had its own handpicked man for the district. This was GOP country: take the primary, and you take the seat. Its man, John Grotberg, enjoyed the perks of outside money: campaign flyers glimmering with expensive ink and headquarters in rented office space.

But Dad commanded an army of volunteers who were mostly new to the political process, and they fanned out far and wide. He knocked on door after door, walked up driveways long and short, across farm fields and industrial parking lots and subdivisions, talking with anyone who'd listen, sometimes carrying me piggyback. He was young, energetic, and owned by no party.

In one of my first memories, people are cheering and clapping and jumping with excitement on election night 1984. The Citizens to Elect Tom Johnson had gathered at the Back Door, a restaurant connected to West Chicago's local bowling alley.

The night was joyous, until its final minutes. He led Grotberg all evening, and as the percentage of reported precincts inched its way closer to 100, a seat in Congress drew within reach of his young hands.

But when the final numbers came in from Kendall County, it slipped away. Grotberg squeaked ahead and clinched the nomination by 662 votes, and the joy drained from the bowling alley restaurant and from many nights and months and years to come. My oldest brother, Soren, then nine, collapsed into tears beside my mom and asked, "How could God let this happen?"

My dad dealt with the loss with stoicism and repression, traits honed and inherited from generations of Swedes. He had gambled a big piece of inheritance on his dream and came tantalizingly close—close enough for it to feel tangible. In the basement war room, he wedged a dolly under each of the filing cabinets, which were swollen from two years of campaign plans, volunteer lists, registration forms, buttons, bumper stickers, and brochures, and wheeled them across the field to the barn, where he stored them in a stall adjacent to the chicken coop. In the general election that fall, Grotberg sailed into office, and my dad returned to the one-story brick building that housed his small law practice and began to move on.

And then, Grotberg suffered a heart attack and slipped into a coma while receiving experimental treatment for cancer, knowledge of which was kept to his inner circle during the campaign. The GOP would hold a special election to fill Grotberg's seat, and my dad was now the most prominent Republican in the district. The phone began to ring with his supporters, excitedly urging him to put his name on the ballot.

But the Republicans were wary of my dad. He had never taken any money or favors from them and therefore owed them nothing, which granted him an intolerable independence. As the family legend goes, the party convinced Grotberg's wife to keep him on life support long enough to move their new man into the district. Their new man's name was Dennis Hastert, a state representative from another district.

My dad's political organization was reactivated, ready for a race. The filing cabinets were wheeled back into the house, which again buzzed with enthusiastic young volunteers.

But this time the buttons and brochures were worthless. The electorate for a special election was composed not of farmers and the families he had won over in the previous campaign, but of party insiders. A handful of county chairmen, committeemen, and other assorted Republicans held the key to his election—a number even smaller than the narrow margin by which he'd lost to Grotberg.

The Republicans of the Land of Lincoln scorched my father from the field. Their tactic was as simple as it was ancient: they set fire to his reputation, calling my parents John Birchers, far-right loons who were secret members of a secret cult. They whispered that he and my mom had attacked abortion clinics.

The party leadership made it clear that Hastert was its man. In a brief meeting with a senior staffer to Governor Big Jim Thompson, my dad was told, "Tom, forget it. You're out. It's never going to happen." My dad had only one thing that they wanted: his name. They wanted him to withdraw from the ballot, suspend his political operation, and give Hastert his endorsement.

He drove home and told my mom. An anonymous committeeman had just called to ask if she was really a cult member. "Only if the Protestant Evangelical church is a cult!" she cried before hanging up and bursting into tears.

"What are you going to do?" she asked my father.

"The game is fixed, and we're not the winners."

The GOP was offering a judgeship and all manner of sinecure if he endorsed, but he had only one demand. In exchange for his withdrawal from the race and endorsement of Hastert, the senior Republican state senator, Pate Philip, and each of the party chairmen had to publicly apologize for the lies that had been spread about him. They would also have to sign a letter to the same effect.

The apology letter was issued. The local newspaper ran a short piece. My dad clipped it out and put it in the filing cabinet. Hastert sailed into office and went on to become the longest-serving Republican Speaker of the House in American history. Pate Philip became president of the Illinois Senate. The others who apologized each went on to control the levers of the party for decades.

The black vines of depression wrapped around my father in the ensuing years, but he held on to his pride, however faintly it burned.

What I Knew

I grew up on a dead-end street that has never seen a tank and never will. We were surrounded by animals, tamed and wild, oftentimes obliged to keep the two apart. We had a small barn in which my older brothers and I tended to the chickens and kept Joe the horse fed and made sure the water in his trough didn't freeze during winter. When Pepe the goat chewed free from his tether to head-butt the neighbor kids, we had him dehorned and replaced his rope with chain. To fill the coop, we ordered Rhode Island Reds and White Giants and Barred Rocks through the Murray McMurray Hatchery catalog, along with a rooster that my oldest brother named Clucker. The post office called when the chicks arrived, and we brought the large and peeping box home. As they grew, Soren, Derek, and I slept summer nights in the loft above the coop, a BB gun at hand to shoot at groundhogs that burrowed in to steal their feed, or at the fox that shimmied through the groundhog tunnel to feast on the chickens. Soren rigged up a black-and-white TV, and we watched *The Twilight Zone* while the birds slept.

I was too young to comprehend the impact of the campaign on our family. What I knew of the world's badness was limited to the snapper turtle lurking in the muck of the pond out back. In the excited company of a brace of White Pekin ducks, my brothers and I paddled around in tiny square boats sawed and hammered and caulked together by our dad, while the fowl gorged on duckweed algae multiplying across the pond's dark surface. After losing a race one muggy afternoon around the egg-shaped perimeter, I drifted toward the ducks just as one disappeared from the surface with a horrific squeal, dragged to the bottom in the prehistoric jaws of the snapper. The others swam on blithely.

Later that summer, as the sun disappeared behind the towering four-hundred-year-old oak, we spotted the snapper crawling across the yard and ran to get Dad and his rifle. From a great distance, he fired a bullet into the turtle's jaw. We approached it tentatively and saw blood seeping from a bullet-shaped opening in its carapace. We asked him to show us his marksmanship badge, still pinned to his Vietnam uniform.

We knew that Dad had been in Vietnam, but he kept those years sealed off from us. He never went to the VFW. I heard that before his deployment, he and his antiwar brother bled each other in fistfights over Vietnam, but not much more. Once, when I was eight, he put on his uniform, and mom dug out her wedding dress, and they posed for a picture on their twentieth anniversary.

In a dim hallway in the basement, there's a picture of him in a Huey helicopter. He's skinny and smiling. I always thought that he was a helicopter pilot, and imagined harrowing missions over Vietnamese jungles and rivers borrowed from *Apocalypse Now*, burned-out cigarette wedged at the corner of his swearing mouth.

I didn't bother asking him about the war when I was young. The picture said enough, and he wasn't offering up any more.

In the nineties, West Chicago was news. Our little railroad town was aglow in radiation, our bodies sick. For decades, from the 1930s until the 1970s, the Lindsay Light and Chemical Company maintained a Rare Earths Facility on Ann Street in the center of town. My high school was a football toss from its gate.

The plant heap leached thorium from ore for use in gasoline lanterns; the radioactive material gave mantles their glow. The process created a mountain of tailings, so once a month, the gates would swing open to the citizens of West Chicago, who lined up with wheelbarrows for free dirt for their gardens. Radioactivity spread by our own nurturing hands and hoes, our tomatoes and tulips sprouted in toxic soil.

The Lindsay Light Company, which was subsumed into another corporation named Kerr-McGee Chemical Corporation, played its own contaminating role in our little play, dumping thorium, radium, and uranium tailings in Reed-Keppler Park near the public swimming pool, Kress Creek, the sewage treatment plant, and the DuPage River, which ran a silted chocolate color through our backyard. My dad taught us to fish in the shade of the small fishing hole overlooking the river. He hacked it clear each spring and set out little chairs for his three boys, and we reeled in catfish and carp with fat night crawlers on Snoopy poles. When I asked him why we always threw back the fish, he shook his head and said, "Kerr-McGee."

In the early 1990s, my hometown organized itself against the plant and fought for help. The Thorium Action Group was founded and organized rallies where we chanted "Hell no! We won't glow!" The governor landed his helicopter on our high school's football field and promised to rid the town of thorium, which accumulated in our bones and lymph nodes and spurred lung, lymphatic, and pancreatic cancer in our citizens.

Men from the Environmental Protection Agency appeared, tiptoeing with wands and gauges over front yards, backyards, sidewalks, and parks, measuring alpha, beta, and gamma radiation. Some of my friends lost their entire front yards in an afternoon as yellow Caterpillar bulldozers scooped the thorium-laced soil into nearby Dumpsters. Bright orange plastic fencing was put up around the ten-foot-deep craters to keep children from falling in.

Railroad tracks were laid to the Ann Street plant, upon which hopper cars trundled away our contamination—twenty-one million cubic feet in all—to a government storage facility in the mountains of Utah. The town's opera house, an anomaly in our blue-collar burg, a half block from the Tastee-Freez, had once been a laboratory for Kerr-McGee; after repeated attempts to rid it of radiation, its foundation gave in. The building was demolished, and the rubble was piled onto the westbound train.

West Chicago obtained Superfund classification and the pitiable designation as one of the most radioactive cities in America. My parents were involved in the effort. In the midst of the struggle, my dad threw in his name for state representative and won, and when I was eleven, he began commuting to Springfield to represent his district.

Henrietta

In the early 1890s, in the town of Skanninge, southwest of Stockholm, my Swedish great-great-grandfather was making plans to bring his family to America. He laid bricks when it was warm, and when winter came, he threshed wheat, pounding grain in the barn out back. He worked hard, enough to own a home with six apple trees and a gooseberry bush in the front yard, but the work claimed him when his heart gave out in his early forties. Burial was impossible that winter, so my great-great-grandmother had him laid out on a bale of hay until the thaw. The next summer, on May 6, 1893, my eleven-year-old great-grandmother and her sister were put on the *City of Berlin*, which churned from Gothenburg across the North Sea, with a stop in Liverpool before crossing the Atlantic. She had the words *Rockford* and *Illinois* written in a notebook; there she picked strawberries and tomatoes for a few years until she became a servant girl in the homes of rich Chicagoans.

Another great-grandfather came from the northern Dutch farmlands of Groningen in 1913, carried in upon one of the last great waves of immigration. Like the other Dutch in America, he worked in the garbage business, hauling ash and cinder from the belching factories of Chicago. His sons took over the business, which boomed in the worst of times; such is the nature of trash. Shortly after my grandpa Bernie met Henrietta, my grandmother, he began to save for a luxury usually limited to the upper class: a good-looking smile. The dentist yanked his crooked twenty-year-old teeth from his young jaws and inserted a shining pair of dentures just in time for the wedding.

I knew none of these ancestors except for my grandmother Henrietta, who lived next door. She grew up in Dutch Chicago on Ashland Avenue just southwest of the Loop, the daughter of a world-class alcoholic who beat my great-grandmother and in a drunken rage struck one of his sons so hard he went deaf in one ear. Henrietta's mother was paralyzed by fear during her father's benders, so my ten-year-old grandmother became a grown-up, locking him out, calling her mother's parents, gathering the siblings' clothing and schoolbooks, and herding the whole family away from Jake. The last anyone heard of my great-grandfather, sometime in the 1940s, he was living in what was then Chicago's skid row, on Lower

Wacker Drive. No one knows where this failed root of the family tree is buried, and no one in our family names their kids Jake.

Henrietta married Bernie, a teetotaler, managed the books for Van Der Molen Disposal, and left Chicago for the western suburbs, where she had six kids. When Bernie died of a heart attack in his early fifties, he left behind a garbage hauling empire that stretched throughout Chicagoland.

When my grammie, a devout Evangelical Christian, was widowed at fifty without great financial worries, she looked to how she could help others. She was fiercely pro-life, and opened her home to forty-six pregnant women whose boyfriends had skittered off or whose families had kicked them out of the house. She fed them, paid their bills, and held their hands while they delivered. When I was little, I thought that only pregnant women were babysitters.

Henrietta then became involved in helping refugees, opening her home to twenty-seven Russians, Ukrainians, and Hmong from Southeast Asia. I never wandered next door without hearing a new language.

Having missed out on the kind of sheltered and burden-free childhood that led others to college, my grammie valued travel over any other form of education. She and Bernie had blazed through the world, snapping pictures of Abu Simbel and Upper Egypt in the fifties before Egyptian president Gamal Abdel Nasser built the dam; Baghdad and Tehran in the sixties; Addis Ababa in the seventies—nearly eighty countries in all.

After my grandpa died, she continued her travels, with a plan to take each of her grandchildren somewhere in the world. When my oldest brother, Soren, was fifteen, she brought him to the Soviet Union. Upon his return, he enrolled in a Russian language class at the nearby community College of DuPage and then went off to pursue a degree in Russian studies in college. My other brother, Derek, started studying Spanish after a trip to Guatemala and Ecuador.

While the sound of Russian instruction tapes blared from Soren's room, I lay on my bed and stared up at a poster of Michael Jordan affixed to the ceiling. By junior high, I had only one dream in life: to go pro and play in the National Basketball Association. I spent hours each afternoon practicing free throws, running lines, praying to Jesus to make me taller, quicker, and stronger. I wore out shoes each summer, attended Crusader Basketball Camp at nearby Wheaton College, blew my allowance on basketball cards, and wallpapered my room with blurry posters from Kmart that shouted Barkley and Shaq in massive block letters.

Only I was short, pudgy, and slow. But with God on my side, though, I'd work around these deficiencies, so I practiced my jump shot at the hoop by the barn while Joe the horse grazed.

The eighth-grade coach cut me. Even Jordan was cut once, I figured, and spent the summer before high school practicing with maniacal intensity, fantasizing about my jersey number. A few weeks into high school, Coach Adamczyk cut me from the freshman team. When Kevin Brewer saw his name on the cut list, he shook and then erupted into a spasm of tears so intense that Coach A said, "Okay, okay, Kevin!" and added him to the roster.

I waited until I was back in my room to cry, and tore down the posters, boxed up the basketball cards, and threw out the Chicago Bulls T-shirts. A few nights later, I sat down my parents in the living room and announced that I was renouncing my ambitions to go pro. I didn't know where my plans would take me, I said, but I knew my future no longer included basketball. They mustered a serious-enough "Well, okay then, Kirk, we'll stand behind you no matter what you end up doing." Years later, they confessed to laughing once I was safely out of earshot.

I found myself exiled into an unfamiliar landscape: no hoops, no trading card stores, no new Air Jordans to save up for, no interest in stats or trades or play-offs or buzzer beaters. The river of worthless shit for which I once pined pooled off into cartons and trash cans and ran dry.

I turned sullen. My patient mother bore the brunt of my angst while Dad was in session down in Springfield. On occasion, I'd ride with him and serve as a page, fetching ham-and-cheese sandwiches for other members and for his office mate, a Democrat named Rod Blagojevich, but they were mostly lousy tippers. Across the rotunda, Barack Obama was also starting out as a state senator.

Into this haze of adolescent defeat sailed my grammie, who pulled her tiny Buick Century into the driveway and honked.

"Got a proposal for you, guy. Howja like to go to Egypt with me this Christmas?"

I shrieked *yes* and ran inside to tell my brothers.

I marked down the days until the TWA flight direct to Cairo on December 20 and memorized the itinerary. After exploring Cairo and Giza, we could cruise up the Nile toward Upper Egypt, stopping at the ruins of Edfu, Esna, Luxor, Karnak, and Abu Simbel.

Within days of arriving, I forgot about basketball. I was entranced by the sound and appearance of Arabic. I constructed a new image of myself as an archaeologist, expert in techniques of construction and burial, hieroglyphs, and the brutal mythology of Osiris, Isis, Horus, and the villain Set, transcribed by the ibis-headed Thoth. I went weak-kneed at the National Museum of Antiquities in Cairo's Tahrir Square.

Grammie and I returned to West Chicago in the dead of winter. On the ride home from the airport, I excitedly asked my parents if I could start studying Arabic and Egyptology. I wasn't old enough to drive but would soon have a learner's permit, so I called up the University of Chicago's Oriental Institute, which agreed to let me sit in on Egyptology classes the coming summer. At the nearby community College of DuPage, where Soren began his Russian studies, I found a listing for a night course in beginner's Arabic.

When my mom picked me up from the first Arabic class, I was near tears. Only one other person had signed up, and college policy set the minimum enrollment at three. Unless someone else enrolled by the following week, the course would be canceled.

The next day, my mom enrolled. I was still adolescent enough to be embarrassed to sit next to her in class, so I sat behind her and beamed as the teacher began to demystify the Arabic script. Although she paid for the spot, my mom never came to class after that. Even though she has more degrees than I do, she still jokes about being a community college dropout. When I exhausted the community college's offerings in the fall of my junior year, I started taking the train two nights a week into Chicago, where I studied with a tutor my mom had found at the Egyptian consulate general.

School changed for me. I traded less in the nervous stock market of popularity and felt as though I had a separate life that none of my classmates understood. The basketball team posted some of the worst records in the school's history. The summer before my senior year, I applied to study at the Arabic Language Institute at the American University in Cairo and skipped my high school graduation ceremony to board a plane back to Cairo for intensive studies. I was seventeen.

War

Abu Khaizaran is a smuggler. Three men, Abu Qais, Marwan, and Assad, are stagnating in a Palestinian refugee camp in Lebanon, and have paid him to secrete them into Kuwait, where they heard there is work. Abu Khaizaran drives a water tanker. He drains the tank and loads his human freight into the back. They drive through Iraq toward the Shatt al-Arab, where the Tigris and Euphrates Rivers meet for a brief moment before tumbling into the gulf. While the truck idles in the inferno of summer, the Kuwaiti border guards give Abu Khaizaran a stack of forms to complete. The paperwork seems endless. Afterward, he sprints back to his truck, worried about his human cargo, and drives down the road into Kuwait before unlatching the seal to the tank. With great effort, he dumps their extinguished bodies alongside an empty stretch of the highway and tries to comfort himself with a thought: *If I leave them here, someone will find them in the morning.* As he climbs back into his truck, his remorse hardens into anger and blame: *Why didn't they knock? Why didn't they call out? Why?*

I had never read a book so closely in my life. The task of translating Ghassan Kanafani's *Rijal fi'il-shams,* or *Men in the Sun,* was the culmination of my Arabic studies at the University of Chicago under Farouk Mustafa, a renowned translator of Arabic fiction. His voice was graveled from decades of Marlboros but still boomed with satisfaction or disapproval over the choices we made with words.

I devoured the university's Arabic courses while working on a degree in Near Eastern studies, the antiquated term used by British imperialists when discussing what we now call the Middle East. I spent the summer before my senior year studying the Syrian dialect in Damascus, and when I returned home, I hadn't yet finished unpacking on the morning of 9/11.

When I returned to campus, it seemed as though everyone was

carrying a first-year Arabic textbook. Before the attacks, the typical introductory course had maybe twelve students. Now the university was struggling to accommodate more than a hundred new registrants. Within months of the attacks, the Central Intelligence Agency and National Security Agency sent recruiters to campus.

I was one of a small number of Caucasians who had reached an advanced level in the language. I agreed, more out of curiosity than any ambition, to be flown to Fort Meade, Maryland, to test at the NSA. In a dimly lit room in the basement of the building, I sat in a cubicle with a cassette player, headphones, a few sheets of blank paper, and a pencil on the desk before me. I listened to the cassette and translated a discussion in Arabic about a dispute between Syria and Iraq over the water rights of the Euphrates. A few weeks later, they sent a letter offering me a job as an analyst. I declined it without much thought. I hadn't studied the language to sit in a depressing government building, translating snippets of conversation between people I'd never know.

After graduating in 2002, I left for a Fulbright scholarship in Egypt to study political Islamist "pulp" writings: cheap tracts and treatises sold throughout the streets of Cairo and the Middle East. Nobody in the United States was paying much attention, but these books were the most widely read in the region, written by uneducated but earnest laymen.

I was supposed to spend the year reading and analyzing these books, but as soon as I arrived, I found myself unable to focus on anything but the imminent war in Iraq. I started moonlighting as an intern at the *New York Times*'s Middle East bureau, where I translated the headlines from the Arabic newspapers each morning for the bureau chief. By the winter, the office was swelling with reporters who were coming into the region ahead of the invasion. I ran measuring tape around the heads of correspondents to order the right-sized helmets and booked their reservations at the Al-Rasheed Hotel in Baghdad. The major Arabic daily paper, *Al-Hayat*, ran a map of the region showing big arrows pointing to the probable points of invasion and listed the individual commitments made by each nation in the "Coalition of the Willing." Iceland deployed two soldiers. Kazakhstan sent twenty-nine. Tonga contributed fifty-five.

I opposed the war on fairly simple grounds. Saddam Hussein was among the most isolated and reviled dictators on earth. Yet America's rush to depose him triggered some of the largest antiwar protests in history and turned long-standing allies against us. If we could not convince like-minded nations of the justness of our cause, we ought to have been humble enough to reconsider the case we were making. Instead, prowar neocons grunted with crotch-grabbing tribalism: skeptics were called sissies, french fries were renamed, and the country backed itself into war.

Many of my friends and professors who had opposed the war were horrified when I told them I wanted to go to Iraq. They believed that no good fruit could spring from a rotten tree, but I felt that despite the unjust rationale for the war, it was unethical to ignore the just and critical efforts to rebuild the country. I was also sick of relying solely upon other sources like newspapers and think-tank denizens to decipher what was happening.

Shortly after the fall of Baghdad, I read an article about the US government's woeful lack of Arabic-speakers in Iraq. I thought I might be able to contribute something and began to apply for jobs in the nascent reconstruction effort. Although I had seven years of Arabic studies behind me, nobody called back: the first year of the war was staffed by the true believers, and my *New York Times* internship likely flagged my résumé in an unfavorable way. And so I waited.

2.

Yaghdan

Years of War

Yaghdan was born into a year of violence, and since 1977, there has been a year of war for each year of peace. Years of peace are used to prepare for more war. On September 8, 1977, his mother delivered him in the Elwia Hospital near their home in Adhamiya, a predominantly Sunni neighborhood on the west bank of the Tigris in central Baghdad.

He was an infant during one of the first major Shi'a uprisings in modern Iraq. The ruling Sunni Ba'ath Party was caught off guard when the Shi'a rioted during their annual *Ashura* procession from Najaf to Karbala'. Thirty thousand Shi'ites protested against their marginalization in the Iraqi government. The response was brutal: more than two thousand were arrested, including many senior Shi'a clerics. A special court sentenced eight clerics to death and imprisoned others. Remaining Shi'a leaders fled, not to return for twenty-five years, among them future prime minister Nouri al-Maliki.

As Yaghdan was learning to speak, Saddam Hussein, already the de facto leader of Iraq with President Ahmed Hassan al-Bakr ailing, formalized his authority with a brutal flourish. On July 22, 1979, he assembled the Ba'ath Party leadership and ordered a camera to record the reading of a list of sixty-eight traitors. Soldiers dragged each man from the room after his name was read; it is rumored that the shots of execution were heard inside the hall. A year later, Hussein began an eight-year war with Iran, a conflict that ranks among the most blood-soaked offered up by the twentieth century. When Yaghdan was in first grade, the sirens wailed whenever Iranian fighter pilots raced in low and fast to bomb Baghdad.

His father hailed from Najaf, where most of the extended family still lived. He was a primary school teacher but took advanced degrees in child psychology and was eventually drafted into the Iraqi Ministry of Education in Baghdad to develop curricula. He was not an ideologue, and his coolness toward Ba'ath Party machinations was noticed by both his supervisors and subordinates. As the war intensified, when Yaghdan was seven and obsessed with English-language cartoons like *Tom and Jerry* and *Casper the Friendly Ghost*, party members regularly dropped by the home in search of his father, hoping to conscript him into the Jaysh al-Sha'abi, the Popular Army. They wanted to send him to the front lines, where bodies piled and lethal gas clouded, but his dad managed to evade them until the war's end.

Mired in a resource-draining war, Iraq's infrastructure—refineries, power plants, water treatment centers, dams, and roads—grew brittle, along with the public's tolerance for Saddam Hussein's rule. Saddam wanted new and better technology and reoriented Iraq away from the Soviet bloc and toward the West, particularly America. He invited US firms like Bechtel to carry out massive infrastructure projects to solidify relations with the West, which gladly threw its support behind him as a check against the Iranian revolutionary government.

And then there was no more war with Iran. Eight of the first ten years of Yaghdan's life had been punctured by missile fire. On 8-8-88, the date of the cease-fire, Iraqis pooled into the streets to celebrate. He was in sixth grade. No longer would the futile war suck the youth from the cities and the men from their families. But the triumphant monuments to war that Saddam erected throughout the country were not enough to obscure the true cost: at least one hundred thousand dead, three hundred thousand wounded, and a material loss to the nation's coffers of a staggering $435 billion, a significant portion of which was bankrolled by Kuwait.

Two years and a month passed before Saddam reignited the engine of war. The Kuwaiti government had refused to forgive the debt, so the Iraqis invaded and took more from them. Cars were driven north, gold seized, the nation looted, and, in twenty-four hours, Kuwait became Iraq's nineteenth province. Though driven by economic desperation, the war—more an aftershock—was presented to the Iraqi people as a form of anticolonial justice. The British had carved out Kuwait from its rightful place in Iraq, and now Saddam aimed to take it back.

The West recoiled, and a coalition was formed. American troops were loaded onto airplanes and ships, and within six months more than half a million troops were positioned for war.

On January 16, 1991, America started a six-week program of bombardment in advance of ground troops. Once Iraqi military targets were destroyed, the United States targeted the nation's infrastructure, hitting power plants, water, and roads, and setting back industrial production to levels last seen in the 1960s. Gone to rubble went the Bechtel projects and others carried out by the West only a few years earlier. One senior administration official admitted that the targeting of key infrastructure—bombing seven of Iraq's eight dams to ruin access to clean water, for example—was a deliberate plan to increase "postwar leverage." Potable water vanished with the power, and access to food became unreliable. Disease spread, and sewage flowed untreated.

The tide of Iraqi soldiers receded from Kuwait nearly as quickly as it had flooded in. On February 15, George H. W. Bush addressed the Iraqi public on Voice of America: "There is another way for the bloodshed to stop: and that is, for the Iraqi military and the Iraqi people to take matters into their own hands and force Saddam Hussein, the dictator, to step aside, and then comply with the United Nations's resolutions and rejoin the family of peace-loving nations." A CIA-funded radio station in Saudi Arabia, Voice of Free Iraq, reinforced this message by broadcasting a speech from a high-ranking defector in the Iraqi military: "Rise to save the homeland from the clutches of dictatorship so that you can devote yourself to avoid the dangers of the continuation of the war and destruction. Honorable sons of the Tigris and Euphrates, at these decisive moments of your life, and while facing the danger of death at the hands of foreign forces, you have no option in order to survive and defend the homeland but to put an end to the dictator and his criminal gang."

The Shi'a community again rose up, believing that the American president would support it. Cities throughout the south—Najaf, Karbala', Basrah—soon fell to local rebels, but Saddam was prepared, maintaining his Republican Guard for such scenarios. "*La shi'a ba'd al-yawm*"—"No more Shi'a after today"—was spray-painted onto the side of their tanks.

Within weeks, the rebels were crushed. Fifty thousand Shi'a refugees fled to Saudi Arabia, others to Iran, and still others to the swampy marshlands in the south of Iraq. In the north, the Kurds also revolted, but retaliation was swift and complete. Hundreds of thousands fled across the border into Turkey and Iran, blistering with a feeling that the American president had just turned his back on the uprising he had encouraged.

After the rebels had been turned into refugees, the UN passed a Security Council resolution creating no-fly zones in the north and south, but tens of thousands were already dead.

Sanctions were imposed in order to extract good behavior from Saddam. Before Iraq would be permitted to import freely, Saddam would have to repay the Kuwaitis, give up his missile capacity and weapons of mass destruction, and cease the repression of his citizens.

And so the economic siege of Iraq began, when Yaghdan was thirteen.

Sanctions

Following his previous wars, Saddam had drilled money from the deep pools of oil below Iraq's blood-soaked crust to clear the rubble and repair infrastructure. After the Gulf War, though, the international community declared Iraqi oil off-limits and banned the importation of chlorine, vaccines, tractors, fertilizer, and anything else that could be converted to military ends. Pepsi was banned, wheat and sugar imports cut. The sanctions committee found danger in the most quotidian needs: a pencil has lead, lead can be used for war, and so pencils were banned. In one of the more ostentatious breaches of the embargo, a convoy of Jordanian trucks sped across the border to ferry millions of pencils into Iraq.

If Saddam could be prevented from rebuilding, the Americans argued, his country would turn on him. The more that Iraqi civilians were deprived of basic services, the greater the loss to the legitimacy of his rule, and the more leverage the United States would have in its dealings with him. It was a simple equation.

The drop in oil production—85 percent, by most accounts—meant that the Iraqi government had less money to import food. Although Iraq was the land of two rivers, it could not feed itself, unable to coax enough food from its soil when its tractors were broken and pesticides and fertilizer were illegal.

A humanitarian crisis developed. The infant mortality rate doubled, due in large part to the proliferation of disease caused by untreated water, a result of the ban on chlorine (which could be used to make explosives). When, in the mid-1990s, the *New York Times* reported that as many as five hundred thousand Iraqi children had died as a result of the harsh sanctions, Secretary of State Madeleine Albright told *60 Minutes,* "The price is worth it."

Haifa

He had known Haifa only as a friend and classmate from the Physics Department at Baghdad's Mustansiriyah University. Yaghdan hadn't seen her since their graduation two years earlier, but when he bumped into her at a mutual friend's lecture in the summer of 2002, he saw the woman he wanted to marry. He was twenty-five.

Yaghdan had opened a small shop on Sina'a Street with a partner. They sold computers, monitors, and software and repaired broken computers brought into the store, which was just across the street from Al-Technologia University in eastern Baghdad. Business was good, despite the economic throes of his country.

Yaghdan hired Haifa at the shop so that they would have an excuse to be near each other, and their love unfolded steadily over the fall and into the winter, oblivious to the revving sounds of war. They saw no pictures of troops massing at their border and heard no speeches from George W. Bush. The United States had threatened Iraq with war on countless occasions, Yaghdan figured, so if a war came at all, it would probably start and end with a couple cruise missiles and another bombed-out military installation.

Two days before the invasion, they were in the store, taking coffee breaks, making dinner plans with friends. Haifa's father had heard enough rumors down south in Karbala' to be convinced, though, and pleaded with his daughter to leave Baghdad. She laughed and said, "There is no war! Are you kidding?"

But Haifa decided to oblige her father and made plans to spend that last afternoon with Yaghdan. They strode around the Mansour district. He bought her ice cream, and the Egyptian pop singer Amr Diab's song "Ana 'Aish" warbled from the window of a passing car. They joked about her anxious father. There was no gravity to their good-bye that night; Yaghdan knew he'd see her in a couple days, after the war had come and gone.

On March 19, 2003, Haifa drove an hour south to Karbala' and teased her father about his "war." Yaghdan and his parents passed a normal evening in their small home on Street Number 2 in the al-Jihad neighborhood in western Baghdad. They had a dinner of rice and fish and went to bed.

Hours later, bombs tore apart the city and burned the night sky in the early morning of the twentieth. At first Yaghdan hoped it was only a demonstration strike, but the bombs fell all night, and in the morning there were more. He felt his ears about to burst and worried that his parents would perish, if not by the bombs, then by heart attacks. At around ten o'clock, the bombers relented, but for how long, he didn't know. He ran out to the driveway and checked their Volkswagen Passat. There was a half tank, more than enough to get them to Najaf if the roads were in one piece.

There was smoldering rubble everywhere, columns of smoke rising from Baghdad. The road out of the city was a mess, thronged with dazed Iraqis piled into cars and trucks and walking alongside the highway, heading anywhere away from the Shock and Awe. Yaghdan had grown accustomed to bombs: there was once a time when his country was not at war with the world, but all he knew was that every few years, the skies over Iraq opened up and showered ruin.

But now, just as he was starting to grasp the edges of a life for himself as a young man—a steady business and a woman who loved him—here it came again. The electricity vanished in an instant, followed by Iraq's antiquated landline telephone network. He had no way of finding out what had happened to Haifa in Karbala'.

In Najaf, he braced for the second night, which passed without attack. He figured that the Americans would not bomb the holy city, but the ferocity of the first day gave him second thoughts. Najaf sits on a hill, so when Yaghdan climbed to the rooftop, he could see American troops, tanks, and Humvees gathering, churning up massive clouds of dust on the outskirts of the city. He heard the sound of a helicopter before he saw it bearing down on him. Alone on the roof, he waved with exaggerated movements at the chopper, which hovered, circled around, watched him. It flew on, over the city, in search of indications of resistance.

June approached. The Americans had taken Baghdad. Iraqi policemen and soldiers, once iron fixtures of his life in Baghdad, had melted away in the first hours of the war. Looting was rife. Government buildings were stripped of their veins of copper piping and any fixtures of value. Cars were stolen and shops emptied. Old feuds were settled.

Yaghdan wanted to return to Baghdad to protect his business. He drove back north, leaving his father in Najaf.

He and his business partner, Mohammad, reopened the computer store with zeal. Yes, there were looters and a breakdown of order in Baghdad, they reasoned, but the American troops would soon settle and take control. He found Americans everywhere in the streets and could tell when they were lost, offering them directions.

There were plenty of reasons to be optimistic in June 2003. He had heard through a mutual friend that Haifa was safe and would return to Baghdad soon. His shop hadn't been looted, and the fall of the regime meant the end of sanctions, allowing him to import new technology and computers without submitting to a review board. He and Mohammad talked with excitement about the coming year, when American companies would surely return to Iraq. He heard that the Bechtel Corporation was returning to build power plants and repair their infrastructure. They'd have better electricity, cleaner water, and a free economy. The Americans would leave in a year, he thought, just as they had after rebuilding Kuwait.

On Sina'a Street, Baghdad's high-tech boulevard, business was coming back. New technology flooded into Iraq, and suppliers ferried crates of computers and monitors down the street to vendors.

At the end of the workday on his third Thursday back in Baghdad, Yaghdan and Mohammad locked the outer door to the shop. Yaghdan carried a white plastic bag stuffed with the week's receipts, which he intended to tally up over the weekend.

Mohammad started his car, a white Toyota Crown sedan, but it was sweltering inside, so he got back out and left the doors open to air it out. Yaghdan leaned against the hood of the car, the receipt bag around his wrist.

With a wail of engines and screeching tires, a black BMW and another Toyota skidded up onto the curb alongside them. Their doors flew open and six men poured out. They carried weapons: four AK-47s and two 9 millimeters.

Without exchanging a word, they began pummeling Mohammad, who lunged back into the car in a futile effort to escape. They dragged him out and told him to hand over the keys. Three men surrounded Yaghdan, who shouted, "Why are you doing this?" A gunman approached him. He was short, at least six inches shorter than Yaghdan. When he reached for the plastic bag, Yaghdan shoved him away.

Yaghdan fell to the ground. Someone had shot him in the leg, right through his kneecap. The short gunman yanked the bag of worthless receipts from around his wrist, jumped into Mohammad's sedan, and sped off.

As he lay there, he thought he was a dead man. A bullet through the knee was not necessarily lethal, but everyone knew that the hospitals were in dire shape. In addition to being looted, they had run out of blood and medication from treating those wounded during the invasion. Doctors were scarce.

The sun was unforgiving. Cars and trucks drove by. A neighboring shop owner raced out and saw a puddle of blood forming around Yaghdan, who lay there quietly.

An ambulance arrived forty-five minutes later, and the pool of red had turned into a small pond. Medics hoisted him onto a stretcher and sped off. Soon someone came by with a bucket of water to wash his blood from the sidewalk.

Yaghdan found that he was not as patient as he liked to think. He still hadn't seen Haifa, and wondered if she and her family were okay. Under strict orders from the surgeon not to move without his crutches, he sat in the corner of the living room in his home, tormented by boredom and heat, which made the skin under his cast itch.

He didn't know who had shot him, but didn't even bother calling the police. There were none to call. He could hobble out and locate some American soldiers, but what would he tell them? What could they do?

His impatience churned with frustration until he decided the surgeon must be wrong and it was okay for him to walk, just four weeks after his knee was shot to bits. He stood up without the crutch and felt something tear apart in his knee. He fell back into his chair and called an ambulance, which arrived after two hours to shuttle him back to the operating room.

Yaghdan's cell phone rang loudly from the other room. Summer was easing into fall, and his knee was finally on the mend. He hobbled on his crutches to take the call from Mohammad, who updated him on business. He mentioned in passing that Haifa had come back to work, and Yaghdan's mind raced happily. "I think I'll try coming in soon," he said, trying to mask the excitement in his voice.

In the three months since he was shot, Iraq had fallen quite ill, stricken by an insurgency that seemed to be equal parts criminal enterprise (kidnapping for ransom, hijacking cargo trucks) and anti-American uprising, fueled by a widening furor over America's inability to restore order.

In the beginning of the war, he and his parents saw massive helicopters carrying tanks and Humvees—sometimes two Humvees suspended from a single helicopter. It was just a matter of time, they believed, before they would see generators hanging from the helicopters.

But the summer passed, and the electricity was weaker than ever. Sewage pooled in the streets, which teemed with US soldiers who never had any answers for the Iraqis who came up to ask about the power and water.

Even though it was September, the house was a furnace. He turned the faucet handle to splash some water on his face, but nothing came out. He didn't care: today he would finally go back to work, to see her. He locked the house door behind him and hobbled past the garden that his mom once tended. There was little hope for the flowers this year, but still they sprouted, sickly but alive.

He lowered himself into the Passat. He could still drive with his good right leg. There were several checkpoints that had sprung up between his house and Sina'a Street, one run by American soldiers, the others by Iraqis. What was once a fifteen-minute drive now took over an hour, but he would not be fazed. He smiled as he handed his identity card to the American soldier and said, "How are you today?" Startled, the soldier smiled, handed back his papers, and waved him through.

He saw Haifa's eyes flash with happiness when he walked into the shop. Yaghdan tried to make small talk with the other employees, but he spent most of his time with her. They made plans to see each other the next day.

As thrilled as he was to see her, he wrestled with the realization that between the checkpoints and the throbbing pain in his leg, he was not yet ready to return to work.

An American organization, Creative Associates International, was looking for Iraqi employees. The recipient of a $62 million contract to revitalize Iraq's schools, the company was hiring Iraqis to help on a range of projects. Millions of schoolbooks needed to be drained of Saddam and Ba'ath Party ideology and reprinted. Over a million schoolbags were filled with pencils, pads of paper, and calculators and given to every Iraqi child. Tens of thousands of teachers were trained.

Suhair, a friend of Yaghdan's from the university, had started working with Creative. She called Yaghdan and recruited him for a massive data-entry project compiling the results of a countrywide survey about the needs of Iraq's schools. He planned to work for the Americans from home for a couple months until he could return to Sina'a Street to run the computer shop.

But he soon began to see how his work was impacting the lives of his fellow Iraqis. He felt that he could do more good with the Americans than with his computer business, so what started as a temporary job became full-time. When he was well enough to walk without crutches, he began commuting to work at the Creative Associates compound in the Karrada neighborhood of Baghdad, just across the Tigris from the Green Zone.

The well of Yaghdan's optimism was filling once again. Although he walked with a slight limp, his knee had healed. Haifa was back in his life, and they had begun talking about marriage.

He went to Haifa's father and asked for his blessing. The wedding took place in January 2004. Haifa moved into his home on Street Number 2, and the pair lived happily alongside his parents.

Eight months later, in the fall of 2004, officials at USAID, which oversaw the Creative Associates contract, noticed Yaghdan's work. He accepted their offer of a job working directly for the US government at the agency's compound in the heart of the Green Zone.

3.

Incoming

EXCERPT FROM:

A SHORT GUIDE TO IRAQ
1943

*For use of Military Personnel Only. Not to be republished, in whole
or in part, without the consent of the War Department. Prepared by:
Special Service Division, United States Army*

You have been ordered to Iraq (i-*rahk*) as part of the world-wide
offensive to beat Hitler.

American success or failure in Iraq may well depend on whether
the Iraqis (as the people are called) like American soldiers or not.
It may not be quite that simple. But then again it could.

The best way you can do this is by getting along with the Iraqis
and making them your friends. And the best way to get along with
any people is to understand them.

That is what this guide is for. To help you understand the people and the country so that you can do the best and quickest job
of sending Hitler back to where he came from.

And, secondly, so that you as a human being will get the most
out of an experience few Americans have been lucky enough to
have. Years from now you'll be telling your children and maybe
your grandchildren stories beginning, "Now, when I was in
Baghdad–."

MEET THE PEOPLE

But don't get discouraged. Most Americans and Europeans who have gone to Iraq didn't like it at first. Might as well be frank about it. They thought it a harsh, hot, parched, dusty, and inhospitable land. But nearly all of these same people changed their minds after a few days or weeks, and largely on account of the Iraqi people they began to meet. So will you.

The tall man in the flowing robe you are going to see soon, with the whiskers and the long hair, is a first-class fighting man, highly skilled in guerilla warfare. Few fighters in any country, in fact, excel him in that kind of situation. If he should happen to be your enemy—look out! Remember Lawrence of Arabia?

Differences? Of course! Differences? Sure, there are differences. Difference of costume. Differences of food. Differences of manner and custom and religious beliefs. Different attitudes toward women. Differences galore.

But what of it? You aren't going to Iraq to change the Iraqis. Just the opposite. We are fighting this war to preserve the principle of "live and let live." Maybe that sounded like a lot of words to you at home. Now you have a chance to prove it to yourself and others. If you can, it's going to be a better world to live in for all of us.

D o you still want to go to Iraq?"
   "Yes."
"Good. Can you go in two weeks?"

The phone call that finally came in December 2004 was brief but exhilarating. I stared down at the half-completed practice Law School Admission Test in front of me and grinned. Law school could wait.

The job was with the US Agency for International Development, an entry-level position in the Baghdad mission as an information and public affairs officer. I knew little about what I'd be doing, but I had read that the agency was working with nearly $6 billion in reconstruction funds.

First, I had to complete a two-week training, the Diplomatic Security Anti-terrorism Course, or DSAC. On a wintry December morning, my class of fellow aid workers and foreign service officers were shuttled to a government farm in West Virginia to undergo explosives training, which consisted of standing in an observation tower and watching demonstrations of various explosives: det. cord, C4, PETN. When the instructor asked for a volunteer to press a button on his remote control, I eagerly raised my hand and blew up a late-model Oldsmobile Cutlass Supreme. As a twenty-four-year-old male, I would have gladly paid for the first week of the course.

I shredded a target with climbing bursts of fire from a sweltering AK-47 and grinned. Next to me, a plump forty-something woman named Doris, who was headed over to do secretarial work in the Republican Palace, struggled to lift her shotgun. She fired one shell, lost her grip in the kickback, and the shotgun fell dangerously to the ground. The instructor glared as he picked it up, and Doris fired no more.

We drove around suburban Leesburg and Reston, Virginia, for hours in a Defense Department minivan and tried to determine which cars were tailing us (usually those with Pentagon parking decals affixed to their windshields). I couldn't help but think that whoever developed this part of the program had seen a lot of bad spy movies and probably hadn't been to Iraq. As I soon learned, you don't really study who is tailing you when rolling around in a quarter-mile-long convoy of three up-armored Suburbans, two or three Humvees, and two Little Bird helicopters engorged with Blackwater gunmen protecting us from the sky. And if I ever found myself in a situation where the highly trained marines and mercenaries around me were killed, leaving it to me to pick up a Kalashnikov or M16, I'd have been better off pointing it at myself. At least I now knew how to find the safety on each rifle.

We received emergency medical training. I learned not to patch a sucking chest wound with the plastic wrapper of a cigarette pack like they did in Vietnam: the cellophane had become thinner since then, thin enough to be sucked right into the chest.

A hostage negotiator taught us that if we were going to be killed in captivity, it would almost certainly happen within the first ninety-six hours. If we survived the first four days, he told us, it was best to pass the time by writing a book or building a house in our head. If our captors ever made us sit in front of a camera and condemn the United States for a propaganda film, we should use our face as a map to point out clues as to where we thought we might be. Our forehead was north, our chin was south. Our nose was Baghdad.

The second week of the course was designed to teach us about Iraqi history and culture and took place in a conference room at the Foreign Service Institute, a small redbrick campus in Arlington, Virginia. Although I had a degree in Middle Eastern history and Arabic and had already spent a lot of time in the region, I went into the second week without pretense, eager to learn what the US government considered the most essential information for its foreign service officers and aid workers.

Entrusted with this duty was a brash woman with smoke-scarred vocal cords who introduced herself as Dr. Mansfield. She claimed expertise on Iraq and fluency in Arabic and was going to prepare us for the coming year of work, with an emphasis on interacting with Iraqis.

She dove right into cultural differences between Iraqis and Americans. "Iraqi women who lose their virginity before marriage will tell a villager to go out and kill a pigeon on the day of their wedding," she explained, before adding that the bird's liver would be extracted, filled with pigeon blood, and inserted in her vagina shortly before the consummation.

Wide-eyed at the absurdity and inaccuracy of the claim, which she presented as the cultural norm throughout Iraq, I looked around the room as my classmates shook their heads in disgust. Shotgun Doris blurted, "I'm sorry, but that is just gross!"

Dr. Mansfield worked her way through Iraqi history: "You may not know this, but Baghdad used to be a great city until the Mongols took it over in 1258."

> Doris: What important things happened there after 1258?
> Doctor Mansfield: Not a damn thing.

Doris nodded slowly and wrote in her notebook, I imagine something like "Iraqi history, 1258–2004: nothing of importance."

Dr. Mansfield seemed to like me, offering advice such as "Grow a beard! Nobody over there will respect you because you're young." I smiled and wrote *beard* in my notebook.

On the final day, Dr. Mansfield focused on gift giving. This knowledge would equip us, she said, to get the most out of our Iraqi employees. I had received Mansfield's permission to record the class, under the pretense of being better prepared.

"Can we get them clothing?" asked a classmate.

"That's a tough one. You probably shouldn't, but you should congratulate them if they have a new shirt. Now, we wouldn't congratulate ourselves on having a new shirt; we know that, since we talked about this yesterday, 'cause we have clean clothes. Okay? But it can be a big deal for some people in the region to get a new item of clothing. Very big."

A British contractor who had just come back from a three-month stint in Baghdad jumped in: "Take a digital camera! They *love* photographs, printed. I'm trying to remember, we had one of these color laser copiers, and we went through something like—and I'm not kidding—fifteen hundred bucks' worth of toner in a month! Somebody went 'click' and printed a picture. Every single Iraqi in the office had to have a copy of that picture."

Dr. Mansfield nodded. "Write that down. That is a great idea."

Doris wrote in her notebook.

Leaning back with a smirk, the Brit exclaimed, "A color picture! A color picture—now, we'd think nothing of it, but they are thrilled with that sort of thing!"

Doris: Do we use, like, regular paper or glossy paper?
Brit: They were *thrilled* with ordinary paper!

I had accepted the job offer only a week earlier: it hadn't yet occurred to me that I'd be working alongside Iraqis at the agency, but to hear them characterized in such prehistoric terms was jarring. We were not a group of invading soldiers in need of desensitization training but civilians who would assume important positions in administering and rebuilding the country.

Apart from *beard*, my notebook was empty. When classmates asked Dr. Mansfield how to ask "Can I take your picture?" in Arabic, her response was as confident as it was incorrect. I guessed that she might have had a year of Arabic lessons decades ago. I could find no record of her ever having received a doctorate.

Later that afternoon, I rode to the outskirts of Washington to Fort Belvoir, where my dad was once stationed, to be photographed for a Defense Department Common Access Card, which would get me in and out of bases and helicopters.

I flew back home to Chicago for Christmas. The suburbs were cold and blustery, and in the freighted days before my departure, my brothers and I reverted to young boys again. Derek and I set up lights around the pond, which Soren and I had shoveled to form a hockey rink. Mom brought us popcorn and hot chocolate, and we watched the steam wend its way from our lungs in between goals. Dad appeared at the pond's edge for a few moments, exhaling Borkum Riff bourbon-flavored pipe tobacco and surveying the game quietly. We stayed away from the deep end that Derek had fallen through when we were little. Splayed down on the ice, Soren had fed him a hockey stick to pluck him from the terror below. I scrambled up the steps two a time, looking over my shoulder and screaming, "*Dad! Dad, Mom! Dad!*"

My dad and I meandered through a shopping mall, making last-minute purchases. Where mom wore her worry on her face, he wore excitement. He once told me, when I was home from college, that he had hoped I'd join one of the services to develop a sense of discipline. I didn't talk to him for months. Now, as I prepared to go over as a civilian employee of USAID, he indulged in what appeared to be a mild fantasy about my job.

I picked out a pair of gray convertible pants. "You guys don't wear that color over there."

"You got any special deals for my son?" he asked the high school girl working the register. "He's off to Iraq next week! Here, Kirk, let me pay for your gear." Embarrassed, I dumped my "gear" onto the conveyor. Spotting a pair of green Carhartt jeans, he jabbed a finger into them and said, "Army issue!"

He found an old army rucksack in the basement for me to use, but I told him the canvas was too worn out.

Although I can scarcely remember him rushing to answer the phone when I was younger, now he seemed to *want* to talk with everyone who called. "Yeah, well, you know our son Kirk is off to Baghdad next week, so we're all trying to spend as much time with him as possible. What's that? No, it's a ten-month tour."

I was stuffing my Arabic dictionary into a suitcase when he wandered in and asked, "Where do you think you'll take your R&R? I did mine in Hong Kong. That was right after the Tet Offensive."

He ignored my attempts to correct his terminology. "Are you going to deploy with anyone else in your same unit?"

"Aid workers don't deploy, and we don't have units," I told him. "I'm flying over alone. They bumped me to first-class sleeper the whole way; should be nice."

Later that night, he walked into my bedroom with a legal pad, closed the door behind him, and said that he needed to ask a few questions for my living will. I was twenty-four, and hadn't given any thought to how I'd want my vegetative body handled. An hour later, he came back up with a typed version for my signature.

"Sit on the left side of the plane if you want a good view coming in. Only if you don't get airsick, though," an attractive young woman working for USAID volunteered encouragingly. Below us swirled pillars of dust, ten stories high and dancing across the desert expanse. The props felt as though they might choke as the tiny Embraer EMB Brasilia twin turboprop plane chartered by the agency to shuttle incoming AID workers climbed through the clouds. I fidgeted with my MP3 player and settled on Radiohead's "I Will." The pitch of the turbines settled, and the plane nosed onward.

It was hot on the plane. There was no door to the pilot's deck. The sun glared, and the glass faceplates of the instrumentation systems flashed light like watch faces. A small pink Energizer bunny twirled on a string tied to an unused switch. As Thom Yorke's voice cooed about lying down in an underground bunker, I realized I had picked a lousy song for the moment. The copilot turned around and announced we were one hundred kilometers from Baghdad International Airport.

The clouds broke, and the Euphrates ribboned darkly below. Weary-looking farms unfurled from its banks, and sand piled over the edges of the fields. We hurtled toward the dusty pall of Baghdad, and the song looped. The plane banked left abruptly and jammed its nose downward. In a frantic approach, the turboprop corkscrewed its way down as though swirling toward a drain, hoping to avoid rocket-propelled grenades. The emergency system began to blare, but the pilots ignored it as the engines clamored and the Energizer bunny circled furiously. At the last possible moment, they straightened the wings and the plane smacked into the runway, bouncing a few times as the copilot welcomed us to Iraq.

Inside the customs hall, I smiled at the bored-looking Iraqi official inspecting my official passport, but he didn't bother looking up as he thudded my entry stamp. A stocky man in his late twenties wearing a faded Metallica T-shirt hurried over once I cleared passport control. He was the first Iraqi employee of USAID I would meet, and he introduced himself to me as Kirk. I stared in blank confusion.

"No," I said, "my name is Kirk. What's yours?"

"Kirk! Well, it's Muhanad, but that's too hard for the Americans, so I use Kirk. As in, Hammett? Metallica, dude!"

In Arabic, I told him it was too weird to call him Kirk, and that I'd call him by his real name, if that was okay by him. He beamed his assent.

Black smoke columned upward from sputtering power plants and IED blasts as the Blackhawk ferrying us from the airport into the Green Zone swooped low over the city. The former ministry buildings were charred and collapsed from the JDAM bombs of Shock and Awe. The Republican Palace was soon below us, and we touched down at Landing Zone Washington. I clambered out of the Blackhawk and followed the woman from the airplane toward a white unarmored van. An Iraqi driver working for USAID drove us the final stretch to the gates of the agency's compound, where Nepalese Gurkhas patted him down and rubbed paper on him to test for explosive residue. Bomb dogs sniffed around his legs as we waited in the van.

Sprinklers spattered tiny eight-by-ten lawns in between rows of gray mortar-proof houses. An Iraqi in a golf cart gathered my belongings, depositing me in the corner of the compound at my assigned house in row A, block 2, unit 4.

I flopped on the couch and felt my exhaustion for the first time that day. The house was surprisingly comfortable, with a separate bedroom, a well-equipped kitchen, a satellite TV, and a DVD player. I wandered into the bedroom and began unpacking. Opening the bed stand drawer, I found a folded wad of papers. I spread them open to discover a receipt and schemata for a penis enlargement system, left behind by the previous occupant. I crawled into bed and slept.

4.

USGspeak

As the drone flies, the USAID compound was situated upon four scabby acres on the dorsum of the nose-shaped Green Zone, its eastern edge carved by the quiet waters of the Tigris. After the fall of Baghdad, when the embassy and the Pentagon split up the opulent Republican Palace, and the properties of the Green Zone were divvied up by various agencies and contractors, USAID laid claim to the former headquarters of the motorcycle division of the Republican Guard and built some of the finest living quarters around. Our bombproof homes lined the northern half of the compound; sardine-can trailers serving as offices clotted the southern half. A massive structure was emerging from the ground in the northeastern corner, built by Iraqi day laborers who were bussed in to pour concrete and stack bricks. AID workers called it the NOB, short for New Office Building, and we eagerly awaited its completion so that we could work in mortar-proof peace.

At nine o'clock on my first morning there, January 3, 2005, I wandered over to the Public Affairs Office and found my new boss in the middle of a tense phone conversation. Doug's hair was disheveled, his clothes rumpled, his right shoe untied. He peered through thick lenses at me, nodded, and pointed at my cubicle, just beside his. I sat down and waited nervously.

"I don't *care* how Washington went, you're scheduled for Basrah tomorrow!"

Through the phone's handset, I heard the voice of a young woman yelling back at him.

Doug took a sip from a white Styrofoam cup and sighed, and the odor of whiskey crept out into the morning air. The woman's voice was still shouting through the phone as he hung up on her. He took off his glasses and rubbed his eyes.

"Are you Kirk?"

I shot to my feet and extended a hand. "Yes, happy to meet you."

"You, too. Look, you gotta go to Basrah tomorrow to show a *Times* reporter our projects down there."

"I'm sorry?"

"The girl who was supposed to do it is refusing to go, and I can't do it."

"But I don't know anything about our projects down there. Don't I need body armor and stuff?"

He thought for a moment, then reached for his cup.

"Yeah. Go down to the warehouse and get your armor."

I raced out of the office in search of the warehouse, a barn-sized building in the far corner of the compound formerly used to repair the Republican Guard's motorcycles. A team of Iraqis issued my body armor, a helmet, a cell phone, and a walkie-talkie. As soon as I turned it on, it squawked with the sound of an American requesting an Iraqi from the maintenance department to fix a problem with her air conditioner. A mess of sweat and fine dust, I slung the armor over my shoulder and hurried back to the office, wondering how to get to Basrah and what I was supposed to do there. I walked in just as my new boss was getting ready to leave, a scowl on his flushed face. "Forget it. I'm going now. Just get yourself set up here, and we'll talk when I get back in a few days."

The Hierarchy of Armor

"Oh, their names are so tricky and hard to remember! Just call them Ahmed or Mohammad, that's what I do, and it sure seems to do the trick."

Sandy, the USAID executive officer, a plump woman in her fifties with sausage fingers and turkey jowls, answered a question about Iraqis in her welcome briefing to orient the half-dozen Americans who had arrived in the previous week. Sandy was the third-highest-ranked American in the mission and supervised the ninety Iraqis who worked for the agency in its Green Zone compound. Of them, only three were named Mohammad or Ahmed.

By the end of the first week, I struggled against an impression taking root that life in the USAID compound and the Green Zone was more high school than front lines. The cliques were recognizable within days: jocks, overachievers, bad boys, the jaded and embittered, the excluded. The jocks were now armed mercenaries, 'roided up on drugs ordered from a Cyprus-based website and lumbering around in a first-person-shooter video game fantasyland. Young professionals were skipping rungs on the career ladder by volunteering for service in Baghdad; they wore crisp button-ups and ties and kept the dust from their shoes and the booze at a minimum. Down-on-their-luck types came for the danger pay, hoping to chip away at debt back home. Still others escaped midlife crises, running to Iraq from crumbling or ruined marriages.

It was clear who was at the bottom of the heap. As I walked into the dining facility, the scene summoned another unpleasant memory from my high school, where whites and Latinos sat in separate sections with little mixing. None of the Americans were sitting with the Iraqi employees. On the second day, I sat with some of them, and a few Americans at the next table over stared at me. Over American food prepared by Nepalese employees of a Halliburton-KBR subsidiary, I eagerly copied out Iraqi slang and vocabulary into a small black notebook.

The war was nearing its third year when I arrived in the first days of 2005, a few weeks before Iraq's first parliamentary elections. The delusions and optimisms of a quick victory in 2003 were now distant memories, abraded by the rise of the insurgency and our torturous response in 2004. By 2005, the violence was fixed in a seemingly permanent state of escalation, each month rivaling its predecessor and challenging its successor. The threat of incoming rockets and small arms fire was high enough that the US Regional Security Office (RSO) issued a directive in January requiring Americans to wear their body armor and helmets at all times inside the Green Zone. Ordinarily, AID workers didn't wear armor to walk the hundred yards from their homes to the cafeteria or the office within the security of the compound, but the security office anticipated a spike in mortar and indirect small arms fire.

During one of my first mornings there, a series of mortars landed in quick succession near the compound, followed by the Voice of God, a loudspeaker broadcasting a recording of a 1950s-sounding American newsreel telling us to "duck. And cover. Duck. And cover." Across the walkway, a woman screamed. "And cover. Duck." The sky was soon freckled with scrambling Blackhawk and Cobra helicopters. In the next office over, separated from ours by a thin piece of corrugated metal, a percussive marching melody erupted: "My eyes . . . have seen . . . the glory of . . . the coming . . . of the Lord." The lieutenant colonel in the US Army Corps of Engineers kept the CD spinning in his computer's drive for such occasions. If he was going to go, it'd be with his own soundtrack.

Then the mortars stopped and the Voice of God and "Glory, Glory, Hallelujah" disappeared, and the computer dinged with a new email from Washington.

The RSO emailed its directive about the body armor the following morning as I was getting ready to leave the house, so I suited up. As soon as I stepped outside, I came across an Iraqi maintenance worker, adjusting the sprinkler out front. Another Iraqi pushed a broom, sweeping the dust from the alleyways between the houses. Neither wore a vest or helmet. "Where's your armor?" I asked in Arabic, and they just smiled and shrugged.

The armor and helmet suddenly felt like a clown costume. As I walked to the office, I saw protected Americans milling about among unprotected Iraqis. At lunch, I quietly asked an Iraqi across the table whether or not he had any armor, and he laughed. "No, of course not! USAID said they do not have any for us."

I stopped wearing the armor after lunch, more out of shame than any principled stand. When the head of security for the compound saw me, he reprimanded me for ignoring the directive. I asked why the Iraqis didn't have any, and he snapped, "Do you have any idea how expensive these vests are?"

Americans were king of the compound, but within the broader Green Zone, USAID staffers nursed badly wounded egos, damaged by their increasing marginalization in the efforts to rebuild Iraq.

In the first weeks of the war, USAID's administrator, Andrew Natsios, had confidently told an astonished Ted Koppel on *Nightline* that the postwar reconstruction would cost America only $1.7 billion, at which point Iraq's oil would pay for the rest.

> Natsios: This doesn't even compare remotely with the size of the Marshall Plan.
> Koppel: The Marshall Plan was $97 billion.
> Natsios: This is $1.7 billion.
> Koppel: All right, this is the first. I mean, when you talk about 1.7, you're not suggesting that the rebuilding of Iraq is gonna be done for $1.7 billion?
> Natsios: Well, in terms of the American taxpayers' contribution, I do. This is it for the US . . .

When it soon became clear that the true costs would run into the tens of billions, constituting the largest aid program since the Marshall Plan rebuilt postwar Europe, the public affairs team deleted the transcript of the interview from USAID's website.

Despite this, I assumed that USAID would lead the efforts to rebuild Iraq. Created by President John F. Kennedy in 1961 as a way of consolidating America's various aid programs into one federal agency, USAID had decades of experience, with missions in scores of countries throughout the world.

Of the initial $20 billion, though, only a quarter went to USAID, while the rest went to a newly created Projects and Contracting Office, or PCO, which operated out of the embassy. Another tranche of funds was managed directly by the Department of Defense, which had limited experience of its own in reconstruction work. Another entity was created at the State Department to "coordinate" these competing efforts, called the Iraq Reconstruction Management Office, or IRMO. Senior USAID officials sat castrated in embassy meetings with State Department contractors and soldiers who had little prior experience but now operated with greater funding and authority. Back at the compound, they spoke wistfully about an indeterminate point in the future when the military would withdraw, State would return its focus to matters of diplomacy, and USAID would have the true lead on reconstruction efforts. One mission director, upset with what she perceived as insufficient status, spent roughly $250,000 each on a small fleet of armored luxury Mercedes-Benz SUVs to shuttle her ostentatiously through the half mile of secured Green Zone to the State Department's palace. Because of their top-heavy design, they were determined unsafe for use outside the Green Zone, which itself did not require up-armored vehicles.

But USAID's identity crisis in Iraq was not entirely the result of losing a bureaucratic turf war. In the 1980s and 1990s, the agency had undergone seismic changes, riding the privatization wave that swept through the Pentagon and countless other federal agencies, leaving employees to focus more on the management of contracts and grants rather than on actual fieldwork. The fuel for career advancement was no longer mastery of a region or a country and its development needs but of the minutiae and paperwork required by a swamp of regulations and directives found in government binders with names such as the *Code of Federal Regulations, Federal Acquisition Regulation,* and *USAID Acquisition Regulation.*

USAID thus became more of an administrative agency than a development agency. Its energies turned to assessing which contractors were capable of delivering what type of deliverable, the time frame for said deliverables, the projected impacts of said deliverables, the mechanisms for contract close-out or early termination, the format and clearance process for issuing requests for proposals, the point systems for grading proposals, the format and clearance process for listing new positions, the point systems for grading candidates for new positions, the timeline for requesting, reviewing, and replying to reports generated by contractors and implementing partners, the schedule and guidelines for conducting performance evaluation reviews of subordinates, the guidelines for . . .

Nevertheless, when USAID received its $6.4 billion share of the funds set aside by Congress, it established the largest aid mission in the world.

One of my primary responsibilities as a public affairs officer, I discovered, was to facilitate the agency's boasting of its reconstruction efforts by digging up any good news from the soil of ten thousand projects in every province and disseminating it in a two-page report called the *Iraq Daily Update*. With a distribution list numbering thousands of bureaucrats, Capitol Hill staffers, journalists, and contractors, the *IDU* had become a small gremlin that needed feeding each morning, and I was now its caretaker. The Public Affairs Office was small: only three people in total when my boss wasn't sleeping off a hangover. While I poked away at the *IDU*, he and my other colleague spent their days fending off journalists investigating potentially embarrassing projects.

My work required me to be on good terms with everyone in the compound if I was to extract any good news from his or her office. "Christ, that goddamn *IDU*! Why don't they make it weekly? Or monthly!" boomed one of the economic development officers. Nobody liked the *IDU*. When I walked into someone's office during work hours, I'd usually find a pained but polite expression. "Sorry. Don't have anything for you today."

My outgoing predecessor noticed my bewilderment when I came back empty-handed the first day. "Don't worry," she said. "Just go back into the archives a few months and grab one of those; maybe refresh it a little. There are tons of them, and nobody remembers."

And so I did, poring through reams of *IDU*s. "USAID Funds Beekeeper Initiative in Dohuk." "Sewing Shop Provides Jobs and Hope in Kirkuk." The photos accompanying the updates had an extortionate quality: the Iraqi recipients pictured never had more than the faintest of smiles.

To learn the language of the *IDU* was to learn the language of the US government—USGspeak—which as early as 2004 had already evolved to tamp down expectations. The $1.7 billion certainty of 2003 was long gone. No more absolutes in word choice. A single page of the update was spayed with verbs such as *developed, improved, assisted, worked with, provided a framework for*, all trailing off into nothing that could be held against them in the future. "Yes, we improved the statistical analysis procedures at the US central bank; there was a two-week training course at the Federal Reserve in New York. Here's a picture of some of the attendees."

USGspeak was not limited to its official reports. In meeting after meeting, we resolved to "look into" and "get a handle" on things. Sometimes we were directed to "begin ramping up" our efforts. This coded yes/no language offered an escape path in case something went wrong as well as a trail of bread crumbs in case something went right and we wanted to take credit. If things went right, we could say that we had started ramping up our efforts in anticipation of this *long ago*. If things went wrong, we could say that we *had* started ramping up our efforts but hadn't received enough funding. Failing that, there were always contractors or the mess of competing acronyms over at the palace to blame. And failing that, there was always the laudanum of "the security situation," which could numb even the harshest critics: our efforts would have been a smashing success if Iraq wasn't such a violent place. But because of unreceptive Iraqis and their mortars, we needed the help of private security firms, which proliferated algae-like and soon claimed thirty cents of every reconstruction dollar.

I countered my cynicism with a little deferential sobriety: the amount of knowledge and expertise required to run a country was massive—far beyond what anyone in the Bush administration had prepared for—and beyond the capacity of Iraq's civil society, most of which had fled, or was being de-Ba'athified into prisons or exile.

And so one could look at the USAID-ARDI (Agriculture Reconstruction and Development for Iraq) program—budgeted at $100 million—with derision or respect, depending on one's mood. In its September 1, 2005, update, a half page was devoted to the training of fourteen officials from the Iraqi Ministry of Agriculture in the installation and operation of sprinkler systems. "This training is the first in a series to train 48 MOA officials to operate and maintain a variety of irrigation systems, including drip irrigation." The improvement of Iraq's irrigation infrastructure seemed both hugely important and wildly inconsequential.

"USAID trained 183 Iraqis in beekeeping basics in an effort to help vulnerable groups gain a sustainable income. Participants included 44 widows, 79 poor farmers, and 41 people with disabilities." I wondered whose job it was to tally off the characteristics of the grantees. Mine? Could someone from the disability column also have been a widow or a poor farmer? The need to quantify the outputs and to tally up the deliverables seemed desperate: 183 beekeepers, 44 widows, 14 officials. Did these mean anything in a country of 25 million?

No matter. A couple years later, another release about USAID's help buying jars and natural wax for another beekeeper ran under the title "Bee Venture Brings Sweet Success."

Sometimes the language was so punctured with USGspeak that it was drained of meaning: "ARDI is providing NGOs with training in facilitation, or guiding participatory decision making, in order to improve their capacity to solve problems and reach agreement through building consensus."

It didn't take long for the distaste of the work to settle in; to realize that I was the person in charge of churning out little scraps of propaganda with tenuous ties to reality. It was enough, though, for the believers in the mission. Appreciative emails from recipients, mostly neoconservatives back in the United States, flooded in shortly after I sent out each day's *IDU*. "Why doesn't the liberal media ever cover *this*?! Not bloody enough for them?" they exclaimed, not recognizing that they were reading a "success story" about training on sprinkler systems that had been repackaged from a year earlier.

A week into my new job, I knocked on the door of the Education Sector trailer in search of a good news story for the *IDU*. A bespectacled young Iraqi with a soft smile stood up and extended his hand and said, "Hi, my name is Yaghdan."

5.

Raise High the Blast Walls

Chaos was the law of nature; order was the dream of man . . .

—Henry Adams

The Americans cared for the Green Zone like a prisoner tidies his cell. As the insurgency gathered force throughout 2005, the true enemy was not some inchoate militia but unpredictability. And so we did our best to make things predictable. We hired fleets of Iraqis to banish the dust each morning from our tiles, sheets, windows, and toilets, and then once again in the afternoon. Pizza Express and Burger King served up grease and cheese to absorb the hangover from the previous night. We hired a French chef who emailed the cafeteria menu each morning: potage Saint-Germain, grilled steak with herbs, batter-fried sole fillet, gratin potato dauphinoise. Iraqi chauffeurs drove us to and from the Bunker Bar, where the bartender was required to ask if you were packing before he poured. The embassy ran three-on-three basketball tournaments in the parking lot behind the palace and announced theme days to boost morale. This Friday: Talk Like a Pirate Day!

But every now and then, the war on the other side of the concrete would open its maw and spew forth some aged mortars or indirect AK-47 rounds and ruin a perfectly good party. So the blast walls grew taller, the parties moved indoors, and the checkpoints multiplied. We paid exorbitant sums to a security firm to produce a daily *Safe Report*, which lassoed the horrors outside—severed limbs, demolished convoys, exploded marketplaces—into neat charts analyzing thirty-day trend lines and forty-eight-hour "activity levels." We learned that "the number of incidents in Baghdad yesterday fell slightly (from 15 to 14). There were only three VBIEDs, vehicle-borne IEDs, compared to four the day before. Yesterday's activity accounted for 18% of the Iraq total (from 17% the day before)." We nodded knowingly, but we secretly knew nothing.

My friends and I found ways to make the Green Zone our own. Late at night on March 15, the eve of the first session of Iraq's Transitional National Assembly—the precursor to its first parliament—several friends and I piled into a USAID van and headed over to the convention center on the edge of the Green Zone. I had heard rumors of a Steinway concert grand piano in the assembly hall where the TNA would meet, but my previous attempts to get in had been stymied by overzealous Gurkhas guarding the entrance. This time, though, I slipped a twenty into the guard's palm, and he ushered us in. Inside, Iraqis were at work hanging a massive banner over the stage emblazoned with an excerpt from the Quran that extolled the virtues of consultation and cooperation. They shrugged when I asked nervously if I could play the piano, which was hiding behind the main stage curtain. My friends piled into the front-row seats designated for the prime minister and the president while I worked through blues and boogie standards by Fats Waller and Albert Ammons. On the way back to the compound, a friend likened the night to a group of Brits goofing around in Independence Hall in 1787, and I laughed guiltily. When CNN and Al-Jazeera gushed out reports on the opening session the following morning, the legs of the Steinway peeked from below the backdrop like a partly exposed secret.

Our world was gray and etiolating, domed with blast roofs and walled with concrete, made frigid by industrial air-conditioning, and in the alleys of our pale blue cubicles we pecked out reports for headquarters and called contractors who were sealed away in another compound a block over. On our computer desktops we kept our copy of the ubiquitous BaghdadDonut.xls file, in which a doughnut-shaped progress bar reflected how many months, weeks, days, hours, minutes, and seconds you'd been in Iraq and how many months, weeks, days, hours, minutes, and seconds before you could board the Rhino Runner, a steel-reinforced armored bus, back to the airport.

Electricity and Unrest

Yaghdan and I became friends, a friendship limited by his departure from the compound each day at five. We weren't able to socialize after work; I didn't know where he lived, and only knew Haifa's name. But in the kiln of the summer heat, he often showed up an hour early to rest his eyes in USAID's air-conditioned building. He had been working with the Americans for nearly a year, and his job brought him into the nerve center of the reconstruction efforts. In the chilled air of the cafeteria, he told me his work in the agency's education office was fulfilling but that it felt peripheral to Iraq's primary need, which was electricity.

Back in August 2003, when Yaghdan was recuperating from the gun-shot wound, the Coalition Provisional Authority's viceroy, Paul Bremer, broadcast a message to the people of Iraq: "About one year from now, for the first time in history, every Iraqi in every city, town, and village will have as much electricity as he or she can use; and he will have it twenty-four hours a day, every single day." This was meant as a rebuke of the electricity policy of Saddam Hussein, in which power produced in the Kurdish north and the Shi'a south was routed to benefit the Sunni center of Baghdad; now everyone would be expected to share. But as soon as USAID engineers repaired the 400-kilovolt transmission line connecting the grid in the southern provinces to the Sunni heartland, Shi'a plant managers in the south dispatched employees to blow it up. So long as the line was inoperable, Basrah and other Shi'a cities couldn't be asked to share and would enjoy the benefits of full power.

And so when the brutal summer of 2005 baked in, with temperatures consistently approaching 120 degrees, only a few hours of electricity flickered through Baghdad's grid each day. No water flowed from the faucets, forcing many to dig crude wells in their backyards to drink and bathe in the fetid groundwater. Water-borne illness spread, along with infant mortality due to conditions such as diarrhea.

Our well-fueled arsenal of Green Zone generators kept our power steady and water pure, insulating us from the only metric that counted: the number of hours of electricity each day, the truest barometer of violence and insurgency. Without power, businesses couldn't stay open past sundown, newborn babies couldn't be incubated at hospitals, schoolchildren couldn't find relief from the heat during class, and, most important, other essential services, such as water treatment plants, couldn't operate. Throughout the country, local entrepreneurs purchased medium-sized generators and sold access to a meager current of electricity: enough for a small fan but not a refrigerator. Before long, messily bundled arteries of makeshift power lines were everywhere. I backbenched a meeting at the palace in which military officers pleaded for speedier progress on electrical projects: they were tired of sweeping up bodies each morning of Iraqis who had electrocuted themselves trying to tap into the informal grid of generators.

As the war trundled along, many Iraqis began to see the American failure to restore power as something deliberate, part of a plan. How else could one explain why the superpower's helicopters never ferried in generators? The Iraqis' disbelief turned to anger and a rapidly winnowing trust in the motives of the occupying American troops.

Soon after I arrived, I was invited to an ornate conference room in the palace for a weekly meeting with a council of public affairs "professionals" representing the State Department, the military, IRMO, PCO, USACE, and other acronyms I hadn't yet deciphered. On the wall was a large indentation that once held a portrait of Saddam Hussein. In its place hung a satellite map of Fallujah.

The chair of the meeting, a State Department official, started with an exclamation: "Goddamit, we need to show the world that we are making progress on the power and water!"

The public affairs working group in the embassy wanted to deliver some good news about America's progress in the power sector, and since USAID was in charge of nearly $3 billion dedicated to electrical generation under a contract with Bechtel, I needed to find a project to showcase. Back at the compound, I wandered into the Infrastructure Office in search of the tough but jovial Texan named Dick Dumford. He cleared some papers from a chair by his desk and swung it around for me. "Whaddya wanna know, kiddo?" he barked. Above his desk was a massive poster of a Siemens V94 turbine generator. I pointed to it and asked, "What's that?"

"That's MOAG!" he cried. "The Mother of All Generators!"

The V94 was purchased for around $50 million in 2003. With a weight of seven hundred tons, it could not be flown in by helicopter: the generator was so fragile that it could be transported only on a special 120-tire truck at a maximum rate of five miles per hour. When USAID purchased it, the V94 was at the Syrian port of Tartous, and plans were made to construct a $178 million power plant in the northern Iraqi city of Kirkuk. A base camp was created, and a housing structure for MOAG and its transformers were installed. All that remained was the generator.

The generator truck reached the Tishrin Dam on a bend in the Euphrates east of Aleppo. When the US government imposed sanctions on the Syrian government, Damascus responded by refusing to let the generator cross the dam. USAID made the decision to reroute the V94 through Jordan and then through Iraq's volatile Anbar Province, adding months of delays.

For most of 2004 and early 2005, the generator sat near the Jordan-Iraq border, costing USAID $20,000 each day to hire a security firm to protect it. In order to bring it to the base camp (which also cost USAID dearly to protect), the agency needed to transport the generator through the most violent geography of Iraq, but before that could happen, roads needed to be repaved and low-hanging power lines had to be cleared away. The steel girders sent out by the agency to reinforce a bridge were stolen before they could be affixed. A single Kalashnikov round could ruin the entire generator.

When the convoy finally moved, it was heralded as the single largest troop movement in Iraq since the invasion. Three hundred marines and private security contractors accompanied it, supported by Cobra attack helicopters. Weeks after it crossed into Iraq, two years behind schedule, and tens of millions of dollars over budget, the Mother of All Generators arrived in Kirkuk.

By one count, the amount of money spent on the security firm to protect it nearly equaled the cost of the generator itself. For the same amount, USAID could have purchased scores of smaller generators and had them inside Iraq within weeks, but these don't provide as dramatic a ribbon-cutting ceremony. In the end, MOAG would theoretically add only 6 percent to Iraq's battered and besieged electrical grid.

I flew up to Kirkuk with a handful of Iraqi and American journalists as part of the public affairs campaign to "create a new narrative" about the progress of the reconstruction. We swept low in our Blackhawk, slinking beneath telephone lines and scattering camels and sheep. There was no designated landing zone when we arrived, so the chopper hovered indecisively for a minute before setting down on the middle of a road a mile away. Gunners hopped out and raised their rifles at the cars now backed up in either direction.

Two armored SUVs hurtled out of the plant, churning up a wake of dust as they jostled across the field toward us. A short man in wraparound Oakley shades with a machine gun emerged from the passenger door of the lead car and shouted, "Which one of you is USAID?!" I raised my hand and was swiftly deposited into the back of the SUV with a protection security detail (PSD) team, which sped off, leaving the journalists behind on the baking road.

Mack the driver used his turn signal even though every car pulled off to the side of the road at the first sight of us. Riding shotgun with a Colt rifle, a South African sat nearly sideways in his seat with his weapon at the ready. Everything on the road elicited a warning over his mic to the backup vehicle trailing us.

"Parked. Five hundred meters."

"Parked, door open. Three hundred meters."

"Carcass. One hundred meters."

"Two trucks merging left. Two hundred meters."

"Donkey crossing upcoming bridge."

We roared into the Kirkuk power plant. Before I could open the door, a private security detail materialized by the window. When I stepped out, he said, "Please stay close." Four other mercenaries formed a circle around me. I stood there, confused. After a few beats, I started walking toward the rickety bus that had been dispatched to collect the angered journalists, and the covey of PSDs moved fluidly with me. "Pacing west," I heard in the earpiece of the closest guard. When I stopped, they stopped. I tried to apologize to the journalists from within my protective halo but found it difficult with my guards' rifles pointed at their kneecaps.

USAID's manager of the Kirkuk power plant led the journalists on a tour like a carnival barker, reciting the dramatic story of MOAG's journey. "Two hundred sixty megawatts! Seven hundred tons! Six hundred forty miles! Three hundred marines!" But the journalists, especially the Iraqis, knew that hardly any power came out of their outlets, MOAG or not.

What they didn't know was that during the costly years of delay, nobody had bothered to train the Iraqi plant workers in the proper operation and maintenance of the state-of-the-art turbine. Within months of finally going online, the generator was broken. USAID quietly spent millions to bring in a Siemens repair team, which needed expensive private security while it worked on repairs.

A few puff pieces came out of the media junket, which surely cost the US government tens of thousands of dollars, factoring in the cost of mercenaries and the military's Blackhawks. "Great stuff, guys, this is big!" the public affairs chief said excitedly in the next meeting at the embassy, holding up a printout of a short *Washington Post* article buried on page sixteen. My boss at USAID was thrilled with my work, and the mission director started to bring me along to high-level meetings.

The Iraqis on the other side of our blast walls didn't appear to have read the article. The insurgency worsened as the power plants sputtered.

Trapped

Yaghdan picked his way along the crumbling, trash-strewn sidewalks of his neighborhood, periodically stopping to take in the changes. Boarded-up windows, char marks, and rubble. The August sun ovened out molten light so intense that the frames of his glasses grew hot. For the first time, he thought seriously about quitting his job with the Americans.

In the beginning, Yaghdan thought that the world inside the Green Zone would eventually lose its blast walls and expand to cover all of Iraq. When he first set foot in the buzzing fortress of the Green Zone, Yaghdan thought, *This is what American life looks like! This is what they want Iraq to look like. This is how comfortable it's going to be if we continue working hard.*

He and his colleagues made the decision to work for USAID during the innocent early days of the war, when those who stepped forward as informal interpreters were thanked by their neighbors who had no other means of communicating with the Americans. Back then, their sense of optimism allowed them to overlook the daily indignities of working beneath the Americans. In his first week on the job, a mortar traced a parabola into the USAID compound as Yaghdan and his boss walked toward the cafeteria. They both dove to the ground; only she was wearing armor. That made him uncomfortable, but the work was too important to make a fuss over a helmet and a flak jacket. Yasser, a brilliant Iraqi in the procurement office who was prone to quoting Shakespeare if anyone bothered to talk with him, spent hours each week scouring dangerous neighborhoods in search of a particular type of low-fat strawberry yogurt for his American boss, who disliked the cafeteria brand that was trucked in from Kuwait by KBR, the Halliburton subsidiary managing billions of dollars' worth of contracts for logistics support for the US military. Tara, an Iraqi woman from Sadr City working to help USAID refurbish health care clinics, was too polite to register her disgust when a semiferal Iraqi cat taken in by her boss would jump up on her lap while she worked at her desk.

In April 2004, *60 Minutes II* ran a report detailing the extensive use of torture at the Abu Ghraib prison west of Baghdad. By the end of the first year of the occupation, whatever goodwill America had earned by toppling Saddam Hussein had been squandered on a spree of endless checkpoints, wrongful detention, incompetent reconstruction efforts, and now torture. Before long, a stigma germinated and surrounded the Iraqi "traitors" who worked alongside the Americans.

Instead of spreading across Iraq as Yaghdan once dreamt, the Green Zone contracted, a prison into which he and the others sneaked each morning. By 2005, their optimism was tattered. They were trapped: there was no hope of finding a job elsewhere if it ever became known they'd worked for the Americans.

Distrusted

But as their countrymen came to see them as traitors, we came to see them as possible insurgents. As the insurgency developed, American civilians ventured outside of the blast walls of the Green Zone less and less. The only part of the Red Zone that appeared each day, other than an occasional mortar, were Iraqis like Yaghdan, who looked more and more dangerous to the bunkered-in eyes of American civilians.

At some point in 2005, someone in the embassy filled out a requisition form for polygraph examination machines. Then someone drafted a policy memorandum requiring all Iraqis working for the United States in the Green Zone to submit to lie detector tests. Then somebody filled out a requisition form for a bomb residue spectrometer, which came with little fortune-cookie-sized slips of white paper that the Nepalese mercenaries guarding the AID compound rubbed on Yaghdan's arms once he had finally made it past the militiamen searching for traitors like him at the outer checkpoints. The paper was fed into a slot in the machine, and a smiling man with a rifle stood in Yaghdan's way until the large green light blinked.

Three months into his job, he emerged from a Green Zone checkpoint and found a white Opel idling, with two bearded men watching him. As he walked, it shifted into gear and trailed him. He sprinted up a narrow alley, hoping to lose the Opel, which had earned a reputation as an assassin's car. He ran through his own streets like a fugitive, and then realized that his safest option was to return to the Green Zone, so he bolted down another alley toward the Assassins' Gate and flashed his USAID badge at the guard. He emerged from another exit an hour later and sneaked home to Haifa.

He was promoted and assigned to the cubicle next to mine, managing a contract for the agency that examined USAID projects throughout the country and ensured quality. This gave him access to a sensitive database that listed the GPS coordinates of thousands of projects, an insurgent's dream. He was proud of his position. He had reached a higher level of responsibility than all of his Iraqi colleagues and even some of the Americans. He felt valued, trusted by the agency.

Still, the indignities mounted. In the first week of his new position, he stepped outside the front gate of the USAID compound for about thirty seconds to greet and escort two American contractors who were reporting to him. They were waved through, while the guards rubbed the paper slips on his clothing to feed into the bomb residue machine; he had never stepped out of their sight. Frustrated though he was, he enjoyed the new job too much to resign over it.

Yaghdan left for work earlier and earlier each morning. He and other Iraqis like him were called spies by their countrymen during Friday sermons at mosques throughout Iraq, in newspaper editorials, and on television. Now, in order to get to work on time each morning, they had to act like spies. He carried a bag with different articles of clothing: a *shemagh* to wrap around his head, a hat, a light jacket, sunglasses. He changed his shape, wearing baggy clothes, grew and then shaved his beard, and hid his USAID and Green Zone access badges in his shoes. Although it would normally take only twenty minutes to head directly to the Green Zone, he took a bus in the opposite direction. And then another bus to a different neighborhood. And then a taxi, and another taxi. Every day, a different route: sometimes from his home in the Jihad neighborhood to Baya, and then from Baya to Bab al-Sharji, where he entered through the gate on the bridge. Or from Jihad to Nafaq Shurta, and then a bus to Allawi, and from Allawi to the Assassins' Gate entrance.

But when the lie detector machine arrived in the compound, he'd had enough. Iraqis who had worked for the agency for years, since the first hours and days of the war, through mission director after mission director, through countless arrivals and departures of Americans, were summoned into a room with a polygraph machine and asked about their loyalties. Sometimes they were asked if they had ever had an affair or slept with someone of the same sex. One long-serving Iraqi emerged from the test with an armed guard behind him. He wasn't permitted to gather his belongings at his desk before he was escorted out. Others resigned before submitting to the test. The security officers saw this as a confirmation of the polygraph machine's value: it was weeding out untrustworthy Iraqis. Why else would they resign?

Even though he wanted to quit, Yaghdan knew he was bound by a contract that was inescapable and unalterable, penned in American English and signed at another time in another Iraq, one that was now at the bottom of a swamp of insurgency, wrongful detention, errant targeting, and an unholy marriage of mistrust and codependence. Despite the polygraphs, the bomb machines, the lack of body armor, the attempted assassinations of his Iraqi colleagues, he was wed to America and knew that it was not a marriage of equals. His unease climbed whenever the executive officer or someone else in management called him Mohammad.

In July 2005 Suhair, the friend who'd helped Yaghdan find the temporary job when he was recuperating from the shooting, hurried into the USAID compound and asked for a meeting with the mission director. She and her two sisters worked for the agency. The night before, someone pulled up to their home in a black BMW and unloaded several AK-47 clips, raking the walls and doors and windows with gunfire. Suhair and her family had been visiting friends, so when the armed men jumped over the fence and shot open the front door, they found no one inside. She came home to bullet slugs lodged in the walls of her living room and bedroom.

The mission director and the executive officer said there was nothing they could do to protect Suhair and her husband, who also worked for the agency. When she pushed them, they told her, "Your safety is not our responsibility." She fled the country a few days later, and her sisters moved into different neighborhoods. Not long afterward, the home of another Iraqi, named Talal, was fired upon. Yaghdan never told Haifa about the Opel or Suhair or Talal or any of the other dangers. He didn't want to scare her.

These dangers were known to US government officials. Iraqi employees requested special access badges which would allow them to enter the Green Zone more quickly, rather than waiting in long lines which were routinely sniped at by militants. Request denied. They asked for permission to move into the Green Zone so that they would have some security. Request denied.

In the fall of 2005, an internal State Department cable about the worsening situation for the LES—USGspeak for Locally Engaged Staff—was leaked to Al Kamen of the *Washington Post*: "Two of our LES employees have been gunned down in execution-style murders, and two others barely escaped a similar fate in August. Our LES employees live in fear of being identified with the Embassy of the U.S. . . . The reality is that the embassy can offer them little protection outside the International Zone (IZ) and is not in a position to grant their repeated requests to house them and their families within the IZ."

Rather than divert any of the massive resources flooding the largest

American embassy in the world to provide even a basic level of protection for its Iraqi employees, the US government came up with a different solution: hire Jordanians to do the Iraqis' jobs. The complications with housing our Iraqi colleagues in the Green Zone did not apply to these new hires, as Jordanians, under the classification of Third Country Nationals, were permitted to live in the Green Zone.

I heard about the attack on Suhair's house the morning she requested help from the mission director. We all gossiped about it in the cafeteria that day, and that was the end of it. I had an uneasy feeling about how the Iraqis were treated in the compound, but the news of her flight filtered into my mind in macro terms: Iraq was going to hell, and we weren't doing a lot to stop its descent. I didn't think much about what her situation meant in personal terms. Could USAID have done more to help her? How would she get to where she was going? After a few weeks, someone else had replaced her, and apart from an email bounced from her now-defunct agency address, her service faded from memory.

Four months into my work, my boss was fired. He had chased enough mortars with whiskey and slipped up, allowing T. Christian Miller of the *Los Angeles Times* to poke around an unfinished water treatment plant without doing any advance work. (Such is the term for a public affairs officer's scouting of a place to anticipate any potential scandals.) Miller found millions of dollars of unused parts and most of the plant absent or asleep. An embarrassing but accurate report about the total lack of operations and maintenance training that had contributed to MOAG's swift demise appeared in April 2005, prompting a flurry of meetings within the agency with the pointless goal of damage control.

Management waited until my boss took a one-week R&R to Cairo to fire him. He didn't find out until he arrived at the regional airport in Jordan and was told by the airline that he was no longer cleared to fly into Iraq. Iraqi maintenance workers were dispatched to his house in the compound with cardboard boxes, which were filled and shipped back to the United States. Someone tacked *-ed* onto his last name, which was then used as a verb for the act of firing someone while he's on vacation, a much more clinical approach than a messy confrontation. Three months later, his replacement—my new boss—suffered the same fate, and his name became the new verb for a Baghdad-style termination. All of us were uneasy when scheduling our vacations.

People came and went. Some were fired, some simply finished their year. Some started to slip mentally from the stress of the workload or the environment and were allowed to return home. Every week, there was a hail-and-farewell party to welcome in the fresh blood and send off the old. Iraqis came and went, oftentimes without our knowledge. I shuffled around old *Iraq Daily Updates* and helped the mission director respond to taskers from Washington: "Urgent: the Administrator has a lunch with the Chaldean American Chamber of Commerce tomorrow. Please tell us how many Chaldean Christians have been helped by USAID projects, and describe the projects." We dropped everything to write a response, a sentence of which would be lifted for a speech in front of grazing Chaldean businessmen. The mission director left, and another one came in. Nothing was permanent, just a flurry of booze and paperwork.

I had fun, made a lot of friends and threw a lot of parties. But after six months, a gnawing guilt settled in. Nothing I was doing resulted in anything of value. If I disappeared from the compound, another body would be assigned to my desk and move into my house within two weeks.

General George Casey, commanding general of all forces in Iraq, was coming to the USAID compound for a meeting. For weeks leading up to it, I was in charge of assembling the PowerPoint presentation that our mission director would deliver. In addition to providing an overview of the agency's work in Iraq, the presentation had a not-so-subtle appeal for the general's help with securing new funding for USAID, either from Congress or from the DOD's own massive well of money. We had conference calls with Washington, debated and consulted and conferred on verb choice for a particular slide, and ran mock presentations. I spent bleary hours over many days tweaking the PowerPoint animations of sliding arrows that reflected the potential of "dramatically increased impacts" if further funding was received. I half believed the charts: maybe Sadr City really was just a hundred million dollars' worth of projects away from raising American flags in appreciation.

In a planning meeting, the USAID management began to speak about the need to seek sustained funding for education programs. "You think the kids are bad now, wait and see how the insurgency looks after another decade of sporadic access to schooling!" I diligently took notes but then stared down at what I had written: "In ten years, more kids in insurgency." My face clouded. We were supposed to be the good guys, and here we were casting five-year-olds as future insurgents and terrorists as a way to secure new funds.

A week later, General Casey walked into the newly constructed USAID building's conference room, which doubled as our panic room. (In the event that the compound was overrun by insurgents, all Americans were to run into the conference room, which had a bombproof vault door that could not be opened from the outside. There wasn't enough room for all of the Iraqi employees.) He was surprisingly short and traveled without a retinue; just a young soldier who sat next to him. He opened up a small day planner, the kind on sale at Staples, said, "Shoot!" and the mission director began her presentation. As rehearsed, I pressed the space bar to advance the slides and their animations. He scribbled a couple notes into his planner.

"This is great stuff, guys. Really impressive." After the bromides, he volunteered an explanation of how he thought the situation in Iraq would play out. He drew a couple lines on a dry-erase board, reflecting troop levels and violence. He shook our hands and then left, and that was the last anyone in USAID heard from George Casey or his pot of money.

I had lost forty pounds within a few months of arriving, heading to the small gym in the compound most nights to try to burn off some of the stress, but it was no use. I wanted to leave.

"I'm having a bit of an existential crisis."

I was sitting in the living room of the mission director's home late one evening after the presentation to General Casey. I had sent an urgent note asking for a meeting.

"Oh yeah? What's going on, Kirk?"

"Well, I'm not doing what I came here to do. I don't want to be in the Green Zone anymore."

I paused, and then said the line I had practiced on the way over: "I need to be out in the field, in one of the provinces, or else I'm going to head back to the States."

She nodded and scoured my face for a few seconds before responding.

"Uh-huh. How'd you like to go to Fallujah?"

I blurted out, "Yeah, that sounds perfect," without thinking or hesitating. She poured two glasses of wine. "Well, I don't want an answer yet. This is a decision you need to sleep on. Tell me tomorrow." We clinked our glasses.

6.

Fallujah

There is a Viking saga about a wise lawyer named Njáll Thorgeirs-son, who lives in the hinterlands with his wife, Bergthora. In a story about honor, he is one of Iceland's most honorable, endowed with the gift of *forspar*, which allows him to see into the future. The counsel and predictions given by such men are unbreakable.

Njáll shares with his dear friend Gunnar a forest, from which each periodically logs timber without discord, until one of Njáll's loggers is slain in a dispute with one of Gunnar's men. Life and limbs were valu-ated by the Scandinavians according to the rank and measure of the man, and Njáll's lowly logger is valued at twelve ounces of silver. Gun-nar pays gladly to keep the peace.

But the silver does not quiet the dispute for long. One of Njáll's men, acting without his knowledge, thrusts a vengeful spear into the belly of the man who had slain the logger. Njáll returns the twelve ounces of silver to Gunnar, and the peace is restored for a season. Discord rings once again when the killer of the killer is killed, and the price for peace rises to a hundred ounces of silver.

With obsessively detailed attention to gore—an ax into the collar-bone, a hand cut off midswing, a shield cleaved by a sword—the saga recounts an ever-expanding battle claiming sons, husbands, cousins, tribes, regions. Peace conferences stall the war for short periods, but the conflict grows with a logic and will of its own. At the peak of the blood-shed, the war spills across Scandinavia and into mainland Europe, but nobody remembers why they're fighting, other than to avenge the most recent offense. In the end, an army of men lay siege to Njáll's home and deal him the fate most horrid to the Vikings, setting fire to his walls and doors and burning him alive.

"The Saga of Njáll Burned Alive" ends with a dark portent, in which the promise of peace has been obliterated by endless war. In the village of Caithness, a man named Daurrud comes upon a cottage late at night. He dismounts from his horse and peers through the slit of a window to find wraithlike women at work on a demonic loom: men's heads used in place of weights, intestines as the weft and warp, a sword as the shuttle. They sing a song as they weave the fate of man:

> See! Warp is stretched
> For warriors' fall,
> Lo! The weft in loom
> Is wet with blood;
> Now fight foreboding
> Our grey cloth waxeth
> With war's alarms,
> Our warp bloodred
> The cloth is woven
> With entrails of men
> The warp is hardweighted
> With heads of the slain
> Spears blood-besprinkled
> For spindles we use
> With swords for our shuttles
> This war-cloth we work;
> So weave we, Valkyries,
> Our warwinning cloth

نكسـب الشـباب لنضـمن المسـتقبل

Capture the kids, and we capture the future

—Saddam Hussein, 1977

In the heart of Fallujah lies an amusement park. The paint on the rides in Jolan Park is faded and chipped away. There is an aquatic-themed whirly-go-round. A ten-foot-tall octopus the color of moldering lime looms at the hub of the ride, extending his swirling tentacles outward over the small cars, which are made to look like severed heads of fish. They scowl as they bake under the Fallujah sun. A motorless Ferris wheel slumbers nearby, a monument now, its bucket seats piling up with years of dust.

Before the marines came, the insurgent leader Abu Musab al-Zarqawi held sway over Fallujah, and his fighters reportedly repurposed a cluster of maintenance shacks within the park into torture cells. A grove of trees once shaded the rides, but Fallujans cut them down for firewood while the marines laid siege. Splintered foot-tall stumps remain, dusted pikes stabbing up through dead soil.

The fighting was fierce in the amusement park when the marines carved their way through. The dead were held in the potato storage facility on the eastern outskirts of town. During the siege, the Fallujans ploughed the children's soccer field into a burial site. When that filled up, they decided to convert the amusement park into a cemetery.

We have to win this war in Fallujah

One neighborhood at a time.

We're going to do it on our terms,

On our timeline, and it will be overwhelming.

—Brigadier General Mark Kimmitt

In Fallujah, we fought upon the war's most miserable plateau, on terrain shaped not by the metrics of insurgents killed or jobs created or schools built but by the raw and rootlike emotions of our primitive selves. In these nine square miles just west of Abu Ghraib, we fought for *honor*, against *terror*, and for the *upper hand*. We would do anything necessary to lug our matériel and forces and barbed wire, no matter the cost in treasure or youth. Amid a berserker fever of absurdity shimmered an omen: if Fallujah—this city the size of a middling American suburb, which a few months prior was completely unknown to every American citizen—was allowed to remain "in insurgent hands," then the entire war would be lost. It was a city to be lashed and crushed and retina-scanned into obedience, and in the heights of Fallujah, America fought a savage fight.

The true benefit of the high ground is often misunderstood: its value is not moral superiority but rather the strategic advantage it confers for attacking those beneath you. And determining who had the high ground in Fallujah depended mostly upon where in the whole gory timeline you started. If you started with the assassination and burning of four Blackwater mercenaries on March 31, 2004, you might feel that the reeking maw of evil had just opened wide, and no amount of artillery was too much to pound it shut. If you began your timeline on April 28, 2003, when nervous soldiers fired upon a throng of civilians protesting the military's occupation of a school, you might feel that the Americans were up to no good in Fallujah and needed to be kept out. If you started with the angered confusion of an eighteen-year-old from Ohio wounded by an IED, you might feel resentment at such a reception from people you thought you'd just liberated. If you squinted all the way back to the day the first of an endless convoy of American trucks appeared, straining under the weight of sixteen-foot slabs of concrete, which were unloaded not far from your front door to direct your movement as though you were Iraqi water in American pipes, you might wonder with a little bit of anger about the true intentions of your liberators. But before all that was Saddam and the deceptive worry of a mushroom cloud. And before that, 9/11. And before that, sanctions. And the Gulf War before. And before that, the Iran-Iraq War. But who can remember that far back?

Of Course We Have a Strategy

My arrival coincided with a shift in war strategies. At first the strategy was to topple Saddam and find the WMDs. When we didn't find any weapons, the new strategy was to install some Iraqi exiles as leaders, rush the public to the polls for a quick election, and then celebrate as democracy and a free market bubbled forth. When that failed, in part by inadvertently forcing Iraqis to organize into sectarian voting blocs, the new strategy was to rebuild the infrastructure and institutions necessary for democracy and economic growth. When that failed due to corruption and an expanding insurgency, the new strategy was to build Iraq's security forces so that "when they stand up, we can stand down," so we dumped billions to quickly train and arm men against the militants. When that failed, in part as a result of those very militants infiltrating the hastily assembled security forces, the new strategy was called the "ink-spot" approach: rather than confront the problems on a national level, build teams of experts to "clear, hold, and build" areas on the local level. Clear, hold, and build enough of them, and the ink spots of security will grow in diameter, and one day the country will be covered in ink. I imagine it made for pretty PowerPoints in the Pentagon. My job was to help with the "build" portion of the Fallujah ink spot.

I was also sent to Fallujah to confront the pervasive opinion back in Washington that an unacceptably large gap had opened between the civilian and military efforts in Iraq. This gap was unacceptable for different reasons, which depended upon where you worked: those in uniform felt that the State Department and other agencies weren't really in the fight but, rather, partying in the Green Zone. Those in State and USAID understood that the Pentagon was becoming the true driver of US foreign policy and that in Iraq and Afghanistan it played an increasingly dominant role in aid and development work, so it made vital sense to get as close to that source of power and funding as possible. A hand-in-glove relationship was the mantra of 2005. My presence as the agency's first representative in Fallujah allowed USAID to claim that it was in the fight. "We have a man in Fallujah, after all."

It was still warm at around two in the morning when I left the comfort of the Green Zone. The only activity was an occasional *thump thump* of a medic Blackhawk, swooping to gather the wounded and rush them back to the Combat Support Hospital. I looked around the pleasant home I'd lived in for the first half of the year, to make sure I hadn't left anything behind. All I found was an Iraqi ant, dragging and struggling with a bit of a Doritos chip on the tile floor in the kitchen.

I was supposed to fly to Fallujah the previous evening, but a sandstorm had rolled in and turned the sky deep orange and the air too hot to breathe. The war paused on days like these; the helos couldn't fly, and the insurgents couldn't aim mortars or spot convoys. Everyone just stayed home and watched TV, resting until the sky cleared up enough to kill again.

By the next night, the sky had cleared. Luayy, an Iraqi friend in his midthirties, worked in the motor pool and was still awake when I radioed for a ride. I had a code name, "Viking," that I was supposed to use for security purposes in case an insurgent was listening in on our radio network, but I never understood why "Viking" was any safer than saying "Kirk." Luayy pulled up in the USAID van and helped me load two large bags, and we headed off in the direction of LZ Washington.

"Fallujah, man, you crazy? Why are you goin' there?" His voice carried the concern of an older brother as we turned through the dead streets of the Green Zone. A lo-fi cassette of the Scorpions' greatest hits warbled through the speakers. "You think I shouldn't go?" I murmured.

Not that I would change my mind. In Fallujah, I would live with the Second Marine Expeditionary Force and oversee more than $20 million of aid as a new member of the agency's senior staff. No more *Iraq Daily Update* or Green Zone grunt work: I was finally in a position where I might contribute something tangible. A couple weeks earlier, friends at the compound had thrown a twenty-fifth birthday party for me and joked in toast after toast that it might be my last.

We pulled into the LZ, a vast expanse of concrete the size of a Home Depot parking lot upon which helicopters would wobble and shiver down for a few minutes at a time before creaking upward. Luayy gave me a hug and drove off.

The marines mostly flew at night. I dragged my bags through the noise toward the droid-like crew member who beckoned with a flashing green light. My face felt like it was blowing away, and once I made it under the warmth of the rotor span, the marine grabbed my hand and pointed a flashlight at it. I opened it to show him the *CF*—Camp Fallujah—I had inked with a Sharpie over the creases of my palm, confirming the destination. He pointed the flashlight at the chopper, and another marine plucked my bags from me and threw them into the CH-46 Baby Chinook. Many of these birds did time in Vietnam. I crawled up the ramp in the backside and found a half dozen weary marines, some with downturned sleeping heads, others with chins on the butts of their M16s. I wondered how many of these my dad had flown in, as I settled into the gurney-like seats and fidgeted with the seat belt.

The Chinook lifted off and wind whipped in through its paneless windows. Down below, the Green Zone drifted from sight as we nosed westward over the knotted skein of dimly lit neighborhoods. In a few minutes, Baghdad was behind us and the Euphrates below us, reflecting moonlight like mercury, deserted fields unfurling from its banks. The bright lights of Abu Ghraib looked like a small city below us. Twenty-five minutes later, we touched down at Camp Fallujah.

Removing Rubble

Seven thirty, and already the sun sat up there like a deep bruise, faintly yellow at the core and melting into an ugly blue sky. I'd stupidly left the window open a crack my first night there, and a shadow of dust had crept in, lightly coating my cheek and chin and eyelids. My new home was in the BOQ—bachelor officers' quarters—of a military base once home to the Mujahedeen-e Khalq, a militant Iranian opposition group cultivated by Saddam Hussein against the regime in Tehran. I was assigned to a room with four bunk beds and a couple roommates, a collapsible table, the fetor of unwashed bodies and clothes, and a strip of fly tape. I once saw an Iraqi fly land on it and pry itself loose in about three seconds, unfazed.

I was nervous as I got ready for my first day on the job. The word in my title, regional coordinator for reconstruction in Fallujah, summoning my dread was not *Fallujah* but *coordinator*. I had spent enough time in the US government and drafted enough scraps of public affairs pabulum to know how potentially toothless the verb *to coordinate* could be.

Before my arrival, USAID had programmed roughly $15 million for projects throughout the city, which was still at about half of its prewar population level of a quarter million. I had been armed with an Excel spreadsheet that listed the projects, color-coded by the USAID sector (education, health, infrastructure), along with exact dollar amounts. I studied the language of the list warily. Primary and secondary schools were "rehabilitated," the hospital and local clinics received "supplies," the directorates of municipalities, communications, housing, and other local potentates received "support." Furniture and Equipment for Mayor's Office: $62,135. Fallujah Veterinary Clinic Rehabilitation Phase I: $98,000. Phase II: $70,000.

Since these projects were in the "restive city of Fallujah," as the public affairs professionals were wont to label it, nobody from the agency had ever gone out to check on the work until now. The money was given to a contractor, who took a piece and gave the rest to an Iraqi or Kurdish subcontractor, who maybe used another subcontractor or maybe kept it. The Americans at the agency overseeing all of this were called CTOs—cognizant technical officers—who maintained their cognizance by reading one- or two-page reports periodically emailed into the Green Zone by the contractor, which sometimes included a picture of an Iraqi man holding a cardboard box, supposedly the veterinarian of Fallujah or a doctor at the hospital. Upon receiving the report, the CTO could then modify column N of the Excel sheet to reflect a status of "completed" instead of "in progress." In my previous job, I would have then written up a paragraph for the *Iraq Daily Update* about the completed project and included the picture.

Most of the completed projects were carried out by the agency's Health, Education, and Infrastructure Offices, which had an excruciatingly slow turnaround from conception to implementation. A school refurbishment project could take a year or longer, to the great impatience of both the Iraqis and the US military.

There was a separate office in the agency, though, called the Office of Transition Initiatives, which was fast moving and well funded. OTI could move millions of dollars in weeks, not months or years. Rubble removal was its darling and was categorized as "conflict mitigation." On paper, conflict was mitigated by an assumption-weakened chain of assertions:

1. Iraqis were joining the insurgency because there was no work for them.
2. If they were given the choice between an honest day's work and fighting against the Americans, they'd choose the former.
3. A make-work program to clear rubble, at the pay rate of about $7 a day, would
4. sap the insurgency of its strength,
5. clean up the city (dovetailing nicely with a $110,000 public awareness campaign run by USAID, in which a picture of a sleeping Iraqi baby was plastered on billboards with the caption "My dream is of a clean city"), and
6. stimulate economic growth, all at once.

If we could just get a shovel and a wheelbarrow into their grenade-prone hands, point them to any of the houses that had been reduced to abandoned fields of rubble, and dangle seven American dollars, we might start gaining the upper hand on the insurgency. At the very least, doing so would contribute to a new narrative, one that ran counter to the unpleasant metric of nearly 50 percent unemployment throughout vast swaths of the country. A simple spreadsheet presented month-to-month "progress": forty thousand Iraqis hired in June, fifty-two thousand Iraqis in July. Someone in Washington would read these impressive figures and murmur, "Well, at least USAID's got this covered!" Maybe a congressman would notice and appropriate more funds for USAID to *build on this momentum*! This line of thinking led to many tens of millions of wasted dollars.

After all, in the swamp of unemployment, the insurgency had nurtured an economy of its own. Some estimated that a third of all cargo trucks from Jordan passing into Iraq through Anbar Province were hijacked by insurgents. Oil and gasoline were smuggled, the children of wealthy Iraqis were kidnapped for ransom, and old-fashioned robbery kept their coffers swelling. In my first few days in Fallujah, a marine told me that the going rate for paying kids to plant an IED along the roadside was $50; $100 if he acted as a spotter for incoming American convoys; and $150 if he successfully detonated the IED as they passed. How would our $7 compete with this? I was doubtful, but I resisted forming any opinions until I had seen the projects under way.

I was equally unsettled by the fact that I didn't have discretionary authority. I couldn't write checks on behalf of USAID. If I wanted to fund any new initiative, I would need to win over the backing of my bosses in Baghdad. And most of the remaining millions allocated for Fallujah were already pledged to rubble removal.

In an attempt to orient myself during my first day, I copied out the Excel spreadsheet into a green canvas notebook and studied a satellite map of the city to identify their locations so that I could conduct a small audit of the projects listed as completed.

Convoys

I never knew which half I represented in the hand-in-glove metaphor, but the skepticism of the marines I was now living with was evident as I walked around the base and introduced myself. Of the few that had even heard of USAID, most thought it was an NGO, not a federal agency. All they saw was a kid without a weapon whom they now had to protect, which was not part of their mission. So when a group of marines in the Civil Affairs Group, to which I'd be attached, made plans over lunch to head over to the firing range in Camp Fallujah, I blurted out that I'd like to join them.

At the range, a lance corporal called me over to fire the M240G machine gun, a twenty-five-pound weapon that can be mounted on tanks. I watched two teams fire at a plywood target in a syncopated rhythm, getting the guns to "talk to each other." I got into a prone position, and a marine crawled halfway on top of me and said he was going to aim. I tensed up as the belt of a couple hundred 7.62 mm rounds was fitted into place. "Keep the shots below the berm," someone behind me warned.

I squeezed the trigger, and my brain shut down. I released the trigger. A cloud of dust from behind the plywood was snaking into the air. I pulled the trigger again and let go again, trying to find the target in the sight. A lieutenant colonel shouted, "Kirk, this isn't one of those types of guns! Your A-gunner is your sight. Just get it in the general area, pull the trigger, and hold it down!"

I pulled the trigger and held it. My head was a jarring mess. The marines yelled, "Go, go go!" while the marine on top of me pushed my shoulder to help aim the gun. The flaring red tracer shots struck the plywood, set fire to it, bored through it, and flailed around in the berm. A massive plume of powder rose from behind the target. I released the trigger, and they were clapping, stooping down to pat me on the back. I smiled, and didn't realize until a few moments later that several of the scalding spent shell casings spat from the gun had landed on the exposed skin of my arm and were now melting their way in. I brushed them off with a grimace and could smell burned skin. "Great shooting, sir!" one of them said.

Later that afternoon, in a poorly lit room with satellite maps of every major city and town and base in Anbar Province, I met with Major General Stephen Johnson and told him of my plans to conduct an initial review of the projects USAID had already funded throughout the city. He nodded and said, "Just get yourself over to the CMOC to get started."

Eight weary miles separate Camp Fallujah from the CMOC, the Civil Military Operations Center, in the center of the city. Before my first convoy run, the captain gathered everyone around to assign the PAX, passengers, to their vehicles. He extracted a laminated map from a pocket, handing a corner to a nearby marine to display a satellite image of the city. Running the group through the route, he outlined alternate routes and rally points in case of attack. Rules of engagement: hand motions, rocks, or water bottles (thrown in the direction of the approaching vehicle as a startling measure), a round in the ground, one in the grill, one in the hood, then shoot to eliminate. Any of these steps may be bypassed depending on the distance and speed of the approaching threat. He turned to me, the only civilian in the group, and asked, "Who are you, and why don't you have a med pack?"

I nervously blurted out my name and USAID.

"Okay, I don't know what that is, but whatever. Who has an extra med pack for Mr. Johnson?"

Someone lobbed over a small canvas sack that contained gauze and some packets of powder, which I assumed were for sterilizing an open wound. I climbed into the back of a "tub," a Humvee with a pickup truck bed framed with armor plating. Beneath our feet ran a patchwork of heavy green fabric—essentially a blanket of flak jackets woven together to stop IED shrapnel from blasting up through the bottom of the bed.

As we approached the border of the camp, the convoy paused, and the cold sound of M16 clips snapping into place filled the air. I tugged at the straps of my helmet in futility. In the previous few days, two Iraqi boys had thrown grenades at marine convoys. One managed to get a "ringer," as the captain put it: when it landed in the tub, its blast took with it several fingers and limbs and incinerated necks and palms.

"Johnson, you're the swatter," grunted a marine across from me, as the convoy lurched toward the city.

"What's that?" I asked.

"It's simple. You see a grenade comin', swat it back."

I sat silent for a moment. He grinned a little. A lieutenant colonel chimed in, and said, "Look, if you miss it, just throw yourself over it to save us, okay?" At this, the other marines in the back of the tub burst out laughing. I smiled a bit and looked back at the first marine, whose grin had disappeared back into a blank face. "Seriously, though, if you see one, swat it back."

I stared at my hands as the convoy emerged from the floury desert road and onto the hardball asphalt heading westward into Fallujah. As we passed below a pedestrian walkway, each Humvee in the convoy swerved violently, an evasive tactic to avoid any grenades dropped from above, jostling me against the marines on either side of me, who raised their rifles over the edge of the tub like the legs of a spider crawling from a drain.

In such moments, every Iraqi looks like a killer. We move at thirty miles per hour—any faster, and you wouldn't be able to spot an IED or VBIED—over roads that have been renamed by the Americans. Route Michigan. Mobile. Huskie. Irish. Fran. Denver. The Arabic names were too difficult for them. Along with the marines, my eyes dart around in search of unusual piles of trash along the road that might conceal a bomb; bits of wire running up tree trunks that might lead to a bomb; unusual amounts of layers of clothing that might conceal a vest bomb; the direction of a car's tires, which might suggest whether it's about to accelerate a bomb into you. I glare at three Iraqi children, no more than eight years old, who stand alongside the road as we pass. One of them wears flip-flops and kneads a soccer ball back and forth under his foot.

The years of my life spent studying the language and living throughout the region drained swiftly from the tub that day. It meant nothing that I spoke Arabic or understood their history and religion. The only thing that mattered was that these kids stayed away from my vehicle and that they not make any quick movements when I passed by. They needed to freeze.

We snaked our way through the chicanes at the entrance of the CMOC, and I jumped from the Humvee with a heavy thud, armor tugging at my shoulders.

Solatia at the CMOC

The citizens of Fallujah lined up outside the CMOC, the nexus of interaction with the Americans. It was previously a youth center where kids came for after-school sports, clubs, and tutoring. In the area where the marines guarding the center slept at night hung a funk of sweat and fatigue made worse by the fact that the windows were sealed shut. In a small courtyard in the middle of the CMOC loomed an elevated boxing ring, three ropes and all, with punishing wooden floorboards.

At the heart of the CMOC reigned a large theater with a stage that looked as though it was set for a performance of *Stalag 17*. Ten-foot-tall stacks of sandbags were piled in front of every window, all of which were lined with strips of duct tape, meant to minimize the shattering effect if a mortar hit. In the center of the stage was a large easel that displayed a four-by-four-foot satellite image of the city. Down in the auditorium section, a T-shaped array of collapsible tables and flimsy white stacking chairs hosted the daily proceedings between the Fallujah city council leaders and the marines. Very frequently, the two groups climbed up to the stage to point at a particular intersection on the map, arguing over a checkpoint here or there. Another easel nearby was papered with American-made posters touting the "heroes of Fallujah": the nascent Fallujah police force. They looked the same as the insurgent posters that had plastered the city between April and November the previous year, using the same language of *heroes, martyrs, defenders, lions of Fallujah, sons of Fallujah.*

As winter approached and I settled into my job, I came into town for regular meetings at the CMOC. A week before Thanksgiving, I sat with a young marine by the boxing ring, smoking a cigarette and watching a gaunt turkey that had been picked up in some village outside of town. It strutted around the ring, pecking its beak inquisitively at cigarette butts and bits of trash left over from MRE packs. The marines assigned to the CMOC were planning to cook it for the holiday.

The city was on edge: a schoolboy had been killed the day before. An Iraqi sniper fired an errant round at a marine foot patrol, striking the boy instead. The Fallujans believed the marines had killed the child, and they were now keeping their children at home and out of school for fear of losing another.

"They're accusing us? They probably already know who it was!" The young marine flicked his cigarette toward an ammunition case that someone had repurposed into an ashtray, which overflowed with hundreds upon hundreds of butts. It smoldered for a half minute before burning out. The turkey strolled by in another lap around the courtyard.

The marine had a rucksack by his feet, and after looking around, he gestured at me to take a look inside. With a boyish excitement, he flashed open its contents: large shrink-wrapped bricks of $100 bills. A couple hundred thousand dollars' worth, I guessed. "What's that for?" I asked.

"Fuckin' condolence payments."

The institution of solatia and condolence payments had become systematized by the war's second year: once a month, the Fallujans stood in line with their grievances. Someone's husband was killed. Someone's arm was shot off. Someone's car had been shot up. Someone's door had been kicked down in a night raid.

The rates were fixed:

- $2,500 for a dead Iraqi,
- $1,500 for a serious injury ("resulting in permanent disability or significant disfigurement"), and
- $200 for a minor injury.

Lieutenant General Peter Chiarelli explained to National Public Radio that the practice "is common in this part of the world—it means a death payment; a death gratuity, so to speak—it is part of life over here." A Government Accountability Office briefing to Congress on the practice offered a helpful explanatory scenario on slide 16: "Two members of the same family are killed in a car hit by US forces. The family could receive a maximum of $7,500 in . . . condolence payments ($2,500 for each death and up to $2,500 for vehicle damage)."

Not all life is valued equally by our bureaucracies: a dead Afghan ran only $2,336. A permanently disabled or disfigured Afghan cost only $467.

"Shit, I heard that the sniper team is a pair of fuckin' kids, a twelve-year-old and his little bro!" The marine stood up and parted with his bag of money.

The sniper became an obsession for many of us. In November and well into December, at least a dozen marines were killed. The rumor about the young brothers swirled with other theories, including one in which an elite Chechen sniper had traveled all the way to Fallujah to kill Americans.

One night I hopped onto a midnight convoy running from Camp Fallujah to the CMOC and found myself sitting next to a mannequin. Several more were piled in the Humvee's trunk, to be used by counter-sniper teams that were struggling to get a lock on the sniper's location. The mannequins were positioned on various rooftops throughout the city and propped up with the hope of drawing fire and smoking out the sniper.

I thought back to journalist Nir Rosen's reporting for the *Asia Times* during the interlude in fighting between May and November 2004, when the town was overrun by insurgents. A day after the marines pulled back in their first failed onslaught, the city held a poetry festival in which the "heroes of the resistance" sat onstage. One of them, a twelve-year-old named Saud, had apparently sniped several marines. Mohammed Khalil Kawkaz recited a poem condemning anyone from the city who had stepped forward to work with the Americans, called "The Fallujah Tragedy":

Fallujah is a tall date palm
She never accepts anybody touching her dates
She will shoot arrows into the eyes of those who try to taste her
This is Fallujah, your bride, O Euphrates!
She will never fall in love with anyone but you
America dug in the ground and pulled
Out the roots of the date palm
The earth hugs the destroyed houses
The women burned and the children suffered
Calling to the governing council
You are deaf and dumb, O governing council!
You found honor in meeting him who pillaged Fallujah.
O Euphrates, what happened to you, that you just lay down?
Get up and fight with your waves and swallow this country and the others,
Stand with Fallujah.

Since the poetry festival, we had razed large sections of the city. But maybe Saud the sniper boy was still in action. Because the sniper had once shot at marines in the expansive gravel field surrounding the CMOC, which was supposedly secure, we were instructed not to linger outside. The only time I ventured across the gravel was en route to the cluster of port-o-johns. In the first days and nights, I armored up, but I soon grew impatient and one day burst from the CMOC doors, running in a zigzag line as I juked my way to the bathroom. Its thin plastic doors offered about as much protection from a sniper round as a stick of butter. Once inside, I rocked back and forth, occasionally leaning forward with the absurd hope that this constant movement would reduce the odds of a sniper hitting me. I started wearing armor again and came to despise port-o-johns.

The Transliteration of Arabic

The Fallujans did not line up only for condolence payments. Many came to the CMOC with the names of their husbands or sons or fathers who had been detained as part of the counterinsurgency efforts. Getting PUC'd up, the marines called it: "person under control." It was once standard operating procedure to arrest as many people as possible in the vicinity of an IED blast, with the hopes that the triggerman might be found among them.

Once detained, their eyeballs would be scanned and their names would be entered into BATS, the Biometrics Automated Toolset System, which was implemented in force in the city. One of my roommates back at Camp Fallujah was a defense contractor and lead support technician for the system. John had a pear-shaped belly and long, wiry hair that fell in a bowl-cut over his Coke-bottle glasses. He wore geek T-shirts: "There are 10 types of people in the world: those who understand binary and those who *don't*." Sometimes he peeled his T-shirt up toward his face and blew his nose into it. Sometimes he fell asleep in his bunk with his hand actually *inside* a bag of Nacho Cheesier Doritos, while a samurai movie played on his laptop. His salary likely topped $200,000.

BATS took retina scans and fingerprints of Iraqis and paired the biometrics with names, photographs, address, weight, height, and any additional information (whether or not said Iraqi was in "capture" or "kill" status). This information was then uploaded onto Toughbook laptops for marines in the field and also sent back to the Biometrics Fusion Center in West Virginia, a newly sprouted sapling in the post-9/11 forest of Defense Department agencies and programs.

The BATS system was a significant development. During the first phase of the war, the military relied on scattershot lists and databases, which were never centralized or complete. But what still bedeviled Americans, BATS or not, was the naming conventions used in the Arab world. Arabs don't have middle names: they have a chain of names with patronymics that reflect the person's heritage. US ignorance over this seemingly innocuous cultural distinction had Orwellian consequences.

Take, for example, the following name: محمد حميد الدليمي

Since Arabic is generally written without vowels, the presence of which are intuited both by grammatical rules as well as prolonged exposure to the language, there is no agreed-upon standard for transliterating Arabic into English. So the name could be written "Muhammad Hameed Al-Dulaimi." Or it could just as properly be transliterated as "Mohamed Hamid Aldulaymy."

The iterations and potential combinations are endless. Mohammad. Mohamad. Muhammad. Muhamad. Mohammed. Mohamed. Muhammed. Muhamed. Hamid. Hameed. Al-Dulaimy. Al-Dulaimi. Al-Dulaymy. Al-Dulaymi.

The Hans Wehr Dictionary of Modern Written Arabic, the bible for all students of Arabic, is based on the transliteration standards of the 1936 *Deutsche Morgenländische Gesellschaft*, adopted by the International Convention of Orientalist Scholars in Rome. There are handfuls of competing systems, however, with computerish names such as SATTS, DIN-31635, and ISO/R 233.

Arcane as it is, the consequences of our ignorance of Arabic emerged as soon as we started arresting Iraqis and filling up prisons. Each arrest led to paperwork, which required transliteration. So eighteen-year-old soldiers and marines detailed to detainee intake, with no knowledge of the language, devised transliteration systems of their own.

As a result, محمد حميد الدليمي, picked up thirty feet from an IED on Route Fran in Fallujah, tells his name to a marine, who types "Mohammed Hameed," as a first and last name, leaving out the reference to his membership in the Dulaim tribe of Anbar. The marine next to him might have spelled the name entirely differently. Five months pass, and none of his family members has heard from him. Maybe Mohammed was found guilty, maybe he was being detained until more information could be located, or maybe he was innocent. Unless someone guessed the exact English spelling generated by the eighteen-year-old marine at the time of arrest, Mohammed Hameed Al-Dulaimi was lost in the system, another casualty of the war that Arabic and English waged upon each other.

Not a week passed in Fallujah where I did not witness women asking the whereabouts of family members. I once asked a woman to just tell me the name of a missing relative, and spent about ten minutes transliterating every different combination—over twenty in total. I handed it to a marine. He looked down at it, and, eyebrows raised, put it in his chest pocket and gave me a "Don't expect much" glance.

Down the hallway, the marines hung the quote from T. E. Lawrence's

Seven Pillars of Wisdom that proliferated on the walls of American power: "Better to let the Arabs do it imperfectly than to do it perfectly yourself."

Clearing the Canals

"The most important thing you can do is just be here. Don't disappear on us." A lieutenant colonel in the Civil Affairs Group spoke quietly and locked eyes with me as we talked late into my first evening at the CMOC. The marines were tired of civilians dropping by Fallujah for a day and then leaving. A lot of them were coming just to say they had been there and to buy the Camp Fallujah T-shirt from the PX before they left. That would have been enough of a nuisance, but members of Congress and embassy officials had a tendency to meet with Fallujah city leaders at the CMOC, make lofty promises, and then disappear. The marines were stuck there, left to tamp down the volatile expectations of the Fallujans.

I tried to reassure him. "No, I'm here, at least until mid-06, and then we'll see where we're at." It had taken about eight months to get out of the Green Zone to a place where I might finally do something useful. I knew that I would be only mildly relevant for the first couple months in Fallujah: the city leaders and marines needed to trust that I was there for the foreseeable future, and I needed to know how much I could expect from my own bosses in Baghdad.

For weeks after I arrived, I rode around Fallujah referencing my small map of rubble removal projects. I saw zero evidence that a single stone had been lifted, despite what I had been reading in progress reports and in the *Iraq Daily Update*, now written by the perky young public affairs officer who had replaced me. The marines who drove around on patrol each day hadn't seen any signs of a program. The questions screamed in my brain. *Where is the rubble being moved to? Who wrote these contracts? Why isn't there even a simple mechanism to gauge results? How do we verify that the theoretical Iraqis hauling the rubble are even from Fallujah and not being trucked in from other provinces and creating more strife?*

Even if the contractor or subcontractor had been out there to enforce the rubble removal, it was easy to imagine gaming the system. Why not just move the rubble to a vacant lot down the street and charge USAID another quarter million to move it again in a month?

When I was introduced to an Iraqi engineer with unparalleled knowledge of the city's infrastructure (who called me *il Masry*—"the Egyptian"—on account of my dialect), I asked him about the rubble removal teams. He laughed and said, "What are you talking about? What teams?"

I wanted to end the program, to stop wasting the money. This would require crying foul, informing the USAID cognizant technical officers and management back in the Green Zone that their projects, which earned them a lot of favor with the Pentagon and were part of the whole hand-in-glove craze, were bullshit. And if a project didn't exist, it meant that auditors in the Inspector General's Office might catch on and start poking around in other parts of their work.

There was waste or fraud in nearly every project I looked at. For instance, $62,000 worth of furniture for the mayor's office ended up in the marines' rec room of the CMOC. A radio tower that had been sent to Camp Fallujah for delivery to the city, as part of an initiative to empower a new Iraqi media, never left the base.

Hoping to get a handle on what the city actually needed, I peppered the leaders of the Fallujah city council with questions. I didn't know if any other Fallujans knew who they were, but they were known by us, and were the only men who came into the CMOC to talk. I wanted to be helpful but did not make any promises.

Just off Route Henry, the veterinarian of Fallujah was waiting for me with a proposal for where I might direct some aid money. A tall, hefty man of sixty, Dr. Nazar had a darkly creased face and gold-rimmed glasses that he pulled from a breast pocket before running through a list of supplies and equipment. He had prepared the list with the hope that I might direct USAID funding his way. He needed incubators, vaccines to combat diseases such as brucellosis, refrigerators for the vaccines, generators for the incubators and refrigerators, fuel for the generators. Syringes, gauze, everything. It sounded reasonable enough.

I wasn't sure what information I'd need from the veterinarian, so I wrote down everything I could learn. How many head of cattle are there in Fallujah and the outlying villages? How many animals did he treat a week? What diseases were the most prevalent at the moment? What were the farmers doing without these vaccines? How many chickens are there in the city?

I wedged his list into my notebook and heaved my armored body back into the tub of the Humvee.

"Mr. Krik?" Dr. Nazar called out to me.

One of the marines gave a glance to signal that we needed to move on, so I answered the veterinarian brusquely. We never spent more than a few minutes in each place.

"Yes, Doctor, what? We are in a rush."

"Fallujah needs a working slaughterhouse again!" he exclaimed. Just a couple blocks away, the marines were occupying the old slaughterhouse, which the veterinarian wanted to reopen. He needed a generator to keep it cool. He pointed to the ground at a startling rivulet of dark blood running along the curb, which was stained brown. The stream issued from the gullets of sheep and other small livestock being slaughtered twenty feet up the street. The flow stretched another fifteen feet down before it disappeared into a small heap of rubble and garbage.

"It's not good; it's not safe to handle meat this way," Dr. Nazar pleaded.

The butchers stared at us, blade in one hand, the nape of wide-eyed livestock in another.

"Okay, we need to clear out," a marine grunted, to my relief.

That night, I spent hours deciphering and translating my observations (I never studied the Arabic words for *brucellosis* or *hypodermic* or *hoof*) into a report with a recommendation for my bosses in Baghdad.

But my enthusiasm for helping out the veterinarian stalled when I searched through the database of "completed" projects and discovered that $98,000 in supplies had already been delivered to the city's veterinary clinic. The happy veterinarian had then wheeled them down the street to his private clinic, where he charged much higher rates. I wasn't going to win any battle in redirecting aid from the rubble removal program if my opening gambit was to buy more supplies for a corrupt veterinarian.

It was customary for Americans working in Iraq to react to all of this with a world-weary shrug and shoulder-patting bromides. "Welcome to Iraq." "Hearts and minds, man, hearts and minds." "Welcome to the world of international development." "Just another day in Iraq." "Welcome to USAID, buddy."

But the sheer waste of the chimerical campaign to remove rubble became such a splinter in my mind that I made it the central focus of my first steps in Fallujah. I would absorb whatever wrath came my way from the functionaries in the Green Zone.

Before I could kill the program, I needed to have a replacement project ready. I didn't have to search very long: everyone knew that Fallujah's irrigation canals were choked. These waterways had once irrigated the Euphrates's fields. The canals need clearing every year, or else the water flow diminishes, the soil becomes hypersalinated, and crops can't thrive. I began to meet with sheikhs and city leaders to plan an ambitious new USAID initiative to hire thousands of Fallujans to hack out and hoist the years of weeds and reeds and trash that had clotted the canals since the beginning of the war.

I didn't think that the canal clearing project would turn the city around, but it stood to make a much larger impact than a nonexistent program. I threw every idea I could at the initiative, wishing to be embarrassed at the outset by suggesting potentially stupid ideas rather than waste millions on another failure and blow my chances at future projects. I studied maps of the irrigation infrastructure with agricultural engineers from the area and tried to spread the project equitably across tribal lines. I asked the marines if they could task an observer drone to survey the state of the canals, since Google Earth satellite images were outdated.

A Quick Vacation in the Caribbean

By late December, I had succeeded in winning over the mission director's initial approval for a shift in strategy away from rubble removal and into canal clearing. I had staked whatever credibility I had on the proposal and was excited to think that, after a year of frustration, I might start to fulfill some of the goals that had brought me to Iraq in the first place. No more taskers from Washington, no more public affairs spit-shining of crumbling projects. I had buy-in from key members of the city council, support from the marines, and the money to make something tangible happen.

A Christmas stocking from my mom arrived a week before the holiday. "We hope you'll be able to take your R&R and join us!" The card was signed by my parents; my mom had sweetly forged my brothers' signatures. There was a large family reunion coming up in the Dominican Republic, where my uncle and aunt run an orphanage, and I was the only one who hadn't RSVP'd. I hung the stocking next to my bed on a plastic adhesive hook I'd bought from the PX.

Someone whose face I never saw had moved in and laid claim to the bunk above mine, and the mattress sagged like the hull of a submerged boat just a foot above my head. He annexed a corner of the desk next to the bed for his collection of *Maxim* magazines. Every night, a hirsute forearm would drop down like the claw game at an arcade to retrieve a ruffled issue, and the weary springs of the bunk would squeak for a couple minutes.

I was overdue for a vacation but wrestled with the idea of leaving. My push to kill the rubble program had angered the officers in charge of it, and I worried that the momentum I had mustered for clearing the canals could be quickly scuttled by its detractors. I was also mindful of burnout and knew that I still had at least another six months on my contract, which I had already resolved to extend.

But when I received an invitation to brief the incoming First Marine Expeditionary Force on USAID's work in Anbar Province at Camp Pendleton in California at the beginning of January 2006, I decided to combine it with the family vacation. I packed light, logged out of my computer at my office in the civil affairs building, and left a small stack of my green notebooks into which I had scrawled months of thoughts and notes.

As a civilian, I could never guarantee a spot on a helo, since I flew space-A (as in "if space is available"). I pulled out two refrigerated bottles of Starbucks mocha Frappuccinos that I had snatched up in the PX, slid them into my backpack, and began the couple-mile hike at midnight through the labyrinth of Camp Fallujah's cafeterias, laundry hooches, PX, gyms, officers' quarters, intelligence buildings, and Humvee repair garages en route to the landing zone. When I stepped into the plywood hut that served as the LZ office, I told the lance corporal behind the desk that I was flying space-A to Baghdad and smiled as I handed him and his buddy the Frappuccinos. His tired eyes lit up as he said, "Okay, sir, we'll make sure you get on."

At about one o'clock in the morning, the helos arrived, and I jammed in some earplugs as I sprinted over to the marine waving a green glow stick. The next morning, Christmas Day, I finagled a ride from Camp Victory to the civilian terminal. The USAID charter flight was canceled due to a dust storm, but Iraqi Airways was still flying, so I pulled out a few hundred dollars and bought one of the last remaining tickets to Amman.

I sat in the terminal next to Iraqis biding their time before flights, and realized that after a year in Iraq, it was the first time I had been without body armor or mercenaries or marines nearby. The coil of stress that had been tightening with each convoy run, each missed mortar, tensed just a little. Suddenly my chest cavity seemed naked.

The dividing lines between us and them, white and brown, exposed and hidden guns, air-conditioning and sweltering heat, clean and dirty water, our knowledge that we'd be here only for a while longer but that they were stuck, began to vibrate and jostle in my mind. I didn't drink water from the fountain because I knew how badly we had failed to provide clean water. I couldn't find any relief in air-conditioning because the airport power was strong enough only to run a rickety oscillating fan that surely must have been pushing air around since the sixties.

I looked around at toddlers and smiled at them but encountered little warmth from my fellow travelers. My head hurt, so I shut my eyes for a moment, before thinking better of it. I opened them again and thought, *Just wait a little longer, and you can relax in the Dominican Republic.*

7.

Fugue State

Sweetie, you've lost so much weight!" My mom cried as she hugged me, and everyone gathered close with shocked airport eyes. After over two days of travel—from Camp Fallujah to Camp Victory by the Baghdad Airport; to Amman; to Madrid; to San Juan, Puerto Rico; to Puerto Plata on the northern coast of the Dominican Republic—I was exhausted, but I stayed up late into the first night, talking with my brothers and cousins and aunts and uncles who were filtering in for the reunion. When I finally made it to bed, I stared at the ceiling fan and waited for sleep.

At three in the morning, I got out of bed and walked past the window of my hotel room. Outside, across a small, rocky field of dirt, loomed a dust-colored apartment complex. It was unfinished, with dark openings where the windows should be. My eyes darted down at my body. No armor. "Shit!" I yelled, and dropped quickly to my knees. I peered out the window from just above the sill and wondered how I could be so stupid as to walk past a window without my gear when the sniper of Fallujah was still at large.

I then realized where I was—in the Caribbean—and a shroud of embarrassment dropped over me in the quiet of the room. Had my cry woken up my family? I never swore around them. Nobody seemed to be moving around in the other rooms.

I crawled warily back into bed, and embarrassment gave way to confusion. "What the hell was that?" I muttered to myself, as a great dissonance clanged through my mind. I didn't remember getting out of bed. I had never before been mistaken as to what country I was in.

I woke up a few hours later. Nobody was awake, so I threw on some sneakers and set out for a jog along the beach. I was alone and ran for miles along the coastline. I tried to ignore it, but what had happened the previous night was too strange to repress, and I ran faster and faster until my energy was spent. The shifting sand made my calves ache.

After breakfast, we all went down to the water. I held my baby nephew and ate Goldfish with my niece. Dad emerged from the resort with a football, and my brothers and I raced down to the surf to toss it around with him. I lunged for an overthrown pass, and as I caught it, I felt the ring on my right hand slide off into the ocean.

"*No!*" I yelled.

It had been my grandfather's wedding ring, an heirloom of nearly a hundred years, now lost in the ocean. My brothers waded over, and we peered into the water but could see nothing. The grief was mounting when the undertow lodged something in between my toes. My eyes bulged as I carefully reached down and retrieved the ring. My dad shot me a look of relief, and we stopped throwing around the football. A bright red helicopter heavy with tourists droned overhead. That night, all the branches of the family gathered for lobster.

Before I got into bed, I folded my jeans and placed my watch on the nightstand. Its date read 12 29 05.

Just after four thirty in the morning, Primitivo, a bald and spindly Haitian working the night shift, started his rounds. When he walked past my window, I yelled something and startled him. He didn't understand what I said, but he looked up and found me perched on the ledge of the window. He pointed a flashlight up at me and shouted, "*¡Peligroso!*" I shouted back in a language he didn't know. He began to run around to the front of the building to ring the bell and wake my family, and heard the sound of my fall. I don't know what it sounded like, my body falling to the concrete; I was still asleep.

He ran back and found me kneeling in a pool of my blood. He tried to help me up, but I swung at him and wouldn't let him near. I stumbled to the back door of the condo, but there were iron gates over it and I couldn't get inside. I raised my hand to the window and began tapping my grandfather's ring against it.

A light came on, and the curtain on the other side of the window rose. My dad stared into my face, splayed and pulping blood, and thought I had just been shot. *My son!* He saw Primitivo behind me and roared a primal paternal warning to "get back; get away from my son!" Primitivo spoke no English, but he retreated. My dad raced around the house, which was now waking up from the sound of the commotion. He gathered me, throwing an arm under my shoulders to help me into the kitchen of the condo. Still I was asleep.

My memory began fifteen minutes after I fell headfirst seventeen feet from my window to concrete. Faintly, I began to make out the contours of the room around me, which got brighter and brighter as my eyes adjusted. My dad, my brother Derek, and his wife, Carolyn, were in a panicked half circle around me. Their words sounded like they were underwater. I looked down. I was sitting in a chair and wearing only my boxers, which had been gray the previous night but were now red. As I stared down at them in confusion, I saw a stream of something spigoting from my forehead and splashing in a crimson puddle on my lap.

"What happened?! Kirk, what happened?! Can you hear me? Kirk!" I didn't know.

"I don't know. What happened—" A pain, indescribably fierce, exploded in my mouth as I tried to answer. I shot them a scared look and tumbled into a well of agony. A ravine of flesh ran between my eyebrows. Blood flowed bitter from the nostrils of my broken nose past the shredded remnants of my upper lip and onto my front teeth, which were dislodged from my broken jaw. My chin flapped below it all.

Carolyn sprinted to the telephone and made frantic phone calls in search of directions to the nearest hospital, which was over an hour away. Dad ran to get the keys to my uncle's pickup truck, and Derek, who had once taken a course in emergency medical technician training, stayed with me. Primitivo stood off to the side and spoke with Derek and Carolyn in Spanish. "*¡Se cayó!*" he kept repeating. "He fell!"

I was eased into the shotgun seat of the truck. My brother gave me a towel and told me to press it against my face to keep pressure on the tears. We tore westward from the small resort town of Caberete, in search of the Centro Medico Bournigal in Puerto Plata.

"My teeth are gone," I groaned.

"No, they're not," Derek said firmly. "Keep pushing on that towel."

"Yes they are." My tongue probed the area but retreated after a fresh peal of pain.

It was dark still, and there was little moonlight. The headlights were weak, and I stared through the windshield at the curving road. We came up to a steel bridge painted forest green, identical in construction and color to the green iron Blackwater bridge, where the burned corpses of the mercenaries had been strung up. Fallujah General Hospital was on the other side of that bridge, so I turned in horrified confusion. Everyone was still there. My eyes stung from the blood if I kept them open for too long.

"Awww, Kirk! Buddy, your wrists!" Derek cried out. "Look at them!"

Both wrists were broken. The pain ravaging my face was so overpowering that I hadn't even felt them, and it explained the difficulty I was having with tugging the towel against my face. My hands twisted out in odd, acute angles.

The truck accelerated. After an hour, we were in Puerto Plata, but lost. They had brought Primitivo along to help with directions, but he had never left Caberete and was useless. My brother sprinted over to a firehouse, where some firefighters were dozing, and asked for directions. One of them hopped on a small scooter and led us the final few blocks to the hospital.

It took about an hour and a half before my face was stitched back together. They wheeled me over to a room with an X-ray machine, which was the most high-tech equipment in the hospital, hoisted me onto the table, and left to deal with another emergency. Derek came in and sat next to me while we waited. I looked up and caught a reflection of my face in the polished glass of the machine overhead and barely recognized myself. I let out a self-pitying whimper. My brother, realizing that I could see myself, moved the X-ray away to spare me my reflection.

"Did someone do this to me?" I asked.

"We don't know yet. You still don't remember anything?"

"No. Just going to bed; I remember that fine."

"I mean . . ." He spoke slowly. "It looks like you got hit with a crowbar."

Even though Primitivo had told them his version of events, my family was doubtful. If I had been attacked by someone, it would make sense. My wrists could have been broken in a defensive posture.

"Yeah, maybe! See if you guys can find anything around where all the blood is."

The medical team came in, slid the X-ray plate back into place over my head, and vacated the room while the scans were taken.

A few moments later, a surgeon came in. Derek and Carolyn translated as he explained what was about to happen to me. First, they would put me under. Then they would run a series of small wires around each tooth and bind them to a bracket to wire the jaw. Then they would stitch my lip back together. Then they would break the nose back into place. Then they would set my wrists and put them in casts.

"Okay?" the doctor asked. All I cared about was the first step, relieved that I'd be able to sleep through it all.

"Yep," I mumbled. As they wheeled me off, I looked over at my family and said, "Find the weapon."

My mom and oldest brother, Soren, slept through it all. We were supposed to golf that morning, and when Soren came downstairs in his golf shirt and shorts and found us gone, he thought we'd left without him. My dad eventually called over and explained what he knew, and asked them to go search for the weapon that might have been used on me. They found a small pond of my blood under the window just as a resort employee wandered over with a mop and a bucket of hot water and soap.

I awoke in a dim room. No machines beeped. It was a simple medical clinic. A small box television was mounted high on the wall, almost touching the ceiling. It was unplugged and broadcasted my reflection. I was in an anesthetic haze and couldn't see very well. There was something ringing my vision that produced the effect of looking through a tunnel. I squinted at the TV screen and saw a blue and white mask over my face. I knew something bad had happened but was trying to remember. I groaned.

"There he is! How you feeling, KJ?!" My family had been off in the corner of the room, waiting for me to wake up.

I saw Derek and remembered our last conversation. "Did you find a crowbar?" My hope was unbridled. If it had been another human, someone who attacked me and fled, there would be no mystery. If not, if it had just been my brain and me . . .

I knew the answer before he spoke, revealed in his tightened lips. "Didn't find anything."

My dad's voice quivered when he spoke. "Kirk, do you know where we are?"

"Yes. The DR." I understood the point of his question and suddenly worried about the state of my brain. Given the extent of the trauma, there had been a concern about hemorrhaging, but the hospital had no equipment to check. I silently went through the names of my grade school teachers, grade by grade, testing my ability to recall. I conjugated a verb in Arabic in all ten forms. I remembered the password to my email account. Things seemed to be working.

Except for the fifteen minutes from the night before. What had happened in those minutes held the key to explaining why I was now in the hospital. I searched for them, but they had already fled to an undiscovered country in my mind, and now amnesia had clawed an impassable ocean around them.

My dad squeezed one of the few toes that wasn't bandaged. "Can you feel this?"

"Yes." His posture relaxed. I was not paralyzed.

A nurse came over and spoke very loudly in my ear. I didn't understand what she was saying. She jabbed a needle into my right thigh and injected something. It felt like a billiard ball was lodged in my muscle, just sitting there. She slapped my thigh and rubbed it around, and the medicine dissolved into my body.

"I wanna get out of here," I moaned.

"We know you do, guy. You gotta heal up here first, then we can go home."

I wanted to be alone, desperately—not to avoid my family but to be freed from any demands of social interaction. I didn't want to act positive. I wanted to make sense of what my brain had just done to me. I wanted to feel sorry for myself. I wanted to watch an ungodly string of movies, I didn't care which ones. I didn't want to answer the same questions everyone asked each morning. "No, no new memories. Yes, I can still move my toes."

The loud nurse appeared every few hours and shouted something in my ear as though I were deaf and injected drugs into my legs. I hated her. I tried to glare whenever she came in, but glaring tugged painfully at the stitching between my eyebrows. She wouldn't have seen it underneath the mask anyhow.

I couldn't breathe through my nostrils, which were stuffed with cotton balls. Wooden Popsicle sticks were jammed up my nostrils to help anchor the mask to my face. I could breathe only through my mouth, and since I couldn't chew anything, this meant that I had to take a deep breath before my brothers or parents tilted a can of chalky-tasting Ensure into my mouth.

"I can't stand it here."

It had been only a few days since my fall, but I begged my parents to get me back to West Chicago. If all I was doing was lying around, I'd rather do that back home.

I began a relentless campaign to get out of there, redirecting every conversation back to my wish to go home, until a surgeon strode into the room in military fatigues. He was a medic in the Dominican military but kept a practice at the hospital. He was going to get me ready for the trip to Chicago, he said, speaking through my brother. This meant making some striations in the casts so that my arms wouldn't be crushed when they swelled in flight at thirty thousand feet.

But it also meant removing my mask. I hadn't seen my face in days and was horrified by how I might look. An assistant came in with a steel tray, which she held with white rubber gloves. My eyes flared as the surgeon asked my brother to leave the room. On the tray were two large syringes filled with a broth-colored fluid.

The doctor picked at the medical tape affixing the upper part of the mask to my forehead and tugged slowly. The tape ran directly over the gash between my eyebrows, and the stitches strained to hold it together. The woman with the tray stood there to my right without moving, and I stared at the syringes.

The tape removed, all that held the mask in place were the Popsicle sticks and cotton balls in my nostrils. The cotton had hardened after absorbing so much blood, so when the surgeon gave a gentle tug at the sticks, they didn't budge. I began to breathe heavily when I saw his hand gather one of the two syringes. He didn't say anything as he inserted the syringe and shot the hot briny solution into my right nostril, which loosened the cotton and freed the wooden stick. I roared, "*Motherfu—*" but the rest of the word turned into a choking gargle as the solution flooded into my mouth. With weeping eyes, I spat it out, and the doctor placed one of the two Popsicle sticks on the nurse's tray.

His cell phone rang. He unclipped it from the holster on his hip. After a brief conversation, he snapped it back, and I saw a large smear of my blood on it. His rubber-gloved hand reached for the second syringe, and I began to beg pitifully, "Please! No! *No más!* Please!" I braced for the second blast.

We flew back to West Chicago on January 1, 2006, exactly one year after I had left for Iraq. My dad pushed me through the airport in a wheelchair and pulled my US government official passport from my chest pocket for the Transportation Security Administration official, who stared at me for a second and mumbled "Welcome back" before waving us along. Kids stared at me until reproached by their parents. I tried to swallow a dose of antibiotics and painkillers, but the water just trickled out of my mouth and into the tear across my chin. My dad wheeled me over to the baggage carousel, and I watched the bags loop in silence.

Heaves of snow lined the highway home. I hobbled across the icy driveway and directly upstairs to my bedroom. The door was shut. I tried but failed to turn the knob, which was a rubbery orange miniature basketball I had installed a decade earlier. In an unsteady voice, I called downstairs to ask my dad to come open the door for me. I crawled into bed, took another Vicodin, and fell asleep. I was home.

8.

Human Rubble

INFO MEMO

FOR: SECRETARY OF DEFENSE [Donald Rumsfeld]
SUBJECT: "What Did Not Happen?" (U)

(C) You asked for a list of the things for which we planned in Operation IRAQI FREEDOM that did *not* happen.
- Iraq descends into anarchy.
- There is widespread vigilante justice.
- Shi'a holy sites are damaged or destroyed.
- There are large numbers of internally displaced people and international refugees.
- "Fortress Baghdad" holds out indefinitely.
- There are mass Iraqi casualties.
- Another state (e.g., North Korea) takes advantage of US focus on Iraq.

The Vise Tightens

Yaghdan and his colleagues besieged their American bosses for help, for special badges allowing them to drive into the Green Zone rather than wait in the dangerous checkpoint lines, for promises of emergency housing in case they were targeted by militias. Month after month, year after year, they asked for protection but received none. The Americans wore condolences on their faces while they said they were looking into things.

Yaghdan removed his glasses and rubbed his eyes. He wished the Americans would buy better computer monitors. These were too small, and the resolution strained his eyes after hours of poring through row after row of the database of USAID projects, which would someday become an unimportant digital artifact of history. On the wall of his cubicle hung a picture of Mashael, a young woman beloved by her Iraqi colleagues who had been killed one morning a few months earlier when she stepped out on the balcony after breakfast. A black stripe to signify mourning cut diagonally across the corner of her picture. Nobody ever found out if it was a stray or targeted round.

It had been only a few months since he ran from the white Opel. There was no point looking back now, he thought. The catalog of if-then considerations were exhausting and unsatisfying: in the end, he had made the decision to help the Americans based on what he knew at the time. In his mind, he defended himself against the lethal stigma clouding those who worked for the United States by stressing that he worked for a civilian agency, and not the military, which he felt bore the responsibility for many of the shameful parts of the occupation. But his civilian employer was losing funding and drifting into the margins of relevance.

Down the alleyway of cubicles from him sat Tona and Amina, two young women who worked in the human resources office. They were best friends; they had attended high school and college together and had worked at USAID since its earliest days. Whenever Iraqis were hired, it was Amina who helped them get their badges; her name was on the back of scores of USAID badges as the "signing authority." Whenever Americans were hired, it was Tona who took their pictures with a digital camera and uploaded them into the badging system. American badges were blue; Iraqi badges were yellow.

When an Iraqi colleague was killed, Tona took an empty tissue box from a shelf in her cubicle and collected money for the victim's family.

At the beginning of the month of Ramadan in 2005, Tona and Yaghdan and the other Iraqis working for the United States were invited to a luncheon at the embassy in their honor, hosted by the US ambassador to Iraq, Zalmay Khalilzad. The executive officer called in the Iraqi staff for a meeting before the lunch. "Don't say anything to him," she warned. "Just eat and come back." She knew that anytime the Iraqis were able to get in front of a powerful American, they asked for protection from the militias waiting for them on the other side of the Green Zone's blast walls. "It's not a good time to talk about this. He's being nice to have you over for lunch." So they went and stood quietly in a long line for a picture with a grinning Zal. None of them ever received a copy.

Not long afterward, Tona and Amina walked out of the Green Zone through the Qadisiyya checkpoint, which opens onto the airport road. They had just cleared the American gate when a young man in an Iraqi police uniform stepped toward them and pulled a cell phone from his pocket. As he took their picture, Amina sprinted at him and started to yell, asking him what he was doing. She snatched his phone and ran back to the American soldiers guarding the checkpoint. The cop boldly followed to retrieve his phone, which the Americans were now examining. In addition to a picture of Tona and Amina, they found a video clip of an insurgent attack on an American convoy. They arrested him, interrogated him, and then took him away, but it was no comfort. They had just gotten the cop arrested, but for how long? A day? A year? Surely he'd search for them when he was released.

A Spark in Samarra

As the sun climbed over the city of Samarra on the morning of February 22, 2006, seven heavily armed Sunni militants dressed in Iraqi Special Forces uniforms strode into the entrance of the golden-domed Al-Askari Shrine and tied up the security guards. Visited by Shi'a pilgrims since the year 944, the mosque was of irreducible importance to the Shi'ite community. They carried in a number of bombs, which were strewn throughout the building. Shortly before seven o'clock, the bombs went off, bringing down the golden dome and any delusions that Iraq was not hurtling toward a civil war.

The response was miasmic. Militias laid claim to neighborhood after neighborhood, hoisting their flags over seized checkpoints, at which they checked IDs for Sunni or Shi'a names. In this manner, the once-mixed Sunni-Shi'a neighborhoods of Baghdad and other major cities were ethnically cleansed. More than a thousand bodies a month piled up at the Baghdad morgue alone. Before long, more than fifty thousand Iraqis were fleeing into Syria, Jordan, and other countries each month.

It was a midterm election year in America, so the news from Iraq filtered in a little differently. The only metric that counted in public opinion polling was the casualty rate of US forces, and since fifty-five Americans were killed in February 2006, and only thirty-one killed in March, what were all the war critics talking about? The thirty-one killed were twenty fewer than the number killed in March 2004, and still four fewer than the number killed in March 2005. Yes, there were seventy-six Americans killed in April 2006, but that was a far sight better than the 135 that were killed in April 2004.

Meanwhile, the refugee crisis became the fastest growing in the world, as nearly one in eight Iraqis was running from the violence: the equivalent of 38 million Americans flooding across the Mexican and Canadian borders.

A couple days after the bombing of Samarra, Fox News ran a photograph of the destroyed Golden Dome with the caption "Upside to Civil War?" The subsequent caption: "All-out civil war in Iraq: could it be a good thing?" Later that year, the network's Stuart Varney spelled out the thinking more clearly: "Let me put out something positive about Iraq, if I may, for a second. Look, we took the fight to the enemy. We divided the enemy. The enemy is now fighting itself. America's interest is surely being well preserved and well protected. We are, in fact, in a way, winning and preserving our interests here, are we not?"

The Democrats also saw an opportunity to capitalize on the violence scorching through Iraq. A six-point plan was unveiled by the party, the first of which was entitled *Real Security: Protecting America and Restoring Our Leadership in the World*, which would "require the Iraqis to take responsibility for their own country." They employed the same condescending language as the neoconservatives I knew back in Baghdad. "We did our part; it's up to the Iraqis now to step up," as if the civil war rending the country had nothing to do with us but, rather, resulted from a deficiency in the Iraqi character.

Several months after Samarra, with millions displaced, a controversy erupted when Brian Williams at NBC *Nightly News* declared a civil war under way in Iraq. Katie Couric of *CBS Evening News* could not bring herself to agree. The Bush administration's spokesman at the White House, Tony Snow, laughed at Williams's assertion. It was not a civil war, he claimed, because the "different forces" were not unified: "You have not yet had a situation where you have two clearly defined and opposing groups vying not only for power but for territory." When pressed on the question at a later briefing on December 5, 2006, he continued:

> I spent a lot of time thinking about this last week, and I'm not sure you get any two people to agree . . . if you have as your definition of a civil war as something that involves the entire landmass—north, south, east, and west—doesn't apply. But some people think that the sectarian violence you've seen—centered largely around Baghdad, and you also have some terrorist activity in Anbar, a considerable amount—they think that is civil war. So it depends on which metrics you use for doing it. And frankly, I gave up on trying, because there are any number of people who have different measurements.

It was just another refugee problem, invisible to most Americans and journalists. Unlike other humanitarian crises, Iraqis who fled to Syria and Jordan in 2006 didn't gather in tent communities or cluster in recognizable refugee camps. They crammed into cheap apartments in overcrowded neighborhoods and waited for the civil war to pass or for the international community to act.

But Yaghdan stayed, unwilling to leave his country and the home in which he was raised, confident in his ability to always keep a step ahead of the militants who hunted America's Iraqis.

PART TWO

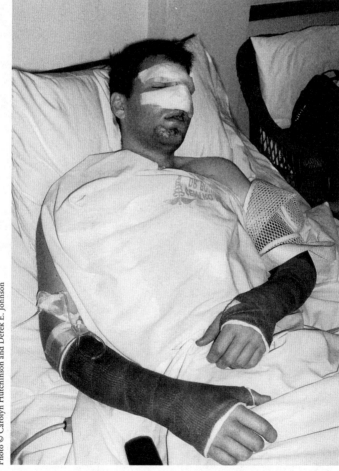

12-29-05

9.

The Insurgent of West Chicago

He who conquers a city is as nothing compared to he
who conquers his own nature.

—David Mamet

It was pointless trying to sleep. I slip out of the hooch into the sprawling mess of Camp Fallujah. I walk in uncertain flip-flop steps over fields of smooth rocks meant to bury the powdery sand, which always found its way up with the faintest encouragement. I pick my way along the catwalk flanking the Cummins generator that churns an end-of-the-world grinding noise, using a small xenon flashlight to avoid waist-high coils of concertina wire. Was there ever a real threat of infiltration?

"Camp used to house some real tough mudders," the marines said. "Saddam kept 'em on the outskirts of Fallujah to intimidate the city, keep it in line."

Now it houses American marines, there to do the same. In clusters of brutalist one-story structures with blacked-out windows operate intelligence fusion centers and logistics teams and endless other functions of HQ. What little rain spatters onto their slopeless roofs steams off. On I wander, over fields of gravel, past an egg-shaped pond with water so dark that three feet looks like a dozen. A single swan glides ghostly across its oil-slick surface. The generator is far behind now; all I can hear is the *ship-ship* of my sandals. I pass through the camp's checkpoint and trudge past the boneyard and its acres of broken-down and half-exploded cars and trucks. The sun is peeking up over the dead fields as I approach the city.

The city wakes, and I hide behind the gnarled remains of a detonated sedan on Route Ethan, weaponless and American. A bowel-shuddering dread seeps in as I watch the darkened blood of a butchered lamb trickling along a nearby sidewalk, dusted with Anbari sand. I want to crawl into the car to hide, but it has been mangled beyond any degree of car-ness: there are no doors, no roof, no tires, only a thornbush of splintered and blackened steel and melted upholstery. I want to crawl under the car, but it grows from the pavement—there is no under. Nearby, a black blossom of char blooms in the middle of the road where the car exploded. The sun is climbing, an executioner's blade overhead, dropping hours of light before I can try to escape under cover of night back to Camp Fallujah.

An errant soccer ball rolls up, stopping at my feet. A Falluji kid races over, his laugh turning into a gasp as he spots me, and then an excited yell. Shoulders and heads appear, forming an ever-tightening clutch around me, their talk turning to shouts and hands grabbing for me. *Fuck. No. No!*

The *No!* lurches me awake into West Chicago. The nightmare waits for me just on the other side of sleep, waiting to replay when I can no longer keep my body awake. There is a wretched pain emanating somewhere from my face, so eclipsing in its fullness that it takes some time to identify the source: I have thrashed my fiberglassed arms against the mob of my nightmare, clocking my broken jaw and severed lips in the process. More blood flows into my mouth and onto my tongue, and I am now irreversibly awake, as another night of potential sleep and recovery slinks from the room. I have wounds to tend, drugs to take. Once back in bed, I turn on the television and stare at infomercials until sunrise and the stirring of my parents downstairs.

In the beginning, despite it all, there was hope. I wanted to go back to Fallujah. I wasn't supposed to be home yet and did not call my friends to let them know I was back. There was no point getting comfortable:

I would heal up in a few weeks, I figured, and be back in Iraq to finish my work.

But I was a wreck. My legs, the last piece of me to hit concrete, were somehow spared, although several of my toes had split open at the tips like small lobster claws. I had to hoist my feet high to ensure I'd clear each step on the stairs, since my big toes were wrapped comically in a tennis-ball-sized mass of gauze. With my casted arms and railroad tracks of stitches across my face, I lurched through the house like a medicated Frankenstein.

It hurt to move. At the slightest movement, an ache would scramble through my arteries up to my head and pause in a menacing stance. If I kept going, it would twist and squeeze different parts of my brain without hesitation. I learned my place, that I could not best it, that I would listen to it, which meant that I did everything with great deliberation and delay. I wondered if this was what I had to look forward to if I ever grew old, which seemed unlikely considering my condition, when a good morning meant I hadn't sleepwalked out of bed.

During the first morning, I ambled down to the basement computer and wrote two emails. The first was to the First Marine Expeditionary Force to tell them that I would be unable to make it to the briefing in Camp Pendleton. Using my index fingers, I typed slowly and did not use any more words than absolutely necessary.

I wrote the second email to management at USAID in Baghdad. I didn't go into much detail about the accident, because I didn't know much. I said I'd need approximately eight weeks before I could get my casts cut off and return to my projects, and apologized for any complications that might be caused by my absence.

I wanted to write a checklist of the things that would need to happen before I could return to Iraq, but I couldn't hold a pen: the distance between my thumb, index finger, and middle finger had been set in fiberglass. No amount of contortions could make them touch, much less grip a pen.

In the basement, I found a roll of duct tape and climbed the twenty-two steps back up to my room like a mountain path, stopping to gather my breath and relieve the pressure in my brain.

I sat down at my desk and placed the duct tape next to a pen. I leaned over and scooped up a sock from the floor, and wrapped it clumsily around the shaft of the pen. It took ten agonizing minutes to free a corner of the tape without the use of opposable thumbs. Sweat beaded and trickled with a sting into my wounds, and I barked, "Goddamn it, does it have to be so hot in here?!" After great effort, I managed to tear off a foot-long piece of tape. Bit by bit, I crudely taped the sock to the pen, its point emerging from the now-thick grip. I lowered my right hand over the sock-pen, wedged it into the space between my thumb and index fingers, and lifted the pen in my hand with a faint smile. I looked at the clock. Thirty minutes had elapsed. My head was thumping, but I had regained the capacity to write.

I called for my mom, who hurried up the stairs, and explained that I needed a sock taped around a knife, fork, and spoon.

Later that afternoon, I wandered to the kitchen with my modified silverware and a faint appetite. I knocked a tinfoil-sealed container of Mott's applesauce from the fridge onto the floor and sat down with my legs crossed before it. The act of peeling off the foil was impossible, so I fitted the sock-knife into my cast, hovered it over the applesauce, and slammed it down, hoping to puncture the foil enough to snake a straw through. But the foil was too strong, and the knife popped out of my cast and onto the floor. Shadow, my cat, walked by and stared for a moment before sauntering over to the open can of tuna my mom had left out for her.

I refitted the sock-knife and tried again. Again. Again. The sweat stung. I figured out how to use my feet to hold the applesauce in place, rested the knife's point directly on the foil with my right hand, and this time bashed the blade through the foil using the cast on my left arm. A quarter of the applesauce slopped onto my feet and the floor. I gingerly pursed my torn lips around a straw and guided it past the foil to feed myself. A couple weeks earlier, I was coordinating tens of millions of dollars of aid. People called me sir.

———

I made a checklist:

- ☐ Stop infection
- ☐ Casts off
- ☐ Unwire jaw
- ☐ Root canals
- ☐ Stitches out
- ☐ Braces
- ☐ Insurance reimbursement

Beneath it all, I wrote "Medical clearance," knowing that I would need a new clearance before being permitted back into Iraq. In every conversation with my doctors, I pressured them to give me best-case scenarios and the most aggressive course of treatment, hoping to be back on a plane to Fallujah in less than two months.

In my childhood bedroom on a dead-end street in West Chicago, I created a war room. I locked myself in and mapped out my return. The floor was soon littered with checklists, timelines, alternative timelines, secondary to-do lists, all with boxes to be checked, printouts of articles, pill bottles, briefing materials for the canceled marines lecture. CNN looped endlessly on mute.

The first week passed, and my bosses hadn't responded to my email. Surely it had been sequestered as spam. I emptied my backpack onto the bed and found the matchbox-sized device that periodically received a several-digit code from a satellite, allowing me to log into USAID's email system to resend the message through my government account.

I woke each morning with a gnawing need to check in on the news, to log into email, in search of some connection with Iraq. I called my colleagues who had returned before me to rant about the lack or quality of media coverage and to trade news about who was being investigated for corruption, which projects were unraveling, who was going to Afghanistan next, who got what plum posting where, who was resigning from the agency in frustration over Iraq. I wrote to the few Iraqis in Fallujah whose email addresses I still had and apologized for my delay in returning.

Early on, friends relayed hurtful gossip pushed by marines and others in USAID and the State Department who barely knew me: the most widely spread version had me drunk and partying out a window. One marine general announced in a staff meeting that I had decided to simply quit so I could stay in the United States, which angered me more than the other explanations for my absence.

Friends who found out about my accident asked me just what, exactly, had happened in the Dominican Republic. I pecked out the number of a neuropsychiatrist friend who worked with veterans at the VA hospital in New York. He listened to my account of what had happened and interrupted: "Kirk, you had a dissociative fugue state." I perked up, remembering the months I'd spent as a fourteen-year-old learning Bach's *Toccata and Fugue in D Minor* on the organ. The act of pedaling a bass line while playing on two tiers of keys was such a leap for my adolescent mind that I had to master the hands so that I could play without looking, focusing my eyes instead on the pedals below my feet and dangling tie. I stared at my casts while he continued.

Over the phone, he read from the *DSM-IV*, the *Diagnostic and Statistical Manual of Mental Disorders*, published by the American Psychiatric Association: "Travel may range from brief trips over relatively short periods of time (i.e., hours or days) to complex, usually unobtrusive wandering over long time periods (e.g., weeks or months), with some individuals reportedly crossing numerous national borders and traveling thousands of miles." A fugue state is characterized by autopilot behavior, which is only sometimes tame. People have emerged from a fugue state to find themselves behind the wheel of their car or in a mall with shopping bags under their arms, with no recollection of how they got there. Incidence of the disorder increases during periods of war.

I hung up, shuffled over to the computer, and typed "fugue" into an online dictionary, and the page blinked back two resulting words. I wedged the sock-pen into position over a notebook and wrote in nervous, oversized letters that filled the page, "Fugue: Flight, Departure."

I had never heard of the disorder before, but each example I found online came as a revelation. I felt as though my accident had trapped me within a kind of John Grisham novel, only a much more pathetic version. There was no pelican brief, no assassinated justices; just some kid who sleepwalked out a window while on vacation from Fallujah. But each sentence seemed as though it were written for my eyes only, as though I had just deciphered some conspiracy in plain sight, the plot to pilot me to my death while I slept.

> The essential feature of dissociative fugue is sudden, unexpected travel . . . with inability to recall some or all of one's past. . . . Fugues are usually precipitated by a stressful episode, and upon recovery there may be amnesia for the original stressor. . . . Once the individual returns to the prefugue state, there may be no memory for the events that occurred during the fugue. . . .
>
> Sometimes dissociative fugue cannot be diagnosed until people abruptly return to their prefugue identity and are distressed to find themselves in unfamiliar circumstances.

I took the words, symptoms, examples, and spread them like plaster over the rupture that had torn open on December 29.

At the end of the second week, I still hadn't heard anything from my bosses. I was growing angry. Didn't the near-death of a senior staff member warrant at least a brief phone call? I didn't know what was happening with my position and wanted to report on my progress, lest they think of giving the Fallujah job to someone else.

I wasn't making much progress, though. The yellow pus of infection colonized healthy flesh as it wept drowsily from the sutures on my chin and forehead. A beard was emerging, and I had the terror-filled realization that I'd need to shave to effectively fight the infection. Once I could no longer push it off, I duct-taped a sock around my razor blade. Each downward stroke tugged at the stitches, and a sickly stream emerged in response. I spent an hour shaving what felt like one whisker at a time until the tear and infection site were mostly cleared. My legs, exhausted, carried me back into bed, where I stared at the silent television screen and tried to sleep.

As I tried to avoid fixating on my bosses' silence, I began to doubt my eight-week estimate. The successful completion of once quotidian demands—feeding, washing, shaving—triggered a wave of euphoria that quickly broke apart into a frightful awareness of how battered I was. I turned my full attention to the maintenance of my body: teeth, bones, face, antibodies, stomach. I was in the cockpit of a heavily strafed bomber, my engine sputtering and coughing, lines leaking, windshield cracked and whistling. My only priority was to hold altitude. In the quiet of my room, I would whimper, and then curse myself for the self-pity: *Oh, you big baby. Least you can walk. Lot of people never wake up. So you have a little dark spell here. Tough shit.* But my high-minded attempts at paying respect to the dead and worse off sputtered quickly. The churn of self-pity grew stronger by the day, threatening to overpower my hope for a speedy return to Fallujah.

My parents, in the thirty-seventh year of their marriage, were struggling with each other like any couple approaching four decades and the imminence and uncertainty of retirement. They had masked any sign of this whenever I'd call from Iraq, but now I was home, and it was unavoidable. And while a trauma in a family brings everyone closer, it also rubs the plates in the tectonic history against one another, resurrecting old tensions and unwanted recollections. I bickered with my dad like an adolescent. That I relied on them to shuttle me to and from surgeries didn't help. I felt guilty for being back in their space at a time when they could have used privacy, and embarrassed that I was home when I was needed elsewhere. I pushed them away, going to great lengths to take care of myself, ruffling my casts into garbage bags so that I could stand under the shower, contorting myself elaborately into my clothes, bashing knifes through tinfoil to eat.

Cockroach

We called the crude web of stitches binding together my upper lip the Cockroach. Whenever my mouth was closed, it looked as though I were chewing on a large dark-brown insect, with partially unraveled stitches for antennae.

I hadn't smiled for weeks. Late one evening, flipping through channels, I discovered *The Colbert Report*, which had aired its first episode while I was still in Fallujah. Two minutes into Stephen Colbert's deadpan dismantling of White House spin about Iraq, wrapped in neoconservative chest-beating pomp, I broke into a grin. The pain flooded in at once. When my lip tightened into a smile, the Cockroach slithered up toward my gums and snagged itself on the wire bracket holding my jaw together. Fresh blood trickled into my mouth, and I raced to the bathroom mirror. I unhooked the mess with my index fingers, returned to my room in a sullen mood, and turned off Colbert. No more laughing until the Cockroach was gone.

The next morning, I pulled on a pair of sweatpants, writhed my casts through an oversized T-shirt and flip-flops, worked my way down the staircase, and slipped out the front door into the numbing winter. The cold felt good on my cuts. I pried open the door to my dad's Buick, lowered myself in, and took off before anyone could stop me.

It had snowed most of the previous night. I hadn't driven in a year, and since both arms were in casts, I had only my fingertips to steer. I kept the radio off, rolled down all the windows, and suppressed a smile. I reached the first intersection, having no clue where I was headed, and again the urge to smile returned. I decided to make only right turns until I was comfortable enough to turn left across a lane.

I imagined piles of snow dumping upon Fallujah. The war would probably come to a halt. I drove up Roosevelt Road, past the grocery store, and turned right onto Joliet Street at my childhood bank, where seven dollars in savings from grade school still accrued interest, a penny a year. Snowplows scraped along ahead of me, spraying a shower of salt in their wake. Snowblowers blasted white arcs from every other driveway. My high school loomed on the left, and I sped past it anxiously. At the next red light, a beat-up Chevy Cavalier pulled up to my right, and a heavy woman stared at me, my casts, and then back at me in alarm.

I pulled into a slippery parking lot and walked into a bookstore to find stacked high in the main display Paul Bremer's book about his year as the head of the Coalition Provisional Authority. I used my casts like chopsticks and carried a copy to the register.

"Ohmigosh, what happened to *you?*" a teenage girl with the pasty complexion of Midwestern winters cooed warmly. I watched her eyes settle upon the Cockroach stitching between my lips and dart away.

I grunted, dumping some bills onto the counter. My first interaction with someone outside of a hospital or my home, and I realized quickly that I wasn't up for it.

"'Kay, here's your change. Hope ya feel better soon! 'Njoy the book!"

I trudged through the snow in my flip-flops. When I got back to the car, I realized I couldn't hold Bremer's book and open the door at the same time, so I dumped him into the parking lot snow. The book was for reading, not for displaying. There he was on the back cover of *My Year in Iraq: The Struggle to Build a Future of Hope,* dismounting a Blackhawk in his idiotic costume of a prep blazer, khakis, and combat boots.

The Buick was in motion. I drove on, past strip malls, gas stations, and hibernating golf courses, following the train tracks until I reached desolate stretches of heavily tilled frozen farmland. I pulled off onto the shoulder just before a railroad crossing. The heater was the only thing audible, save for a periodic rubbery scrape of the wipers. I opened Bremer's book and started to read.

Two weeks later, I blasted out of the driveway and aimed the car at Chicago. Bremer was giving a speech in late January 2006 before the Chicago Council on Foreign Relations (now the Chicago Council on Global Affairs), at the same Hilton hotel where Mayor Daley had unleashed his cops on antiwar protesters during the 1968 Democratic Convention.

I gave my keys to a shocked valet and made my way into the hotel ballroom, passing a constellation of Burberry jackets and mink stoles wrapped around what I supposed was the foreign policy establishment of Chicago—an incongruous concept. I didn't know anyone and didn't bother trying to make small talk, sailing past and positioning myself in the first row in front of the podium. The Chicago cognoscenti stared at me as they wriggled out of their coats and into the seats around me. They did a poor job concealing their whispers. "What do you suppose happened to him?"

My arms were swelling in their prisons, and my jaw was throbbing. I hadn't taken any painkillers all day, because I didn't want a Vicodin haze to roll in while Bremer was talking. I wanted all my senses at the ready.

Bremer emerged to sturdy applause. My glare was surely intensified by the row of stitches between my brows. He spun fantasies from the podium, taking care to blame Iraq's current problems on Iraqis, and to blame future problems on Iraqis, too. A few nights earlier on TV, I had seen him contradict his own account of the decision to disband the Iraqi military in his first days in Baghdad, so I was in the mood for confrontation. When the Q&A session began, I shot up a black-casted arm and held it firm. He looked at me, furrowed his bushy brow, and turned his head to take a question from someone else.

For thirty minutes, I alternated arms when one grew tired, and as time wore thin, raised both at once. "Why doesn't he call on him?" a woman behind me whispered to her husband in a tone of support. As he wrapped up each answer, he looked at me and then called someone else. The Q&A ended, and a hundred-strong line formed to get books signed. I was exhausted, sore, and wary of the hourlong drive through the snow ahead of me. I got into the car, feeling at once foolish and angry, and headed back in darkness to West Chicago, where the punishing roulette wheel of sleep spun over my bed.

As the cold of January hardened into February, it became apparent to me that my injuries were more severe than I wanted to admit. Nobody in USAID management responded to me.

The winter sun set early, not long past four. I drove to the theater to watch movies in darkness with other West Chicagoans and usually fell asleep before the opening credits finished rolling.

My acidic side began to appear at the slightest of provocations and corroded the most unsuspecting and innocent. I watched *It's a Wonderful Life*, still in the DVD player from Christmastime, and laughed contemptuously at Jimmy Stewart's doe-eyed George Bailey, whose dip in the river renews him, opens his eyes to the miracle of life, focuses that which is blurred, straightens that which is skewed. Everything was very tidy for George. I lumbered to the bathroom, knocked a Vicodin bottle on its side, and pinched a pill between my ring finger and pinkie. The pill began to dissolve on my tongue into a bitter metallic strain of saliva.

"Kirkie, there's someone here to see you. Are you decent?"

My mom entered cautiously with a pastor friend of hers "who knows *all* about you, who is one of your *biggest* fans, and wanted to come by just to see *you*." She seemed nice enough, but I was having difficulty separating her words from Jimmy Stewart's. Sensing that I wasn't giving my full attention, Mom muted the TV.

The Vicodin receded for a moment, and her words became clear— ". . . Because the Lord has a Plan for you, you have been Spared for a Reason . . ."—before they were tugged away in a hydrocodone riptide.

Somewhere around the phrase "to not take for granted each day we have," I catapulted a "Ha!" from my lungs and blurted, "Okay! Well, thanks for coming!" I decided it was better to vacate the minister from my room, however rudely, than to subject her to what was roaring through my mind. What did she know of not taking days for granted? I was twenty-five years old and didn't exactly feel that I was wasting my life. What did she know of being spared?

I had grown up on stories in church about the transformative power of a near-death or rock-bottom experience, the turn to Jesus after a drunk-driving accident, after a near-fatal drug overdose: these people realized only after the brink moment that life is short. But I was lying there because I had spent a year in a war zone, and my sleeping mind decided for me that it had had just about enough. I was alive because the mortars that Iraqi kids my age had launched in my direction were duds, poorly aimed, or nudged away by an indifferent gust of Iraqi wind. I was still on earth because I had marines who protected me. I was alive because my wrists had been strong enough to break a headfirst fall to concrete. I was there because I lucked out. I wasn't arrogant enough to find a plan just for me in the tornado of chaos and probabilities that had spat me back into West Chicago.

The minister left with an understanding smile. I apologized to my mom a couple days later.

My grip on Fallujah was slipping. For a year, I had studied thousands of pages of USAID reports, Bechtel power and water plant assessments, aid absorption rate studies, classified marine situation reports, inspector general audits, embassy electricity forecasts that sagged under the weight of their own stats, endless iterations of data projected onto maps of Iraq's provinces. In my early days back, I tried to imagine that I was home for a short period to report in from the field, but the only people I could brief were my increasingly worried parents, brothers, and friends, who had no idea what I was talking about.

As March approached, the possibility that I would not return increased with each week that passed without word from my bosses. I sketched out a briefing book for whomever USAID would inevitably send to replace me, and broke it into sections: Canal Clearing. Agriculture. Health Services. Wat/San. Power. Employment Generation. Audit of Past Projects. Key Persons on Fallujah City Council. Key Counterparts within Second Marine Expeditionary Force. Unsorted Notes on Anbar.

I looked at the checklist I'd made on my first morning back home. All I had managed to do was prevail against the infection and tug the stitches from my eyebrow.

A family friend who was a surgeon at the nearby hospital offered to sink a screw into the broken bone of my right wrist. The liberation of one hand would dramatically increase my ability to take care of myself. Friends counseled me to let the wrists heal naturally, but I had convinced myself that I could return to Iraq with a cast on one arm. Surely it wouldn't be too difficult to find a marine medic to saw it off, but I stood no chance of getting a new medical clearance with both arms in casts, so I leaped at the surgeon's offer to operate.

Nobody could get to the veins on my arms because of the casts. Linda, the medical assistant, shook a WD-40-sized can and sprayed a cold aerosol over the delta of veins and arteries running upon the top of my foot, temporarily freezing the area. A jolting piercing, followed by a sigh. Another piercing. Another sigh, coarsened with exasperation. "Come on . . ." She shot me an impatient glance. She hadn't yet sunk the IV and was looking at me as though I were to blame. Within thirty seconds of meeting her, she had become an enemy.

But then it was in, and Linda was standing next to me with the supreme sleep, blissful and blank, in little glass bottles on her tray. She injected the anesthesia into the tiny veins of my foot, and I loved her without condition for it.

When I realized I was waking, I moaned in groggy protest. Why couldn't they just put me under for a month or so? My eyes rolled around aimlessly until they settled on my mom, who was crying. She wiped her cheeks when she noticed that I had come to.

It took another few moments before I thought to ask, "What's the matter?"

"Oh, I'll let the doctor tell you." She looked anxiously at the door. I was waking up fast now.

"What do you mean? What happened?"

"Honey, I can't explain it like he can. Let's wait for him."

"Mom, c'mon, just tell me. He can tell me more later."

She dropped her head and wiped away fresh tears.

"The doctor made a mistake. He got in there, and—" She looked angrily back at the door. "Oh, this is ridiculous. *He* should be the one telling you!"

"Mom. Please. Don't worry, I won't be upset. Just tell me."

"He got in there, and I guess he had the screw halfway in, and the bone started cracking apart more. Something about the angle of the screw being 'tricky,' he said. He had to unscrew it. Oh honey, I'm so sorry!"

I looked down and noticed a new cast on my right arm. The cuts on my face started to sting, and I gathered that I was crying. "What does this mean in terms of recovery time?"

"He said you can get the cast off in another eight weeks. I know you wanted a different result, dear. I'm sorry."

I imagined holding the surgeon's incompetent hands on the bed stand and bashing them with my casts. For the first time since the ER in Bournigal, I had regressed: my wrist was worse, not better. The botched surgery blew apart the only flimsy bridge I'd been able to construct since my fall, the idea that I was speeding toward a return to the most important job I'd ever had.

The surgeon slid into the room upon a stream of nonsense, suggesting that I shouldn't feel upset. "If anything," he chirped, "the surgery might have stimulated the tissue with positive results." The bill arrived ten days later, topping $6,000. The screw alone was $800, and it wasn't even in my goddamned wrist.

Insurgency

Dead flies and a blue wasp with a broken wing lay in the window casement, entombed by the storm windows my dad put up when I was still in Fallujah.

My descent was rapid after the failed surgery. I lost my grip on the fire hose of information about Iraq, the reports, trend lines, atmospherics, and situation reports, but the need to assess still rumbled within. I could do little to restrain myself. I printed out Google Earth maps of my hometown and began to study its infrastructure. I circled water and wastewater treatment plants, power step-down stations and transfer lines, the hospital, police, and fire stations.

I imagined that I was an insurgent and studied which areas of the city were the farthest from the police and fire stations. I looked up the number of cop cars and fire trucks. I circled gas stations, propane tank lots, and the most vulnerable points in the power, water, and gas lines.

Distracted from my infirmity, I went deeper. I grabbed a couple maps and headed into town, studying them coldly. I looked at population density. I highlighted the tallest buildings and perches in town, among them the windows looking out from the English Department on the third story of my high school. I pulled into the parking lot behind the Burger King and left the engine running as I surveyed the rail yard, through which graffitied coal hoppers and boxcars trundled toward Chicago. Where were the quickest access points and escape routes? How often did commuter rails run?

I figured my hometown could be brought to its knees in a few hours. The basic infrastructure was embarrassingly exposed: in many cases, there wasn't even a chain-link fence around a soft spot. Two simple attacks in opposite corners of town would cripple security. Alarmed and depressed by the thought experiment, I backed away from the rail yard and turned myself into the military occupier of West Chicago.

I imagined my dad's Buick as a brigade commander's Humvee and rolled out of the Burger King parking lot onto Route 59. I dissected the city into manageable quadrants and determined which streets would serve as main and alternate supply routes. I allocated ten tanks and forty Humvees and began to position entry and exit checkpoints at the main arteries into town. On Main Street, in the parking lot shared by True Value hardware, Taco Bell, and McDonald's, I positioned an M1 Abrams tank as a show of force. I placed countersniper teams in the English Department, in the Bible Church steeple, and on the catwalk below the W E S T C H I C A G O letters stenciled in black over the faded blue paint of the water tower. I snarled concertina wire through miles of backyards and bulldozed berm walls to seal off the more vacant stretches in the western third of the city.

The high school would be the seat of my administration, my civil military operations center, providing ample space for condolence payments and meetings between our occupying forces and disgruntled West Chicagoans. In the cafeteria, where I had posed for my yearbook picture, I'd line them up to scan their eyeballs and fingerprints. The town jail wouldn't be able to hold more than eighty if packed, so I designated my middle school as the primary detention facility and suffocated it with blast walls, razor wire, floodlights, and gravel-filled chest-high Hesco barriers. Curfew would begin at eight across the city.

The Jel-Sert factory, which turned corn syrup into Fla-Vor-Ice popsicles, would serve as the morgue. If I applied the Iraqi civilian casualty rate to our population base, the bodies of a few hundred West Chicagoans could be expected each month.

I needed to know the greatest employers, the local powerbrokers, the city's most pressing needs. I printed a year's worth of city council minutes and began to pore through them. I bookmarked the police blotter page on the *West Chicago Press* website. I drove through occupied West Chicago and sensed the coil of hypervigilance tighten, just slightly, when I imagined what an IED would do to the soft-skinned Buick. My mood darkened.

"Whatcha up to, sweetie?" my mom asked when I pulled back into the driveway.

"Nothin' much, just drivin' around."

Surrender

The Vicodin didn't work anymore. Instead of increasing the dosage, I stopped taking it altogether. I shivered in a cold sweat on the bed, passively watching a CNN report on Fallujah. An itch gnawed from deep within the new cast, and I knew that there was nothing I could do to scratch it. I tried to focus on something else, and the crawler at the bottom of the TV screen announced that Sheikh Kamal, the head of the Fallujah City Council, had been assassinated the previous night.

I raced to the computer in search of more news and found a message from a friend in USAID still in Baghdad. "Thought you'd get a kick out of this," he wrote above a forwarded message from somebody in USAID management who had just arrived: "Who is Kirk Johnson, where did he work, and when did he leave?" Someone from IT realized that I still had my Iraqi cell phones and the satellite device for checking email and was urgently demanding their return, lest any inventory be missing. My first letter from management since the accident, and all they wanted were my phones.

The itch was tormenting. I bashed my casts together, hoping to somehow stop it, but it persisted, unfazed. I crawled into bed and turned off the news.

I had resisted it as long as I could but finally submitted to the conclusion that I had failed in Iraq. I had not been good enough or strong enough to keep a grip on things, my brain had tumbled, and now I was obsessing over Google Earth images of my hometown infrastructure.

A sympathetic lieutenant colonel gathered my clothing, toiletries, and the Christmas stocking my mom had mailed to Fallujah and shipped them back in two large gorilla lockers. When they arrived, I pried them open and searched eagerly for my green government-issue notebooks, containing months' worth of notes and contacts, but they had likely been tossed into the burn pit before the Second Marine Expeditionary Force cycled home. The agency never sent a replacement to Fallujah. The canal-clearing initiative unraveled, and its funds were diverted back to rubble removal. Despite all of my efforts, not a single thing remained. It was as if I had never even been there.

I mailed the worthless cell phones back to USAID, threw out my notes for the briefing book, and stopped following the war.

Insurgent maps of West Chicago gave way to cover letters and résumés. I was unemployed, after all, and a huge portion of my savings from a year abroad had been distilled into IV bags, dispensed into orange scrip bottles, and transferred into the bank account of the doctor who mangled my wrist. I was staring at tens of thousands of dollars' worth of bills.

The medical center in Bournigal had prepared a thorough discharge folder for my American insurance provider, Clements International, including doctors' notes, typewritten lists of procedures, X-rays, drugs, and medical supplies. I was comforted by the thoroughness of its records, the thickness of the folder, and was relieved to know that I had insurance from a company that specialized in covering expats and aid workers.

Except: I had neglected to call Clements from the emergency room in Bournigal and therefore failed to obtain a preauthorization number. The customer service representative clucked as he informed me that the insurer would not reimburse me. In an appeal, I FedExed my entire discharge folder to the company, which then indicated that it would not honor any claims because the hospital paperwork was in Spanish. When I called to receive preauthorization for a series of upcoming root canals and a procedure to remove the wiring from my jaw, I was told that my policy covered only medical costs incurred abroad, not domestically. I pulled out the surgical to-do list, estimated the cost of the remaining procedures, and figured I would be penniless in two months.

———————

The horizon of depression is stripped of contour and color. For months, I trudged across its baked fields in search of relief, past occasional mirages of minor achievement (stitches removed, infection subdued), and through a fog of stomach-eroding painkillers and antibiotics and more surgical complications.

While sitting in the endodontist's waiting room, I found a quote of mine in a dated issue of *Time* magazine, uttered months earlier on Election Day in Fallujah, in which I spoke about the fledgling reconstruction efforts in the city. The doctor asked me, "What was it *like* over there?" as he slid a black rubber bit between my jaw and prepared a series of root canals. After several shots of Novocaine, though, he removed the bit from my mouth and told me there was a problem: the scar tissue around the roots of my teeth prevented him from fully anesthetizing the area. If I didn't want to feel a lot of pain, he said, I could reschedule for a general anesthesia session in a month. Sick of waiting for procedures, I told him to just get it over with. He drilled away into my four front teeth while "Love Potion No. 9" warbled through a small speaker overhead and tears streamed down.

After the oral surgeon missed one of the steel wires wrapped around my front tooth as he removed the bracket holding my jaw together, I decided I was done making new appointments and filling out more insurance forms, so I drove up to the hardware store, bought a wire cutter and a pair of needle-nose pliers, and yanked it from my gums.

When my arms were finally exhumed from their fiberglass caskets, they looked as though they belonged to someone else, slender and frail and jaundiced. One wrist made a popping sound whenever I turned a doorknob.

I would need braces once again. The chairs in the orthodontist's waiting room were designed to resemble huge white molars. Surrounded by anxious and acne-besieged thirteen-year-olds, I stared up at the "Before and After" wall and its neat Polaroid rows of patients' smiles, and found my scarred face glowering from within the adolescent jungle. When the orthodontist asked if I wanted any special-colored rubber bands—maybe red and white for the Bulls?—I grimaced my no, and he began to hoist my dead teeth back into place and ensure the postponement of any dating life.

A half year after the fall, my checklist was finished, but I had given up on returning to Iraq. I no longer wanted anything to do with that part of my life, and my cynicism about international development work clouded out the desire to work anywhere else. Why bother?

I decided to disappear into law school for a few years and make a nice salary when I got out. I drove to the library of the community college where I had first studied Arabic and waded through LSAT prep books and practice tests. I was done with Iraq.

10.

Homeboy

Hayder leaned toward the mirror and ran a comb through his jet-black hair. He hummed a melody as he shaved. The pitch was a little off, but he didn't notice and wouldn't mind much anyway if he did. His eyes were deerlike, deep and black and wet. He was good-looking, one of the most handsome guys in his neighborhood, and he knew it.

He never had a problem landing dates. He dressed smartly, and though he was five foot nine, he sauntered through the Tunis quarter of Baghdad's Suleikh neighborhood as though he were six two. He was on his way out for the night, and in a good mood.

The Tunis quarter was once a lousy place to him. He was born there, but when he was four, his father was admitted to a program in international law in Wales, so the family moved to Cardiff. When his dad graduated, he took an important job with Lloyd's of London, the British shipping insurance colossus, so they stayed in Britain.

Hayder was twelve and happy in England, barely spoke any Arabic, and didn't remember anything about Iraq, but two forces beyond his comprehension summoned the family back home. The first was unchallengeable and came from Saddam Hussein's government: when the war with Iran started, the regime ordered all Iraqis studying abroad to come home to serve the country. Although Hayder's father was worried about returning with his family—they had developed habits and customs that might be problematic back in Baghdad—there was little choice in the matter. He was conscripted into the Iraqi Ministry of Transportation.

He tried to make the best of the situation and told Hayder, "I want you to know who you are and where you come from. You have a proud history there."

The second force summoning them back was just as unyielding but altogether hidden from Hayder. His mother, in her early forties, was ravaged with breast cancer and was going home to die.

Hayder was miserable. Gone were the green streets of Cardiff and his friends at St. David's Primary. Now he lived in a city that had enemies, rocketed regularly by Iranians. He used to listen to the music program *Top of the Pops* on the BBC, and Duran Duran, and even knew a few break-dance moves. He hated Iraqi music. He didn't know what they were saying and certainly couldn't dance to it. He wore shorts, and the other kids on the street made fun of him and said he was gay. They stared at his BMX bike, which his father had shipped from England, as though it were a Rolls-Royce. He sat in school and couldn't understand more than three or four Arabic words. The kids taunted him for living in Britain, calling him *ameel, ameel il-ingleez*. When he asked his mom what it meant, she told him to ignore them. She had heard the same thing when she was growing up: her father served as a military officer on the staff of King Faisal, who had been installed by the Brits.

One day his mom told him to take care of his brother and sister and to be good. His thirteenth birthday wasn't far off. He didn't know what she meant. That night, his uncle came to gather Hayder and his siblings for a sleepover that lasted for days. When Hayder returned home, his mother was already in the ground, buried at the Karkh Cemetery on the western outskirts of Baghdad.

Not long after, his father was injured by a bomb blast down south in Muhammara, and Hayder's first year back in Iraq came to a close.

Over time, Hayder adapted. He learned Arabic and found new friends who liked Madonna and Michael Jackson. They traded cassettes, posters for their rooms, and VHS tapes of American movies like *Rambo* and the James Bond series. One of his friends even had a porno on VHS.

Hayder made the Tunis quarter his own. After he graduated from the Oil Training Institute of Baghdad, he found a job as a translator for international companies that came into Iraq to sell products under the UN's oil-for-food program in the 1990s. Russian, French, and Indian companies, they all spoke English and liked Hayder. He made about $5 a day, which wasn't great, but it was work. He spent it on cigarettes and on his dates.

When his little sister was married, his father threw a huge party in their home. After the bride and groom signed the contract in the *katb kitaab* ceremony, he took Hayder aside into the storage room of the house and said, "Look, son, I've invited all of my friends. They're going to bring their daughters with them. I wish you'd pick one, because I want to see my oldest son get married."

Hayder didn't want to get married. "I'm getting married every night to a different girl!" he said to himself, smiling at his joke.

"Son, I want to hug my grandchildren before I die." Hayder bristled a bit and said, "Dad, okay, I'll look."

He walked back into the living room. The ceremony had given way to celebration and feasting and Iraqi pop music. He saw Dina and within minutes made plans to take her out for a date.

There weren't any nightclubs in Baghdad. They went out to smoke narghile by riverbank restaurants such as Qamr al-Zaman and Al-Saha, where they ate kebabs and fish. Dina liked to smoke cigarettes but couldn't in public, so they mostly relaxed at home with his family.

In less than a year, they were married, on March 1, 2001. Hayder was twenty-seven.

Homeboy and the 101st

Hayder and Dina moved into a small home in Dora, on the south side of Baghdad. There was a large refinery nearby and stretches of empty fields. They had a happy year, young and married, and by the middle of 2002, Dina was pregnant. They decorated their home with Louis XV furniture, gaudy and gold, and hung *kharze zarqas*—lapis lazuli–colored amulets meant to ward off the evil eye—on each wall.

When the regime's official television channels switched over to Al-

Jazeera on 9/11, Hayder sensed the approach of another war. Even though Hayder found no Iraqis in the list of terrorists who had hijacked the airplanes, he worried that it would be used as an excuse to attack Saddam. They used to be able to listen to *Amrika al-yawm—America Today*—on the radio, but the regime cut the frequencies as American forces gathered in the Persian Gulf. They knew that George W. Bush had said Iraq was part of an "axis of evil," along with their enemy Iran, but it was hard to know more than that.

Hayder's brother-in-law managed to buy a satellite dish, though it was illegal. When nighttime came, they sneaked onto the rooftop with the Nilesat dish and pointed it up at the sky until the signal from the outside world poured in. They stacked some crates to conceal it and hurried back down to watch CNN, as though they were eavesdropping on a conversation about themselves. American flags always flapped in the corner of the television screen. Before the sun climbed back up, Hayder and his brother-in-law would slip back onto the roof to remove the dish.

For months they gathered to watch the secret news, until it was 2003 and not much of a secret anymore. They saw Iraqi soldiers scampering along the roof of the local grade school, and antiaircraft batteries were soon visible. Hayder and Dina watched as tanks rumbled through the fields of Dora, followed by massive trailers carrying helicopters and aircraft parts. The soldiers were everywhere, blocking bridges, digging ditches in nearby gardens.

Hayder was convinced there would be a massacre. Saddam would never surrender. Turkey had decided against letting American troops invade from the north, so the invasion would surely come from the south, with Dora as the southern entry point. Dina was swelling; the baby was due in seven weeks. He was afraid to move the family in her state.

On the first night of the war, at around five thirty in the morning, their home shivered from an explosion. Hayder ran to the roof to watch the bombers come but never saw them. They flew far overhead and disappeared before the bombs landed.

The ground forces were coming. Hoping to avoid being caught in the cross fire in Dora, Hayder and Dina moved in with her family in a different neighborhood. The regime broadcast a message saying that Baghdad would be an American graveyard and that there were soldiers on every street corner, ready to defend their city.

But the soldiers disappeared. Hayder and Dina were packed alongside five families into one home, where they watched the news without rest. A couple weeks in, Al-Jazeera broadcast the American troops crossing a bridge that was only a block away, and Hayder cried out, "They're here!"

He found it difficult to contain his emotions. The fear that had patrolled most of his life in Iraq surrendered its weapons without a fight. He was overjoyed. The Americans would come, bringing in the best administrators to run the country. They would have democracy, they could start selling their oil again, they would have Kentucky Fried Chicken and Burger King and nightclubs. Microsoft would come to Iraq.

He ran out into the street to celebrate, and found others bashing windows and looting stores. The next day he saw an Iraqi shoot someone in the chest while the crowd continued to loot.

"Can I describe it? You can't laugh at me. It was like watching *Saving Private Ryan*. The convoy was like a mile long. I was watching a movie with American soldiers in it, and they were smoking, making jokes, and someone would say, 'What the fuck?' and 'Shit,' and I turned to Dina and said, 'Is this real, or am I imagining it?' She used to tease me for liking the Americans and Brits so much. 'Here are your people,' she said."

Hayder was standing with Dina and his best friend, Mouayyad, when the first convoy of the 101st Airborne rolled in. Hayder approached the soldiers walking on foot, unsure if he wanted to say hi or thank you, but as he headed over, one of the soldiers raised his rifle and said, "If you come any closer, I will shoot you." Hayder said, "Relax, you don't need to pull out your gun."

The soldier lowered his rifle, shocked at the British-accented English. Hayder was surprised at the fear he saw in the young soldier's eyes. "I just wanted to say hi, guys. We're very happy that you came over."

Dina wanted to move back into their home in Dora now that the

Americans had arrived. They were worried about the looting and didn't want their home ransacked. Hayder told her to wait behind while he surveyed the neighborhood, but she wouldn't listen and got into the car.

They crossed the bridge into Dora and into the gaze of a huge tank staring at them. Hayder got out slowly with his hands up and then Dina, who was due any week now. The tank's muzzle rotated away in deference, and the two got back into the car and drove on.

The house and water storage tank on the roof were punctured from shrapnel, but although the windows were broken, nobody had stolen anything. Hayder excitedly went out and bought a generator and supplies to ready his home for the arrival of their first child.

A Knock at the Door

Dina whispered nervously to Hayder, who was still in bed. "Hayder, there are a lot of Americans in the front yard. I think they just knocked on the door!" He threw on a T-shirt and shorts and opened the door. They were standing out front, laughing at a joke someone must have just made. They turned to Hayder. He read derision in their faces, which to him seemed to say, "Here comes another Iraqi idiot who can't speak a word of English." A soldier stepped forward and handed Hayder a sheet of paper, which had a few sentences in Arabic saying that they wanted to search the house. Hayder handed the paper back and said, "Gentlemen, I don't need this. How can I help you?"

"Holy shit, you speak English?"

"I'm pretty sure I was just speaking English. How can I help?"

Some bombs they had dropped hadn't yet exploded, they said, so they wanted to see if there were any in his yard or up on the roof. Hayder invited them inside, offering a Coke or some tea. The captain of the unit said, "We'd love to have some tea, but we're dirty and do not want to come inside and mess up your house. Maybe we could sit in the garden."

Hayder pulled some plastic chairs from his garage and sat out back with the captain while the others searched for unexploded bombs in the garden. A citrus tree threw a shadow on the tomatoes climbing their wooden stakes, and cactus plants stood guard on the edge of the back porch. They spoke about Iraq and the war and Saddam for nearly an hour. The captain shook his hand gratefully as he left.

Ten minutes later, a soldier named Izzy returned, knocking at the door. "Hayder, the cap'n wants you to come over. There's an Iraqi family telling us something, but we can't understand 'em. Can you come?" Hayder told Dina he'd be back in a few minutes; it was just a few houses down the street. He walked over with Izzy, translated the conversation, and walked back home.

Fifteen minutes later, Izzy was back at the door. "Hayder, can you help us again?" So he went back.

They kept coming for help. He went to twenty homes, throughout the day and into the evening. He was happy. He hadn't met a lot of his neighbors before that day; they seemed so grateful to him for his ability to translate.

The next morning, the captain knocked on his door at eight o'clock. Hayder was still sleeping and grumbled when Dina woke him up. "I'm sorry if we woke you, Hayder. But would you like to work for us?" Hayder was excited but said he needed to discuss it with his wife.

Dina knew Hayder would take the job but worried that it might not be safe. "Where's the risk?" he said. "Saddam's gone!" Everyone was thanking him for speaking English so well.

His friends told him, "Do it, man! You're gonna help us out a lot! Who is going to bring our voice to the Americans?"

They said, "You're gonna help out the neighborhood, bring back the electricity."

Hayder demurred. "I'm not the mayor, I'm just going to be a translator."

They said, "Yeah, but how will they know what we need unless somebody tells them?"

Five bucks a day, cash, that was the deal. Izzy always played Nelly's "Hot in Herre" in the Humvee and taught Hayder how to dance like him. Everywhere they went, Iraqi boys crowded around to look at and flirt with the few females in the company. Hayder felt like he was in the movies. He absorbed their slang and made them laugh.

"The fuck's your name again?" someone asked in the first few days.

"Hayder."

"What kind of shitty name is Hayder?" They busted him like he was one of their own.

"Well, it's a local name."

"Nah, that's too tough for us to remember. We're gonna give you a nickname."

"Okay."

"Let's call you Homeboy." And everyone did.

Mouayyad was with Hayder when they saw the 101st enter Baghdad. They were best friends. When they were in high school, and Saddam was about to invade Kuwait, they worried they'd be trucked to the front lines to fight against Americans. "If that happens," Mouayyad said, "we'll go to Kurdistan, and from there to Turkey. Then to Cuba. And then we'll smuggle ourselves into America."

As soon as he could afford to buy his first car, Mouayyad bought a Chevrolet Caprice Classic. He was crazy about America. He used to kiss his Caprice each morning. "I'm not gonna buy Toyota shit!" Mouayyad said. "I'm buying American."

So when the Americans came in, Mouayyad also stepped forward to help. His English wasn't as good, but he knew engines and machines, so they hired him to work on their bases as a generator repairman. He kept their ACs running and their bases lit. They called him Moe.

The troops that Hayder rode with were there to fight a war, not to become policemen. One evening on patrol, there were peals of gunfire. Hayder knew it was celebratory fire; that someone had just been married. But he could not stop the Americans from shooting back, and Iraqis were wounded.

Some units were less disciplined than others and kicked in front doors instead of knocking. They shouted as they came in, not giving the women of the homes time to cover their hair. Hayder heard them curse the Americans as he translated the soldiers' demands to search their homes.

The people in his neighborhood came by every day with only one question, which they asked relentlessly: "Hayder, when is the power coming back?" He told them that the electricity wasn't controlled by a single button somewhere, but they weren't assuaged. Everyone talked about the massive generator that the Americans brought into Kuwait after the Gulf War. Why couldn't they do that here?

He communicated his neighbors' concerns to the Americans just as relentlessly, so much so that Izzy and the others would sigh, "Oh boy, here we go again. Here comes Homeboy, gonna ask us about the power."

"Well, what's going on with the electricity?" he'd ask. Their answers were vague, and the higher the rank, the loftier the language—"We're going to set things up so that the Iraqi people take control over their own destiny"—and Hayder realized that they didn't have the training, the capacity, or a clue.

Before long, he was lying, and lying all the time. He wanted the Iraqis in his neighborhood to still have hope. He didn't want them to start hating Americans, even though he saw it germinating in the splinters of every kicked-in door, with each passing summer month without electricity. He couldn't fully explain it to himself, but he loved America and got angry whenever anyone spoke poorly of it or called the Americans liars. So when they asked, "Hayder, what did they say about the electricity?" he usually said he forgot to ask.

One evening he came back from work and found Dina's sister running from room to room. "She's in labor! Get your things together!" Hayder and Dina piled into their Malaysian Proton Wira and raced to the hospital, hoping that their doctor would make it there before the American-imposed curfew.

Ali was born around seven in the evening on May 29, 2003. Hayder scooped him up and kissed him as he cried. He felt sorry for his boy, because he was born at the wrong time. He whispered to Ali, "I'm going to protect you until you get big. I will do anything that needs to be done to keep you safe." After a few days, Dina and Ali came back to the house, and they lived like a regular family. Some of the soldiers came by one day to say hi to Ali and take pictures.

Quitting

There wasn't room for him in the Humvee as they rode through the neighborhood of Abu Dasheer, near Dora, so Hayder rode in the back of a commandeered ambulance with some other soldiers. The main street was always crowded because of the small stands on the median, where vendors sold vegetables, cell phones, and watermelons. The ambulance was stuck in pedestrian traffic when someone flung open the back door and tried to fire a revolver. The soldiers leaped on him before anyone was wounded, took the assailant to prison, and told the Iraqis on the street that nobody would be permitted to sell goods in the middle of the road anymore. To underscore their point, they drove their Humvees up onto the median and sent vendors running.

The war was still in its infancy, but things were deteriorating quickly. Hayder tried to help, sitting with the captain each day, discussing alternate routes, and assessing the quality of incoming tips from informants. He drafted a new letter in Arabic for the soldiers to present to Iraqis, which was much more polite. He stopped asking about the electricity, which seemed to relieve just about everyone in the unit.

But a slip of paper and conversations with the captain were just words. Once an RPG sailed past his Humvee and hit the median. Another time a car blew up in front of him. Soldiers in his unit were killed, sometimes by bullet, sometimes by bomb.

Hayder decided to quit. Ali was just a couple months old, and Hayder felt like he was breaking his promise to protect his son. He didn't sign up for this, he told the captain, and walked home.

The next morning, the Americans came by and said, "Homeboy, we can't do this shit without you. You're gonna have to come along with us." They said, "Look, everyone's pissed off over here. You think we're having a good time?"

Hayder said, "Okay, let me grab my clothes." He didn't want to go back, but he loved his unit, Charlie Company of the Eighty-Second Airborne. He was worried that something bad might happen to them or that they might mistakenly do something bad to his fellow Iraqis, so he went back to help, absorbing and interpreting the frustrations of both sides.

Charlie Company knew that Hayder was getting burned out and was starting to fear for his safety, so they started dropping him off at his front door to make sure he got home in one piece. He knew it wasn't convenient for them to turn a convoy of several Humvees up his narrow street, so one day he told them to just drop him on the main road by his house. They agreed but said that they would stay to watch him from there.

As he approached his home, a stranger, maybe twenty years old, was coming out the front door. Hayder sprinted toward him. The Americans in Charlie Company saw something amiss and scrambled over, just as Hayder had beaten the intruder into submission.

"Homeboy, ask him if there's anyone else inside."

Hayder translated the soldier's question about his own home. Yes, there were two more inside.

"Are they armed?"

Yes, they were armed. "They're waiting to kill you," the young man groaned to Hayder.

"Wait here," said the captain, and they kicked in his door. Inside were two teenagers, who dropped their guns the moment they saw US military bearing down on them. Mercifully, Dina and Ali were visiting her sister that day.

During the interrogation, Hayder learned that one of his neighbors had informed the intruders about his work with the Americans. They called him an *ameel*, just like in grade school.

He wanted to leave, but where could he go? He owned a 9 millimeter pistol, but that wasn't much protection. Another friend of his, who worked as an interpreter and lived a few blocks over, was hanged in the neighborhood with a sign around his neck that read "This is what happens to those who work with Americans."

Dina begged him to quit. Hayder wanted to, but he felt that he understood Americans better than the Iraqis ever would and understood

Iraqis better than the Americans ever could. He was the bridge, and even though things were getting bad, he had to continue.

It was a Thursday, the night of August 6, 2003. Hayder was killing time in the Eighty-Second Airborne's compound across the bridge from his home in Dora. While waiting for the captain to come in with their orders, he sat on a worn-out black sofa and played FIFA World Cup soccer on the PlayStation with a soldier named Brian Hellermann, a thirty-five-year-old Minnesota native with a wife and two young children back at Fort Bragg, North Carolina.

The captain came in and said, "Homeboy, we're going out tonight." They needed to go pay the salaries of the Iraqi police and then bring them along on a training mission to teach them how to patrol. Brian paused the game so that they could finish it later. Everyone armored up, except for Hayder, who didn't have any gear.

As soon as they left the compound, at around seven in the evening, a car swerved in front of them and blew up. They set up a perimeter and waited for backup to come and investigate the wreckage.

When backup arrived, Hayder and the guys piled back into the Humvees and resumed their primary mission, heading to the police station. A few minutes later, another car sped up alongside them on the highway, coming closer and closer. "Pull over!" the soldiers shouted before firing at the hood of the car, which stopped quickly.

"Weird fuckin' night, huh?" Hayder said to the captain, who grunted his assent.

They paid the Iraqi cops and started their night patrol. Around a quarter to one in the morning, they pulled off onto the shoulder of Highway 8, alongside a middle-aged Iraqi standing beside his car. "Hayder, go over there and tell that guy he's gotta move his car because curfew's about to start." Hayder translated for the man, who said the car wasn't starting.

"Well, he can't stay here, or else some other unit might detain him. Ask him where he lives. If it's close, we'll drop him off at home."

The bullets blazed in just as Hayder began to translate. The Americans were screaming to get to cover as they fired back. Hayder stood in shock for a moment, wondering where the bullets were coming from.

He needed to run. His Humvee was directly in the field of fire, so running there was foolish. He looked around. He spotted a white Toyota 4x4 pickup truck and bolted toward it. He heard bullets flying past his ears and slapping into the side of the truck.

Something blew up, maybe an RPG. He didn't know what. He was thrown onto the ground, and above the gunfire he heard the captain shouting orders to take cover and shoot back, but Hayder didn't have a weapon and wasn't a soldier.

He was lying there when he saw Brian Hellermann fall to the ground. He knew Brian was shot but didn't know where. Brian's face was turned down toward the pavement, and his radio was on and squawking. He was only five feet away and still in danger. Those were the only thoughts that formed in Hayder's head. He got to his feet and bolted over to drag Brian back to shelter in the lee of the truck.

He made it over to Brian and started to pull him but fell to the ground. Hayder looked down at his body and saw that his right leg was missing. Then another round tore into his left leg. Hayder turned and saw the assailant crouched in a nearby field, spraying sparking shots along the pavement. He looked over at Brian and saw that he was dead.

"Oh my God. What have I done?" Hayder lay on the pavement of a street not two miles away from his home. He wanted to hold his son. "Ali just came into my life, and now he's going to live without a dad? Dina's going to have to go through all of this alone." He looked up at the sky as the fight roared around him. He wasn't religious, but he said, "Hey, Allah, just try to save me here, make this go by as quick as possible."

Someone ran through the fire and grabbed them both, dragging them off to the side.

It was quiet. Someone was carrying Hayder. He looked down and saw that his leg was still hanging by a husk of flesh. They put him in the back of a Humvee tub next to Brian, whose face was purple; a large-caliber round had pierced the Kevlar of his helmet. They piled dead bodies next to Hayder, and then more bodies on top of him. Though he was barely conscious, he realized that they didn't know that he was still alive. His throat was full of fluid, so he couldn't make much noise. As the Humvee raced back to the base, the blood of men above seeped down onto him, and he drifted in and out of consciousness.

The Humvee came to a halt. Someone shouted, "Hey! Homeboy's alive, get him outta there!" Hayder was extracted from among the corpses. A medic appeared, wrapped strong elastic bands around Hayder's legs, and said, "Don't worry. Don't worry. Just stay here. Homeboy! Stay here."

When his throat cleared, he shouted and thrashed around. The medic placed a firm hand on his shoulder and said, "Homeboy, you need to calm down, you're bleeding a lot."

In the Combat Support Hospital, they laid him out and cut off his jeans and T-shirt and boxers and began to clean him. Someone stood at the side of the table with a defibrillator, just in case. A doctor came over to Hayder and gently took hold of his hand. "Son, can I pray for you in the name of the Lord Jesus?" Hayder said, "Yes sir." He didn't care; he'd take any kind of hope. He passed out as the doctors strapped on their surgical masks.

When he woke up, he wanted water, and someone brought it to him. He looked around the room, and on a nearby gurney there lay a soldier whose face was shelled, torn up by gunfire and the blast. When he saw that Hayder was awake, he said, "The others are dead. You and me are the only ones who made it."

The captain came in and smiled a pained smile. "Homeboy, we came to visit you in the middle of the night, and you were a little delirious. We asked you to go to work, and you know what you said? You said, 'Sir, I'm a bit tired. Is it all right if I go out tomorrow?'"

For the first time since he'd woken up, Hayder looked down at his body, but there was a blanket draped over it. He lifted it up slowly and saw both legs there. *My God*, he thought, *they saved it!* There were steel bars and rods sticking out of his right leg, and his left leg was heavily bandaged. He was overjoyed, certain that he would be able to walk with both legs, and thanked Allah and Jesus and anyone else who might have saved him.

He was tired and overwhelmed and went back to sleep. For the next five days, they wheeled him back and forth to the operating room to perform more surgeries. He was heavily medicated, and hallucinated so fiercely that the orderlies were forced to strap him to the bed. He slept for two days continuously while the surgeons worked on his legs.

But they were swelling, growing bigger and bigger despite the operations. One night nearly a week after the attack, the surgeon woke up Hayder and said, "Look, Homeboy, we did our best, but we have to amputate now. You've got gangrene going up your leg, and if I don't take it off tonight, you might wake up dead."

Hayder said, "Okay, let's do it."

When he woke up, the blanket was again draped over him, but this time he lifted it up and the leg was gone.

Dina had not heard from Hayder in a week. She thought he was dead, until another interpreter in Hayder's group paid a visit to pass along the news that he was still alive. They did not believe him or the Americans anymore, though, and were convinced that it was a lie. After two days, Hayder's dad walked up to the military compound where Hayder's unit in the Eighty-Second Airborne Division operated and shouted, "Just give us his body so we can bury him!" The captain said, "No, no, I promise he's alive. We're gonna bring him home soon."

It had been only a hundred days since it started, since the day Hayder watched the 101st Airborne stream into Baghdad like a strip of movie film. Since his neighbors surely knew about his work with the Americans by now, he rented a secret home a few blocks over and hobbled into it after nightfall. There was no prosthetic leg, just a stump, some wooden crutches, and a bag of drugs. Dina's brother brought in a crate of whiskey and slept on the couch with a pistol.

The first three nights, Hayder didn't sleep. He watched three sunrises and thought he was losing his mind. He kept the door locked and watched television and played video games—Tomb Raider, Call of Duty, and Counter-Strike—with his brother-in-law. He drank heavily.

The summer heat was peaking. Since there was no electricity, his neighbors would sit out in the garden for a bit of breeze, but that was too risky for Hayder. He didn't want someone to jump over the fence and kill him, so he bought a generator, installed it in the garden, and stayed indoors. Eventually word spread that a one-legged man was living there, and his neighbors realized it was the same Hayder who tried to save an American, so someone tossed a grenade over the garden wall and blew up the generator.

His father was working in the new Ministry of Transportation and met regularly with American officials. Paul Bremer was in charge of the country and had given the transportation portfolio to a lawyer named Ronald Dwight.

Mr. Dwight noticed a deep despondency in Hayder's father during a meeting one afternoon and asked him privately what was troubling him. He learned about Hayder's situation and said he wanted to help.

There was little left in Hayder's reservoir of hope, but he began to correspond with Mr. Dwight. He was so worried about his spotty dial-up Internet connection that he hobbled out and bought a small pile of dial-up cards and bribed the telephone serviceman in the neighborhood to ensure that he always had a line to the outside world.

Mr. Dwight knew T. Christian Miller, the investigative reporter from the *Los Angeles Times* who had tormented USAID with his exposés on bungled reconstruction projects. T. had the unusual beat of covering reconstruction contracts in Iraq, and he knew the fine print that led to so much corruption and inefficiency in the war efforts. His articles were not about massive car bombs in marketplaces but about sputtering power plants, and they did a lot more to explain the root causes of the major problems rending the country. Dwight introduced Hayder to T., who dropped by quietly for a visit.

T. left with a sheaf of documents and contracts. Hayder had been paid through a San Diego–based defense contractor called Titan Corporation, which received hundreds of millions of dollars from the government to find interpreters, whose average pay was a few dollars an hour.

Hayder didn't really understand the contracts, which were freighted with legalese. After he lost his leg, he had called his bosses at Titan, but all they ever told him was "Yeah, we'd love to help you, Homeboy, but we can't get you out of Iraq." One day they told him to get a passport, and they'd give him treatment in Kuwait. But as soon as he got one, they said they couldn't. When they said they were going to bring him to Qatar, Hayder excitedly packed his bags, but on the scheduled day, they told him they couldn't help him after all.

Holed up in his hiding place, Hayder entered the Internet access codes from the cards he had bought and waited for something to happen. Miller wrote a front-page article about him, demonstrating that Titan had done nothing to help, and suddenly Hayder's boss called to say the company had finally decided to help. His father loaded him into the car and drove him to a small clinic in Amman, Jordan, where Titan would finally provide for a prosthetic leg and treatment.

The first place Hayder walked to with his new prosthetic leg was the Embassy of the United States of America in Jordan. He had brought along a couple letters of support from his unit, along with a certificate of appreciation: "Thank you for your dedicated service to Coalition Forces and the paratroopers of the Eighty-Second Airborne Division. Your tireless efforts have contributed to a brighter future for Iraq. We could not have done it without you. Best of luck in all you do. C Company 2-325th Airborne Infantry Regiment."

He spoke to a young consular officer through the thick windowpane and said, "I am an Iraqi interpreter, and I would like to apply for asylum in America." He thought there would be a form to fill out, but there wasn't. The officer said, "Oh, you need to go over to the UNHCR and register." So Hayder walked to the United Nations High Commissioner for Refugees and registered his family. It was early 2004.

Dina and Ali came to Amman, and the family moved into a small apartment in the Seventh Circle neighborhood. Titan told them that they would have a monthly stipend of $600. One month later, a representative of Titan visited to inform them that the next month would be the last, delivering an ultimatum: "This is the last of the money we can give you. You can either go back to Iraq and work for us or quit, but this is it."

Hayder knew he couldn't go back. The burning of the Americans on the bridge in Fallujah was looping on all of the news stations. He called his dad and said, "The house is yours. Do what you want with it, sell it, burn it, give it away, I don't care. I'm not coming back." Dina sold the jewelry that she had inherited and their computer and television, cobbling together about $2,000.

Hayder couldn't work. He was in Jordan illegally, and if a cop stopped him, he could be deported. There are few protections for refugees in the Middle East. None of the countries has signed the 1951 Geneva Convention Relating to the Status of Refugees, the international agreement according certain protections, chief among them *non-refoulement*: the principle that refugees cannot be forced to return to the country from which they fled. In Jordan, Hayder was nothing and could become nothing, hobbling through a precarious state of limbo.

The two-month stipend from Titan evaporated, and the money made from selling Dina's jewelry was fast running out. Amman was expensive, and the only plan Hayder had was to hope that his refugee petition would get the family to safety in America before they were broke or deported.

T. Miller called Hayder and said there was an American lawyer who'd read the article in the *Los Angeles Times* and wanted to help him sue American International Group (AIG), the insurance giant that had received more than $1.5 billion in premiums from US taxpayers to provide insurance coverage under the Defense Base Act. The act, a World War II–era law, required all contractors working for the US government to provide insurance to their employees, Iraqi interpreters included. But the Iraqis were rarely informed about this right, and Titan, AIG, and other companies didn't remind them. Worse, representatives sent to Jordan pressured gravely wounded interpreters into accepting a onetime payout and signing a waiver of all future coverage. Some were told that they would be sent back to Iraq if they refused to sign.

Hayder was patched into the Houston courtroom during the lawsuit by telephone. The judge asked him questions. AIG fought hard against the lawyer representing Hayder but was ordered to compensate Hayder for the loss of his leg. This was valued at the rate of an American leg: $21,000.

When the bank called to inform Hayder that the wire had arrived, he woke up Dina with excitement. "This will get us started in America!" he said. All that remained was the visa.

11.

The Dog's Head

As soon as my arms were cut loose from their casts, I left West Chicago and drove to Boston with the hare-brained idea that I could work for Samantha Power, the Pulitzer-winning author of *A Problem from Hell: America and the Age of Genocide* and the director of Harvard's Carr Center for Human Rights Policy. A year earlier, when I was still in Iraq, a student of hers had emailed me to see if I was interested in providing research assistance for a book she was writing that examined America's foreign policy "amnesia," since I had once edited a blog called *American Amnesia* on the same topic. Now that I was unemployed and sufficiently healed, I wrote to Power to offer my services, and found a cheap apartment on Massachusetts Avenue in the South End of Boston.

It was a flimsy lead, but it served as sufficient justification to leave home. My parents had put up with enough of my mania, and I needed to be alone, in a place of my own. Power never replied to my email. In my haste to head east, I didn't realize that she was on leave as Senator Barack Obama's chief foreign policy advisor. I sent my résumé to Obama's DC office, and that was the end of that.

I had buried Iraq from sight and avoided the news. Whenever someone new asked what I did, I said I was getting ready for law school. The nightmare of being abandoned in Fallujah visited only once a week now. Apart from visits to the orthodontist, my life was free of hospitals and clinics. When a reference to or memory from the war fluttered past my ramparts, I shooed it away and reset the drill clock to take another LSAT practice test. I tore a photo of Alfred Hitchcock out of an old issue of the *New Yorker* and taped it over the only mirror in the apartment so that the scars on my face wouldn't remind me of the fall. I sealed away whatever triggers I found, repressing a tumorous sense of failure.

Denny

Dennis Hastert has a large frame and tiny, Luxembourgish eyes. When I walked into the Speaker's chambers, he ambled over and shook my hand as though we were close friends. I thought of my father as my hand disappeared into the large grip of the man who had sealed my dad's political fate.

"Sit down, Kirk!" he said jovially, gesturing at a small conference table.

I didn't really know what I was doing there. Hastert had run into my mom at a Fourth of July parade in West Chicago a few weeks earlier and told her that he wanted me to come in for a visit. I received an invitation from his office a week later and rode the Chinatown bus down to Washington.

"So. You're back. Tell me about your time there."

I had done my best to lock them away over the past seven months, but a herd of emotions and experiences and opinions still brayed and clambered inside. Sitting across the table from the Speaker, a man from whom I wanted nothing, I flung open the gates and gave an unvarnished critique of everything wrong I'd witnessed back in Iraq. Hastert nodded throughout, as his foreign policy advisor took notes.

After forty-five minutes, I felt embarrassed for the time I had spent talking, so I stood up and thanked him for inviting me in. We posed for a picture between flags of America and Illinois, next to a display of his collection of model trains, model cars, and model tractors. I smirked, trying not to reveal the shiny braces in my mouth. I caught the next bus up to Boston.

Forty-eight hours later, I received an email marked "Time Sensitive" from a staffer in his office, requesting that I return to Washington.

Hastert was sitting at his desk when I returned a few days later. A muted television broadcast footage of marines evacuating US citizens from Beirut, due to the war that had broken out between Israel and Hezbollah. I hadn't been able to iron the only suit I owned, and felt sheepish. Hastert smiled slightly as he got up to greet me. He put his arm on my shoulder and got in close: "Listen, I want you to sit behind me and just listen. If anything seems really off to you, just lean forward and whisper in my ear. 'Kay?"

"Okay, Mr. Speaker." I had no idea what he was talking about.

He guided me to a door in the corner of the office, which was opened by an aide as we approached. The camera flashes were momentarily blinding, so it took a moment for my eyes to make out the dour face of Nouri al-Maliki, who had just become the prime minister of Iraq.

A dining table was set in the middle of the small room. As we walked in, Senators Ted Stevens, Dick Durbin, and Harry Reid and Congressman John Boehner were chatting in a corner with House Minority Leader Nancy Pelosi. I felt like Forrest Gump as I took my seat behind the Speaker, directly across from the prime minister. The media were dismissed from the room as a light breakfast of smoked salmon and fruit was brought in.

Hastert initiated the breakfast with an affirmation of the US-Iraqi relationship and introduced each of the senior leaders in the room. Al-Maliki's interpreter translated the bromides into the prime minister's ear in a quiet, unobtrusive tone. The conversation then turned to each member's pet issues. Stevens spoke bluntly about the difficulty he would have in appropriating significant funds for any new initiatives. Durbin wanted Al-Maliki to condemn Hezbollah as a terrorist organization. The congressmen spoke more to each other than to the Iraqi prime minister.

Nobody mentioned the reconstruction. Nobody talked about the civil war. Nobody brought up the growing problem of refugees fleeing Iraq. I took notes but didn't lean forward to whisper anything in Hastert's ear. What could I say?

After an hour, the Speaker stood, prompting everyone else in the room to rise and then clear out. He came over to me: "Stick around. I'd like you to hear his address, and I want to introduce you to some friends."

An aide walked me down to an ornate Victorian room and told me to sit there until someone came for me. I walked around the small room, taking in the pale green walls and elaborate inlaid marble, and sat on a couch. I had no idea where, exactly, I was and what in the world was happening.

I was staring at my notes from the breakfast when the door opened and Nouri al-Maliki wandered in. An aide trailing him quickly sized me up. I shot to my feet and said, "*as-salaamu 'alaykum ya ra'is,*" as I backed away and yielded the couch with a gesture. His eyes were forlorn, always fixed on the ground a few feet in front of him. They finally lifted up and fixed on mine. "*W'alaikum as-salaam . . .*" he mumbled, his voice trailing off with uncertainty as to who I was.

We stared at each other for a few seconds. I smiled, flashing my braces at him, and didn't know what to say. It felt as though he were looking through my eyes into the back of my skull.

The room filled with American and Iraqi aides, who prepped him for his imminent speech to Congress. A foreign-policy aide to Hastert came over and whispered, "What are they saying?" She nodded as I translated mundane snippets of their conversation about last-second changes to the speech.

In the scrum, Hastert put his hand on my shoulder. "Come over with me, Kirk." We walked out of the small room. I looked to my right and saw Dick Cheney walking up the hallway toward us. The members of the House and Senate rose as Hastert and the vice president walked in, followed by al-Maliki. Applause. Once in the chamber, Hastert pointed to the left of the dais and said, "Just find a place and stay there. I'll come for you afterward."

As al-Maliki worked through his speech, a large black fly harassed his face and forehead. He brushed it away with his hand with an unchanging face, but the fly persisted. I stopped listening to his boilerplate speech and followed the insect, which flew away from the prime minister in drunken curlicues over Senators John McCain and Barack Obama, Secretary of Defense Donald Rumsfeld, and Attorney General Alberto Gonzales. Up it flew, and my eyes scanned the dozens of relief portraits of famous lawmakers throughout history hanging near the ceiling, settling on a profile of Hammurabi, lawgiver of ancient Mesopotamia. I remembered an *Iraq Daily Update* I'd written about a USAID and State Department initiative to train Iraqis in the rule of law. As the civil war spread, sectarian militias were now implementing extrajudicial court systems, imposing their own rule of law across huge swaths of the country, and judges were fleeing.

Someone in the gallery began to scream.

Protester: Iraqis want the troops to leave! Bring them home now! Iraqis want the troops to leave! Bring them home now!

Hastert: If our honored guest will suspend for the moment, the chair notes disturbance in the gallery. The sergeant at arms will secure order by removing those engaging in disruption.

[*Applause.*]

Protester: Bring them home now!

Hastert: The gentleman may resume.

Al-Maliki [*through translator*]: Hope over fear, liberty over oppression, dignity over submission, democracy over dictatorship, federalism over a centralist state.

[*Applause.*]

Al-Maliki enjoyed a standing ovation. Hastert waved me over to introduce me to Representative Peter Hoekstra from Michigan, the Republican chair of the House Permanent Select Committee on Intelligence. "Talk to him about Iraq like you talked to me." Overloaded with input, I blankly shook his hand and followed Hoekstra into a conference room at the US Senate Select Committee on Intelligence.

My thoughts flitted barn swallow–like as I listened to Hoekstra detail a recent three-day trip to Baghdad. He and Senator Rick Santorum had eagerly summoned a press conference a month earlier to announce to the world that weapons of mass destruction had finally been found in Iraq, suggesting that the controversial decision to invade had been decisively vindicated. They minimized the fact that the sarin and mustard gas canisters were relics of the Iran-Iraq war, rusted-out carcasses decaying for decades in the desert. They peddled this scrap metal for all it was worth until the Pentagon stepped in to repudiate the significance of the find. I smiled at Hoekstra but just wanted to get out of the Capitol and onto a train.

I was about twenty minutes north of DC on the Amtrak when my phone rang. "Mr. Johnson, we have the Speaker on the line for you." A baby was crying a few rows behind me, so I got up and made my way to the snack car. I sat on a stool while a small line of Amtrakkers ordered Heinekens and White Castle–grade cheeseburgers. Hastert's voice cut through the din: "Didja talk with Pete?"

"I did."

"Yeah. Good. Well, listen, I'm not gonna twist your arm. You're gonna do your own thing, but you know, the intel committee's a great job. Think you should come and work for us. That committee's a real sweet position; you could keep your eyes on Iraq, y'know?"

"Boy, I—"

"And y'know, Pete's a sharp guy."

"Okay, well, thank you for that, Mr. Speaker. I'm trying to figure out what I'm doing next, but I really appreciate the chance to talk with you guys. I need to mull it over for a bit."

"Yeah, like I said, you gotta do what you gotta do. I'm not gonna twist your arm, but think it over. This could be a real nice opportunity for you. And you know, I could always use you, too."

The train was hurtling north through Delaware when I hung up, bracing myself on the seat backs as I worked my way back to my row. I was in some strange bubble of opportunity and couldn't understand why. Even though I would soon be broke, I didn't want to work for Hastert or Hoekstra. I couldn't work for the Speaker without feeling as though I was betraying my father, and I couldn't work for Hoekstra without betraying my sense of integrity.

Besides, I was done with Iraq. I was taking the LSAT in another month and needed to submit all my law school applications by the fall. I decided to wait a couple days before politely declining the offers.

A storm rained over Baghdad. Yaghdan couldn't sleep. Just two days earlier, on October 13, a man from his neighborhood had spotted him walking out of the Green Zone. He didn't know the man or his name, just that he lived down the street near the bakery.

He crawled out of bed for *fajr*, the dawn prayer. As he prayed, he heard something rustle the bushes in his garden. *Probably a cat.* He managed a few hours' sleep before the generator sputtered out and the small fan by the bed fell quiet.

Haifa was still sleeping. Yaghdan thought he'd go out and get some bread for breakfast. As he opened the front door, he noticed a sheet of paper on the threshold.

"We will cut off your heads, and throw them in the trash."

He remembered the rustling sound from the previous night and crept out toward the garden, where he found the severed head of a dog.

He woke Haifa, who read the note and began to tremble. "Maybe the storm blew it into our yard!" she said, hopefully, but he shook his head, telling her it had been slipped under their door. He told her about the dog.

He didn't want to believe it was finally happening. Maybe the letter and the dog head were unrelated, arriving on his front step by coincidence, but his mind would no longer be swayed by wishful thoughts. They needed to go.

He wiped his hard drive, removing all traces of his work from his computer. He gathered the papers he'd collected over the years—commendation letters from Creative Associates and USAID and the contracts he had signed with the Americans—and fed them a few pages at a time into the flame of the *mankhalaf* that they used for grilling kebabs outside.

He was angry. He had taken every precaution. His own family didn't even know about his employer. He took a bucket of water and washed away the ashes and the blood from the dog's head. Haifa silently packed her most prized possessions into two large red-and-white-checked canvas bags. There was nothing to say.

He did not burn his badges. He needed them to get into the Green Zone one last time to ask for help. Before he walked out the gate, he told Haifa not to open the door for anyone, not to call anyone, and not to walk by the windows even once.

Yaghdan folded the note into his pocket. The air was foul from the rotting dog. He took a deep breath and flung open the steel gate to the street, not knowing if the authors of the threat were waiting on the other side. He hurried to the Green Zone.

Forty-five minutes later, he entered the USAID compound and headed to the corner office of the Hammurabi Office Building. He strode in, pulled the note from his pocket, and placed it on the desk of Sandy, the executive officer who was given to calling Iraqi staffers either Ahmed or Mohammad. "I need help!" he exclaimed as she peered up from her in-box. She stared at the Arabic on the threat letter and looked up at him blankly.

"It says, 'We will cut off your head!'"

Sandy told him to wait at his desk while she talked with the mission director.

Yaghdan knew about the empty houses in the compound. Several months earlier, when USAID was struggling to finish its annual report on time and needed his help, they had Yaghdan move into one of the houses for over a week until it was finished. The State Department had been encouraging USAID officers to move over to the new embassy compound, which meant even more vacancies. He thought they might let him live there for a couple months while he and Haifa had a chance to change neighborhoods.

Tona and Amina and his other Iraqi colleagues had sensed something was amiss as soon as he walked in. He told them about the threat, and they murmured. He sat at his cubicle and waited for something to happen. He worried about Haifa. What was he doing here? Why did he leave her alone?

The regional security officer, the man with the polygraph machine, called Yaghdan into the safe room of the building and closed the heavy door behind them. Inside, he found the mission director and the executive officer.

The RSO told him that he needed to get out of his house immediately. Yaghdan asked to move into the compound. They must have anticipated this request, since it was declined without hesitation. There just wasn't any way to make that happen, they told him.

What *could* they do for him, then, he asked. The EXO chirped that he could have one month of unpaid leave, which was the vacation time he had earned over nearly three years of service to the agency. If he had not resolved his "problems" by the end of the month, they would give his job to somebody else.

He felt as though he were being fired. Could they help him get out of Iraq? "Oh no," they said. "USAID doesn't control any part of the immigration process."

As he made his way through the Assassins' Gate checkpoint, everything inside him felt tight. Haifa was surely wondering if he was still alive and how much longer she should wait before calling her family for help. He walked as quickly as he could over the bridge without breaking into a jog. He no longer cared who was on the other side; he had already been discovered, after all. The implication was only beginning to take shape: he and Haifa would flee Iraq. They would drive south to Karbala', where Haifa's father lived, but would not stay for long: the longer they stayed, the more they put extended family at risk.

On the other side of the bridge, he took the first of three taxis and eventually hopped out at the end of his street. He walked nervously toward his gate. To his relief, he found it shut, without any signs of break-in. His voice was thin, hollowed out, as he called Haifa, who raced over from the living room and smothered him in a relieved hug. The bags were by the door, waiting.

Yaghdan awoke with a start. He kept having the same dreams, always of a bearded man in a suit. The man in a suit was dragging someone by a rope down to the banks of the Tigris. There were other men nearby with guns, laughing. He saw the face of the person being dragged, and it was his own, and he woke up. The first night after he and Haifa fled, he'd slept for sixteen hours straight, but now the man with the beard kept tormenting him.

But he was no longer by the Tigris. He had paid a couple thousand dollars for temporary business visas to fly into the United Arab Emirate of Sharjah, where they rented a small apartment. They had a month before they would be asked to leave.

He and Haifa went out on long walks together. They went to the cineplex and felt free to wander in peace for the first time in distant memory. There was electricity, clean water, air-conditioning, and people on the street who had never seen war. Even without the death threat waiting for them back home, this might have been enough to convince them not to return to Iraq.

But the idyll of their life in the costly emirate was soon overclouded by the impermanence of the situation. Even if they managed to bribe their way to a pair of long-term visas, they couldn't afford to live in Dubai. They would have to leave again, and they had only one option remaining: Syria, where, due to lax visa requirements, more than a million other Iraqis had poured in since the bombing of the Al-Askari shrine in Samarra earlier that year.

As Haifa repacked their things, Yaghdan ducked into an Internet café down the street, paid a few dirhams for a connection, and began to write an email to me.

PART THREE

USAID's staff, as photographed by the author in January 2005. The faces of Iraqi employees who were forced to flee have been obscured.

12.

Wake Up

A child eating alphabet soup notices that the only letters left in her bowl are one each of these six letters: T, U, W, X, Y, and Z. She plays a game with the remaining letters, eating them in the next three spoonfuls in accord with certain rules. Each of the six letters must be in exactly one of the next three spoonfuls, and each of the spoonfuls must have at least one and at most three of the letters. In addition, she obeys the following restrictions:

The U is in a later spoonful than the T.
The U is not in a later spoonful than the X.
The Y is in a later spoonful than the W.
The U is in the same spoonful as either the Y or the Z,
    but not both.

19. If the Y is the only letter in one of the spoonfuls, then which one of the following could be true?

    a. The Y is in the first spoonful.
    b. The Z is in the first spoonful.
    c. The T is in the second spoonful.
    d. The X is in the second spoonful.
    e. The W is in the third spoonful.

The fates lead him who will; him who won't, they drag.

—Seneca

Yaghdan's message was addressed to a part of me that I had choked off: the part that had piloted me from my hotel window, that still cared about what was happening in Iraq. Nearly a year had passed since my fall.

I read it in ten seconds and then clicked through my other emails. *Poor bastard.* There was certainly nothing I could do. He was halfway around the world, and I didn't know a thing about helping refugees. His email soon slipped from the home page of my in-box; I had law school applications to finish. It was early November 2006, and I was fast approaching the submission deadlines. I had run out of money and had moved into a small room in my aunt's house in Brighton, a hardscrabble town on the western edge of Boston.

Late one night two weeks later, I received a note from an Australian friend named Ann Vitale, who had worked in the education office alongside Yaghdan.

From: Ann Vitale
Sent: Tuesday, November 28, 2006 12:00 AM
To: Kirk W. Johnson
Subject: RE: Happy Thanksgiving!

I don't know if you heard but Yaghdan has had to leave Iraq. A severed dog's head was thrown over his wall with a note attached saying that next time it would be his head.

Poor guy. I have set up a fund to help him, and many of my friends and family are donating to it. Once I've a substantial amount, I'll send it to him. I'm trying other means of getting him out, but of course that is not easy and the queue is miles long.

Anyway, hope you have fully recovered from last December's shocking injuries.

-ann

Shame pounded against the levee and flooded in. Here was an Australian trying to make something happen in a situation for which her country wasn't even responsible. I stared at the law-school-related correspondence in my in-box, embarrassed. I hadn't even bothered to respond to his email. Her modest proposal to raise funds for him suggested something astonishingly basic: of course I could do something more than summoning a few seconds of pity.

I crawled into bed but knew I wouldn't be able to sleep. My mind was surging. I flipped the light back on, cleared stacks of admissions essay drafts from the desk, and pulled out a fresh legal pad. At the top, I wrote "Yaghdan."

I didn't have any money left to send him, but I had a few connections to people who might be able to help him. I began scrawling names. "Hastert." Surely the Speaker of the House would be able to do something. Although I hadn't been in touch with him since the Amtrak call earlier that summer, I thought he might be receptive.

Below "Hastert," I listed names of journalists I'd met through my public affairs job at USAID. I wrote "Op-ed."

A plan began to take shape. My excitement bubbled from a forgotten place, hidden beneath a year of self-loathing, self-pity, self-recrimination, self-everything. Here was something I could do for someone else. If I could help Yaghdan make it to safety in America, I might finally have accomplished something concretely good.

I filled several pages that night, working until four in the morning. In a few hours, I had generated so much work for myself that I could hardly wait for sunlight to come to get started. When I finally crawled back into bed and closed my eyes, I felt, for the first time in a year, eager.

The next morning, I called up a senior staffer at Hastert's office. His listlessness was evident. The Republicans had been drubbed in the 2006 midterm elections, and though Hastert had been reelected, the Speakership had been lost to the Democrats. His staff was preoccupied with packing up its offices and revising resumes. He feebly promised to make some calls on my behalf and hung up.

I wrote to T. Christian Miller, the *Los Angeles Times* reporter, and asked if he would put in a word for me with the editors at the op-ed page of the paper. A day later, I received a warm invitation to submit a piece. I had never written an op-ed before, but the words erupted as soon as I began. I spent hours reading through the basics of the US refugee admissions process, mapping out the key players in the Bush administration, and soon had drafted a piece that called upon the government to grant visas to Iraqis like Yaghdan—whom I referred to as *Y* in order to protect his identity.

Having run out of time on their short-term visa in the UAE, Yaghdan and Haifa had moved to Syria, one of the few countries still permitting Iraqi refugees to enter. In the few weeks since he fled, the only plan he'd devised was to look for a job in another USAID mission somewhere in the region, hoping that his training in the agency's procedures and systems would boost his chances.

So when I wrote back to him with an excited outline of the plans I'd developed, his reply was nervous; he didn't want to harm his chances at working for USAID again. "I don't think an article about this will help. It will make USAID very angry. But I trust you."

I didn't want to undermine his plans to work for the agency again, but I knew that there was no way that anyone would pay attention to his plight if we were deferential or overly polite to the US government. I thought about my own departure from USAID, and how quickly irrelevant I had become to the mission. And I was an American, on senior staff. "I won't publish this if you strongly object," I wrote, "but I think you are wrong. Nobody will help you in the government if they are not pressured to do so."

His response came quickly: "I trust you. Go ahead and publish it."

On December 15, 2006, under the headline "Safeguarding Our Allies," my piece appeared in the *Los Angeles Times,* the first major newspaper to run an op-ed about the plight of US-affiliated Iraqis. Though ten months had passed since the destruction at Samarra and the subsequent eruption of civil war, the discussion in the media centered on bombs and not the aftermath of human displacement. More than three million Iraqis had been uprooted by violence, the region's largest refugee crisis in sixty years, but pundits in the United States were more interested in debating the fate of Defense Secretary Donald Rumsfeld or whether the suggestion of withdrawal was an act of cowardice.

I flew down to Chattanooga, Tennessee, that morning for a long-planned weekend with some old friends from college. When I got off the plane, there was a voice mail from the Hastert staffer, notifying me that he'd sent an inquiry to the State Department on Yaghdan's behalf. Bobby Worth from the *New York Times* had also called to interview me for an article on the subject. I'd met him at an embassy function in Baghdad a year earlier but was surprised to get his voice mail. I returned his call, vented about the situation, and turned off my phone for the rest of the weekend.

I returned to Boston to find a dozen voice mails from journalists and Capitol Hill staffers whose names I had never heard before. I had no idea how everyone was getting my number. When I logged into my email account, I thought at first that my address had been sucked into some Middle Eastern spammer's list: three out of every four emails were in Arabic.

I saw a familiar name and opened the message. Ziad had always stood out in the USAID mission as someone with great ambition and an acidic sense of humor. His ambition had bested him, though: he was fired for trying to organize an informal union of the Iraqi employees to fight for better treatment and more protection. One day we noticed he was gone, and that was the end of Ziad, as far as we knew. He wrote to inform me that he was scheduled to flee within a couple days by way of a smuggler's network and might need my help.

I scanned for other familiar names. One by one, I read desperate messages from former colleagues who were either hiding inside Iraq or had fled to Syria and Jordan and points beyond. My op-ed had nicked a vein, which now gushed into my in-box. By the time I got to the scores of emails from Iraqis I didn't know—those who had worked for the State Department, the military, and US contractors—I was in a cold sweat. Many of the emails had been sent the morning of my op-ed, which I noticed at the bottom of most of the messages: it had been forwarded heavily throughout the diaspora. The subject lines all begged me for help.

Maryam worked for UNICEF on teacher training projects in Iraq that had been funded by USAID. Three months earlier, several Iraqis in police uniforms had knocked on her front door and asked her husband to come down to the station for questioning. She'd begged him not to go, but he smiled and told her he'd be back by nightfall. Since then, she had traveled to every police station, prison, and jail that she could find in Iraq, but her husband was gone. At the end of her search, she found an envelope resting on her front steps. Inside was a death threat and a Kalashnikov bullet soaked in blood.

A man sent photographs of his legs, mangled by a militant's power drill as retribution for his work with FedEx. The militia threw him out of a moving sedan in the middle of the desert and left him for dead, but he survived, fled, and found my email address.

A woman sent photographs that she had taken as she fled her neighborhood in southern Baghdad: dust-covered corpses and exploded vehicles.

Another sent me an email with a video clip attached. I stupidly double-clicked it and found myself staring into the resigned eyes of an Iraqi man about forty years old, hands bound behind him. He was forced to confess to his work with the Americans, after which a militant held his badge up to the lens, which began to blur. The camera lens shuttled back a bit and a US government-issued Green Zone access badge came into clear focus. The man offered no resistance when a balaclava-clad militiaman pushed him to his knees. I should have closed the video, but continued to stare as the muzzle of an AK-47 came to rest a few inches from the man's left temple. He was looking down at a crumbling sidewalk when it fired. He slumped forward.

These people were making a huge mistake. I was only twenty-six. I didn't have a job and couldn't afford my own apartment. I was stealing a Wi-Fi signal from the neighbors on a laptop that had six months of life left in it at most. I didn't have even the most basic answers for any of their questions about how to make it to safety. I had little knowledge of the refugee resettlement process and didn't have any useful contacts with the decision makers within the State Department. All I had done was write an op-ed so that someone else, ideally in the government, would figure things out for them.

I closed my computer, threw on a coat, and stepped out into the frigid Brighton evening. I lit a cigarette and started walking. It felt as though I had just witnessed some kind of crime and had to decide whether to call the cops. I looked over my shoulder and could see the light of my room, where the laptop beckoned like a black hole.

I took a long drag, my heart already racing. What the hell was I supposed to do? I could write a blanket reply to all of them, telling them I couldn't do anything. I'd only been trying to help Yaghdan, after all. But how could I ignore Ziad? I had worked alongside nearly one hundred Iraqis at USAID. What about the rest?

On and on I walked, past Kiki's Kwik-Mart, where down-on-their-luck Brightoners frittered away paychecks on scratch-offs. Losing tickets littered the parking lot, clinging to the tires of departing cars for a few turns before slipping off into the snow. My smoke burned out, but my exhalations were still visible in the cold. After an hour of wandering, I became numb.

I made up my mind. Helping one hundred people was a ludicrous proposition. I was penniless and needed to focus on finishing law school applications. I would draw the line around my closest friends, like Yaghdan and Ziad. The rest were on their own. I could not help someone I didn't know; I didn't even know how I was going to help the ones I did.

Seven more emails from Iraqis had come in during my walk. Most of the subject lines were a variation on the theme of "Please help, Mr. Kirk!"

A guy my age wrote to say that he was holed up in his apartment with his wife and baby daughter. He had been an interpreter for the US Army, but his cover was blown. Someone kept calling his cell phone to say "We will find you, soon." He estimated that he had one month's worth of canned food and rice inside his apartment, where he stood guard by the door with an AK-47. "I have only two clips for the Kalashnikov. We are waiting to die here, please help us Mr. Kirk."

A Christian woman named May sent a long message from Amman. She had worked in the Coalition Provisional Authority under Bernie

Kerik, the former New York police commissioner who had overseen a disastrous early attempt at training Iraqi police, an effort that lasted just ninety days before he packed it up and went home.

May helped manage the TAPS program, an Iraqi version of 911, allowing ordinary citizens to call in anonymous tips about impending insurgent attacks. Shortly after Kerik left, May's fifteen-year-old son had been walking to school when a group of armed men leaped from a sedan, snatched him, and sped off. May's cell phone rang with the demand: $600,000 for the release of her son. Her husband divorced her in anger over the calamity caused by her work with the United States, and paid a large amount of money to the men who had taken their son.

May tried to continue her work with the US government but soon received her own death threat, whereupon she fled to Jordan and applied for resettlement as a refugee at the UNHCR. Her application had been stalled for over a year. Her email to me included scans of her ID badges and several commendation letters, including a note that Kerik had written, which concluded with: "Your courage to support the coalition forces has sent an irrefutable message: that terror will not rule, that liberty will triumph, and that the seeds of freedom will be planted into the great citizens of Iraq."

I found another email from Ziad, recounting a memory about his former colleagues from his days at USAID:

> I remember one day I was so upset when a group of Iraqis asked me about a TV report on Al Jazeera network showing the Vietnamese who worked for the US in Vietnam kicked out of aircrafts evacuating the employees from an American base in Vietnam and I assured them at that time that it was mere propaganda to make us stop working with the US to help our country, how stupid I was and now here I am facing what I lied about.

He signed his email with a quote: "Henry Kissinger once said, 'To be an enemy to the US is a problem, but to be a friend is sometimes fatal.'"

I stopped reading. It was three in the morning, but I was wide awake, with a throbbing headache. I squeezed my eyes shut and listened to the ringing of my ears. I thought about ignoring all of the emails. If I just kept silent, they might stop writing. But I had to reply, if only to tell them that I'd try to find someone else to help them. I was embarrassed to be receiving pleas from sixty-year-old heads of families who told me that I was their only hope. I worried that they would find out how poorly suited I was to help them.

There were simply too many to track. I needed to impose some order on the mounting chaos of my in-box. I opened Microsoft Excel, and in the first field I typed in Yaghdan's full name. Below it, Haifa's. The third name was Ziad. I carefully inputted their emails and cell phone numbers, and created a column to briefly describe their situation.

Below their names, I typed in May's full name. Below hers, the man hiding in his apartment with an AK-47. Below that, the FedEx employee. Below him, Maryam, whose husband had been disappeared by men in Iraqi police uniforms. It became instantly clear that I would need the names of children, spouses, dates of birth, and more specific information about their threats and work history before I could figure out what to do with this list.

I sent scores of emails, telling them that I needed more details. I made no promises other than to say that I'd try to find someone else to help them.

When I woke, I had dozens of responses, laden with photographs of bullet-pierced arms and legs and torsos, death threat letters with Muqtada al-Sadr's rotund and scowling mug in the corner, and scans of US government ID badges. I studied the death threats and found three that were nearly identical, save for the name of the threatened. It was an odd thing to consider that seven thousand miles away some militia member was working away at his own computer, formatting death threats using a list of names supplied by the chewers that waited outside the checkpoints of the Green Zone.

With each round of emails I sent, my messages were forwarded to other Iraqis, who then wrote to me with their own stories. I kept asking for more—more information, more documents, more facts—and the list grew. If I was trying to draw a line around the extent of my involvement, I was doing a terrible job of it.

I stared at the names of a handful of former USAID colleagues on the list and knew that I needed to find out what had happened to the rest. I dug up a warden's list—the HR roster of all USAID Iraq employees, American and Iraqi—took a red pen, and placed checkmarks next to Yaghdan and Ziad. There were over ninety more. Within a few days, I reconnected with nearly all of them: in the eleven months since I'd left, more than half of USAID's Iraqi employees had fled or gone into hiding inside the country.

Within a couple weeks of the publication of the op-ed, I had all but forgotten about law school. I submitted some rushed applications and stuffed the LSAT prep books and personal statement drafts into a box in the basement. Every morning, I woke up and worked with a manic intensity on the list, which grew by a dozen names each day. I'd forget to eat at times, wading through the tragedy of my in-box before collapsing into bed with the following morning's work on my mind.

With each revision to the list, I took the old copy out to the front porch and burned it in an empty flowerpot. There was little risk of any-one in Brighton discovering the names, of course, but I didn't want to take any chances. Several Iraqis told me that a list of embassy employees had not been shredded but instead thrown into the trash, where it was discovered in a Baghdad landfill by a militia scouring American garbage for intelligence. Names of US-affiliated Iraqis soon appeared on the walls of neighborhood mosques under the title "Traitors."

December 29 arrived, marking the first anniversary of the fugue state. I felt something resembling relief to be sleeping without pills or nightmares, to see the scars across my face slowly melting into flesh, to feel less brittle in bone and tooth.

But in the inventory of what might qualify as a return to normalcy, much was missing. An oral surgeon's assistant stunned me by asking me out after staring into the pulp chambers of my incisors and vacu-uming up saliva during root canals. I went on my first postaccident date, but all we talked about were my teeth. I picked at the soft heart of a loaf of bread, still unable to chew or pick up a fork, and tried to muster a smile for her. Before my dwindling bank account evicted me from my tiny apartment in the South End of Boston, I'd lived in an apartment building full of gorgeous dental students who were fascinated by the war zone of my teeth, but I felt too scarred and fractured to ask anyone out.

A full recovery from the fugue meant finding a job again and moving back into my own place. If I lucked into a spot in law school, I'd have about nine months to fill before classes started.

But as I peered into the coming year, all I saw were the names of Iraqis, rows upon rows of fathers and mothers and children and grandparents to whom I had made a vague promise. At some point, I'd have to bring the list to the State Department. Once I handed off the information I'd compiled—all of the names, cell phone numbers, email addresses, recommendation letters—I was hopeful that something would happen. Maybe Yaghdan and Haifa and the others would start getting phone calls and invitations to come to the embassy for visa interviews. They could stop running and start new lives, maybe even in America.

13.

Bureaucrats

Ellen Sauerbrey was not a very gifted politician. After a stint in Maryland's state legislature, she ran twice for the governor's seat and lost twice. After that, she stopped running and started raising funds for George W. Bush. The sixty-eight-year-old's reward from the president was not a sinecure ambassadorship in some obscure Caribbean nation but the reins of the Department of State's Bureau of Population, Refugees, and Migration as assistant secretary of state.

She was nominated to replace Arthur Dewey, a decorated Vietnam War veteran with decades of experience in refugee and humanitarian affairs. As the head of the Refugees Bureau, she would oversee a $700-million-a-year operation to work with various organizations and the UN High Commissioner for Refugees to establish and sustain refugee camps. She would also be entrusted with overseeing the US Refugee Admissions Program, which was still recovering from a total shutdown following the attacks of 9/11.

Not everyone was convinced of her qualifications.

On October 25, 2005, she went before the Senate Foreign Relations Committee for a grilling by Democratic senators who considered her too inexperienced in humanitarian affairs to run the bureau. Senator Barbara Boxer led off: "I don't think we see the requisite experience that we've seen in other nominees."

Sauerbrey responded feebly, "I do have experience managing

resources. I do have experience in managing people. I think these are highly transferable skills."

Boxer: "I'm talking about a résumé for this job, not about the census or other things."

Senator Barack Obama weighed in: "I think the concern here is just that the issues of refugee relief are a very specific and extraordinarily difficult task, and it doesn't appear that this is an area where you have specific experience."

The *New York Times* ran an editorial blasting the nomination: "Ms. Sauerbrey has no experience responding to major crises calling for international relief. . . . This is a post for an established expert in the field."

The editorial board of the conservative *Washington Times* was among the few outposts urging her appointment, implying that the principal factor driving Democratic opposition was the mishandled Hurricane Katrina relief efforts under another inexperienced Bush appointee. "[I]n the wake of the Michael Brown debacle at FEMA, her critics want the Senate to think she's an unqualified crony. In this case, the facts simply don't bear it out." The paper suggested that Sauerbrey was opposed for two reasons: that she was pro-life, and that she was an outsider who might disrupt the status quo: "The other possibility is that the career types might see in Mrs. Sauerbrey another John Bolton. Mrs. Sauerbrey is not a career diplomat or humanitarian-aid specialist; she lacks an establishment pedigree. Worst of all for them, she appears to have strong convictions—which, by the way, are shared by the president. If confirmed, she might upset business as usual in the way Mr. Bolton has at the United Nations."

The White House, anticipating the Democrats' objection, bypassed the confirmation process and installed her as a recess appointee in January 2006, a month before the bombing of the Al-Askari Shrine in Samarra and the start of a several-year miasma of ethnic cleansing and human displacement.

On the morning of February 11, 2007, I woke up with a sore neck and a restless mind, having slept poorly on a buddy's couch in DC. Seven weeks after writing the op-ed about Yaghdan, I was now hours away from my first meeting with the Refugee Bureau at the State Department. I flicked on the TV and saw a crowd gathered by the old state capitol building in Springfield. "Illinois Senator Barack Obama to announce candidacy momentarily" pulsed at the bottom of the screen.

I printed out the list, watching page after page spool out with the names, phone numbers, photographs, and scans of badges that I had spent the past two months gathering. I was nervous. I didn't exactly know what I was doing. Until now, I had kept myself busy with a strategy of gathering details. It was a simple-enough system, allowing me to put some emotional distance between stories of tortured and raped bodies and myself: find a phone number, enter it into column D.

But now I had to do something with these names, and I had no idea what to expect from the State Department. I stuffed the list into a manila envelope on which I wrote "DOS." I walked through a biting chill toward Foggy Bottom and listened to my HELO playlist of clichéd Vietnam War songs, created partly in jest to listen to while I flew in Blackhawks and Chinooks. "The End," "Paint It Black," "Fortunate Son," "All Along the Watchtower" all helped to drown out the thoughts racing through my mind.

At the entrance to the State Department, I was met by a woman who'd spent too many years in the dull light of federal buildings, her skin grayed and her voice hoarsened by what I assumed to be a lifetime of cigarette smoke. She forced a smile and escorted me through security and into a conference room in which four other officials from the Population, Refugees, and Migration Bureau were waiting.

I sized up the room. The black suits and gray dresses sitting across from me created a dynamic that seemed slightly adversarial. I felt uncomfortably young, not unlike during meetings with the command staff of the marines in Fallujah, which only made me more intent on being taken seriously.

The gray-skinned woman started out with a pro forma welcome to the State Department. I thanked them and started out earnestly:

"I have these names of our former colleagues, and have been gathering them so that we can help get them out of harm's way. I know it's difficult to track Iraqi employees of the US government, so I've spent the last two months contacting all of my former AID colleagues, and—"

"And how have you been doing that, Kirk?" the woman interjected. The others stared at me.

"How have I been communicating with them?"

"Yes."

"Well, I have the email addresses for a few of my former colleagues. But to figure out the complete list of colleagues, I used a former warden's list to start identifying those I hadn't accounted for—"

"But it's my understanding that you're no longer working for the US government?"

"Yes, that's right."

"So how do you have access to a warden's list? Those are classified, aren't they?"

A little missile of anger spiraled from one side of my brain to the other. I sat silently for a moment, gathered my thoughts, and then locked my eyes onto hers.

"Look, if this is going to be the tenor of our conversation here today, we're not going to get very far. Warden's lists are not classified, anyhow. I didn't come to explain the mechanics of how I'm connecting with the Iraqis, but to see what you're going to do to help them."

"And we understand and appreciate your help with that, Kirk." Patronizing drips splashed and puddled on their side of the table.

I pulled the envelope from my backpack and thunked it onto the table. The woman unsealed it and began to flip through the pages, pausing here and there, passing sections to other staffers. I watched in silence. I was wearing the only suit I owned, and noticed that I had tracked slush up the back of my pant legs. Time seemed to stretch into hours as I waited for someone to look up from my list and say something.

"Kirk, we are going to have to study this more closely. But we can tell you that we are looking into this issue and appreciate your help in bringing these names to us. If we can, we'd like to be in touch with you after we've had a chance to review things more thoroughly?"

"Yeah, fine." I was itching to get out of there, tense and unsettled in their company. Was I just some kid that they were humoring on a slow day, or would they actually do something? Hoping to add a little pressure, I mentioned the meetings I'd scheduled with the UN High Commissioner for Refugees and with staffers on Capitol Hill, who would all be eager to know what the State Department would do with my list.

After the meeting, I hurried to a café to write down my notes. As I transcribed their comments, it became clear that every answer had been a classic yes/no, a staple of USGspeak, which sounds good enough in the moment but never settles well. In the end, they had only taken the list and committed to "looking into it." I had zero concrete information to report back to Iraqis on the list.

One point of our discussion was particularly irksome: due to confidentiality requirements, they explained, they wouldn't be able to speak with me directly about the particulars of any cases. Was I really not to be trusted? After all, I was the one giving them the list, which was filled with information that the Iraqis had entrusted to me. Hadn't I crossed some threshold of common sense whereby the State Department could tell me what, specifically, Yaghdan would need to do before he could find a safe haven?

The more I considered it, the more I realized what a brilliant policy it was, from a bureaucratic perspective: it allowed them to suggest that they were so concerned with protecting the vulnerable that they were unwilling to communicate with the person who brought them names of the vulnerable, so pure was their commitment to the integrity of the process. It also carried a not-so-subtle message to buzz off. Don't poke around in our process, and let us do this our own way, at our own pace.

A few weeks before my trip to DC, the *Washington Post Magazine* ran a piece I wrote about coming to terms with my accident and failures in Fallujah. I had written it long before Yaghdan and the refugee crisis took over my life, in an attempt to make sense of the accident and the PTSD I'd struggled with back in West Chicago. After the story ran, I received a number of emails from veterans—private first class to general officer—who shared stories of their own freak accidents suffered upon their departure from Iraq or Afghanistan. More than a few tied themselves to their beds each night.

Even though it was not the primary subject of the essay, USAID did not come off particularly well, and no government agency wanted any Iraq-related press by that point. On the heels of my op-ed about the agency's abandonment of Yaghdan, I guessed that some folks in the public affairs office were probably upset. When I was scheduling meetings for my trip down to Washington, I'd sent an email to an old boss of mine, a Bush political appointee, and proposed a lunch when I came down with the list. He called me shortly after receiving the note.

"Kirk, I gotta tell ya, your articles are not being very well received here at the agency."

"Well, I don't know what to tell you. I'm not coming after the agency. You guys can't do anything about the list anyway. This is a State and Homeland Security issue."

"You know what you're pushing here, Kirk; you're dragging the nation back to the rooftop of Saigon! Have you considered that?"

The photograph from the final moments of the fall of Saigon in April 1975, where South Vietnamese employees clambered outside our embassy with the hope of boarding one of the departing helicopters, became the iconic image of the end of the war, printed in every high schooler's history textbook for a generation. I laughed. I had no idea what I was doing, but I knew I wasn't dragging any nation anywhere. I barely had my own life together. My aunt had needed to rent out my room in Brighton to help pay the bills, so I was now sleeping on a mattress by the water heater in the unfinished basement, where I'd dumped my box of LSAT prep books and law school admissions paperwork.

A couple hours after my meeting at State, I headed over to my old employer. I stared at the smiling pictures of Bush, Cheney, Secretary of State Condoleezza Rice, and USAID Administrator Randall Tobias hanging in the lobby of the Ronald Reagan Building, and wondered how they were affixed to the marble wall. Velcro would make them easier to peel off after an election, I figured.

The Bush appointee called out my name from the other side of the security screeners and metal detectors. I traded my driver's license for a "Visitor—Escort Required" name tag and gave him a half smile as I shook his hand.

"Welcome back to the agency, Kirk."

He poked at my silence as we rode up the elevator. "Good trip so far?"

"Going okay. Interesting feeling being back here at AID."

The doors opened, and he escorted me into the Legislative and Public Affairs Bureau. As we walked past the government-blue cubicles that I had last seen in the compound in Baghdad, I noticed my magazine piece resting on nearly every desk. On one desk, I spotted a heavily high-lighted printout of my op-ed about Yaghdan. I felt the aggressive unease of an encircled animal as I followed him into his office.

He sat down opposite me and asked if I wanted any coffee. When I declined, he started off in an irritated tone: "So, Kirk, I saw in your bio in your magazine piece that you were working on a collection of stories about your time in Iraq, is that right?"

"Well, yeah, that's one of the things I'm working on."

"And do you plan on publishing any more of these?"

"Yeah, I'm hoping to."

He furrowed his brow as though deep in reflection.

"See, here's the thing, Kirk: I'm pretty sure you're not allowed to be publishing anything about your time there with USAID. I'm saying this as a friend, because I wouldn't want you to get in trouble for violating any terms of your contract."

His words dissolved like a pill into my bloodstream, the impact immediate.

"I worked for USAID, not the CIA. I never signed any gag order."

He leaned over to a nearby chair, upon which sat a green binder. On its binding, I read "Kirk Johnson." He flipped through what I rec-ognized as my articles, past other pages that I couldn't make out, and pulled out a few stapled pages of paper. He slid them across his desk to me.

"See, take a look at this contract language. It says right there, the sec-tion that talks about not speaking to the media or publishing anything without clearance from the agency."

I looked at the contract and knew immediately that it was not mine. I pushed it back and forced a smile.

"This isn't my contract. I never signed a gag order. Besides, I'm not even working for the agency anymore. I was never fired and never resigned; you guys just forgot about me after I walked out the window . . ."

He showed me his palms defensively and leaned back, away from the alpha stirring in me. I continued.

"I'm a little confused here. I told you I was coming in as a courtesy call to explain what I was doing with my list. And the first thing you do is bring up this contract?"

He recomposed and locked eyes with me.

"I'm telling you this as a friend. We'd hate to see your objectives torpedoed. What I thought would make sense is that you submit your future publications to us, just so we can have a look at it and maybe even help, before you actually publish them."

I put my hands on my knees. "That's not going to happen."

He tried to change the tone of the conversation and asked, "Hey, can I see the list? Fill me in on what's going on."

I stared over his shoulder at a framed picture of the entire USAID Iraq staff in 2005, in the piazza of the compound. I had taken the picture during my first week in Baghdad. I pointed to it and said, perhaps melodramatically, "The list is right there, in that picture. I'm not showing it to anyone other than the principal actors in the resettlement bureaucracy."

He looked over his shoulder at the picture. Half Iraqis, half Americans. There was Yaghdan, his modest smile concealed partly by a bushy mustache. Tona and Amina were off to his right. Of the Iraqis pictured, only a few remained with USAID.

"I'm not going to submit anything to you guys. If that's a problem, then let's see how it plays out. Subtract my medical bills, and I have about a thousand bucks left, and every other person in my family is a lawyer."

He stared back at me, masking any reaction. I was getting too upset. I thought back to a trick I'd used during insufferable meetings at the palace in the Green Zone and imagined that I was arguing with a parrot perched atop a chair. I grinned and stood up. "I'm sorry we had this meeting. I've got somewhere else to be now."

I shook his hand and motored out of the bureau, past my magazine pieces, past stacks of briefing books containing archives of my *Iraq Daily Updates*, past row after row of bureaucrats struggling to spit-shine USAID's projects for an uninterested media and a yawning public.

The awareness of just how little I had to lose had fully dawned on me only when I had mentioned my bank account balance. It was strangely empowering. After all, what was the worst that could happen? That I fail again? That I move out of the basement and back home to West Chicago? It wouldn't be great, but it still seemed trivial compared to what was filling my in-box each day.

I was waiting at the bank of elevators outside the Legislative and Public Affairs Bureau when the Bush appointee caught up with me.

"Let's be in touch, okay?" he said in a hushed tone as he handed me his USAID business card. I didn't understand why, since I already had his contact information.

"And look, if she gets in touch with you, make sure she gets on your list, okay?"

I glanced down at the card and saw the handwritten name of an Iraqi woman.

"Don't worry, it's not like I slept with her or anything. But try to get her help if she gets in touch with you."

That evening, a friend in USAID forwarded me a press release in which Condoleezza Rice announced the creation of the Iraq Refugee and Internally Displaced Persons Task Force. Undersecretary of State Paula Dobriansky would lead the task force, "building on support already provided, to coordinate refugee and IDP assistance to the region and refugee resettlement. The task force will also draw on the Department of State's multidisciplinary expertise to devise strategies for Iraqis at risk because of their work with the US government."

I grasped for meaning in the sentences, but they evaded my best efforts as they fishtailed along: "The task force will focus the State Department's coordination with other USG agencies, the UN, and other stakeholders. The work of the task force will also support the department's participation in existing interagency processes run by the National Security Council."

"Will focus . . . coordination . . . Will also support . . . participation." Whoever drafted it had a mastery of the numbing potential of USGspeak.

Despite the vagueness, the task force was launched with one hard promise: in fiscal year 2007, already four months under way by that point, the United States government would admit seven thousand Iraqi refugees.

I ran the math in my head. In the first four months of the fiscal year, eight, nine, seventeen, and fifteen visas, respectively, had been granted to refugees from Iraq, for a total of forty-nine. I needed a calculator to get at the nut of the promise: for the next eight months, the State Department would have to issue an average of 870 visas each month— a 7,000 percent increase. This suggested an efficiency I had long since come to doubt.

Slouched in the back row of the Chinatown bus back to Boston, I tried to make sense of a stew of conflicting emotions. I was exhilarated by the brush with my old life—the life that I thought had ended when I fell out the window. I wasn't navigating according to any master plan but by echolocation: after shouting about a problem, Iraqis shouted back, and now the government was talking.

But the promises were meaningless USGspeak. I had hoped to dump off the list at the State Department and move on, but I now worried that if I didn't keep the pressure on them, it'd be forgotten, misplaced, used for scrap paper.

I thought about who might be able to help me. The Americans with whom I'd worked in Iraq cheered me on privately, but nobody else stepped forward in any public way because they were still working for the government. One State Department foreign service officer had created a separate Gmail account for the sole purpose of referring the name of an Iraqi colleague to my list. "I am weeping into my keyboard as I write this, with the hope that you can help him," she wrote. When I wrote her back and asked why she felt the need to create a secret account, her response came in one line: "I can't be seen writing you."

But there was one person with whom I was emailing almost hourly, who seemed to be my only ally in turning the screws on the US government. I had devoured George Packer's reporting for the *New Yorker* while in Iraq, reading his book *The Assassins' Gate: America in Iraq* over two sleepless nights on a sagging cot at the CMOC in Fallujah. I'd first emailed him years earlier, in 2004, seeking his advice on how to find a job in the reconstruction efforts, but we started talking regularly after he wrote an op-ed in the *New Republic* about the need to protect US-affiliated Iraqis. We traded each rumor or theory we uncovered about the Bush administration's policy, and when he went to Iraq and Syria to investigate the crisis for the magazine, I introduced him to Yaghdan, Ziad, and several others. If Packer wrote about the list, there was no way the State Department could ignore it.

14.

Journalists

After a nightmarish journey as human cargo, shuttling through Dubai to India, Syria, and then to Egypt, Ziad's smugglers told him they would attempt the dangerous final trek to Sweden. Stockholm, which had no part in the war, had already admitted tens of thousands of Iraqi refugees at a time when no coalition members were opening their doors. Worried about the safety and legality of the final leg into Europe, I begged him not to continue, which might have played a role in his decision to run from his smugglers once he got to Cairo. Soon thereafter, an officer in the *mukhabarat*, the dreaded Egyptian secret police, who was involved in the smuggling network picked him up and took him to a prison beneath the Cairo airport. There he was tortured, mainly by electrical shock. For weeks, he resisted the cockroaches in his cell by wadding up bits of paper and jamming them into his ears and nostrils so that they wouldn't lay any eggs there.

Yaghdan and Haifa were now in Syria, having run out of time on their visitor's visas in Dubai. They had planned to rent a cheap apartment in the Sayyida Zainab neighborhood of Damascus, where many other Iraqis fleeing the civil war had holed up, but Yaghdan was convinced that he'd been spotted by a member of Muqtada al-Sadr's Mahdi Army, which openly maintained an office in the city. They boarded a northern-bound bus to Homs and waited. Either their money would run out or they would get a visa.

It had been a month since I had delivered my list to the State Department, and, apart from a bland email in which it said it would "prioritize" the Iraqis on my list "as appropriate," there was no tangible progress. New names continued to come in each day, and although I'd developed a system of emailing encrypted files to the Refugee Bureau, it was beginning to feel like loading up a car that was missing an engine.

Any illusions I had maintained about the list being a short-term project shattered upon the publication of "Betrayed: The Iraqis Who Trusted America the Most." In March 2007, on the fourth anniversary of the war, George Packer's sixteen-thousand-word exposé erupted with a suffusing outrage in the *New Yorker*. Yaghdan's plight was spotlighted in the pages of one of the most influential magazines in the world. Packer wrote about my accident, the family history with Dennis Hastert, and about my trip to DC with the list.

A new torrent of emails ensued, from foreign service officers, contractors, soldiers, and marines who had read the piece and wanted to refer the names of their Iraqi employees. Some wrote from a place of guilt: "I wish I had thought of doing more to protect him . . . has he written to you? Is he already on your list, and if not, can you find him?" Another wrote perfunctorily: "Please add the following name to your list: Ahmed al-Rikabi."

The flimsy dam that I had constructed to manage the river of emails from refugees was buckling under the new pressure. With each click to refresh my in-box, I found new names and new requests.

A second round of emails came from other journalists suddenly turning their attention to the issue. I assumed that they wouldn't want to talk with me, since Packer had already written about the list, but I soon realized that they had been assigned by their editors to produce their own reports, no matter how derivative. His reporting had bulldozed a path through which the rest of the media now strolled.

It was a strange business. The more that journalists wrote about the list, the more requests I got from other journalists. I found myself fielding one or two calls a day, walking each journalist through the crisis, teaching what I'd learned about the refugee admissions process, and steering him or her to annoyed public affairs officers at the State Department's Refugee Bureau. Although a few had bothered to do some background research before calling, most would kick off the call with, "Okay, I'm recording. Why don't you just start from the top?" as though I were peddling a movie script.

Someone from a reputable paper would call and say, "I'm looking for a woman, preferably in Syria, who worked for the Americans and was attacked." Or, "Is there anyone on the list who is in Egypt, Christian, and had family members killed?" Or, "Yeah, hi, I need someone in Iraq or Jordan who's been tortured and is in hiding." Or, "Do you have any Iraqis who worked for the Brits who fled to Lebanon?" Like ordering a pizza.

If the journalists needed me for a quote, the Iraqis on the list needed them for much more. Beyond the obvious benefits of greater coverage of the crisis, whenever a journalist wrote about someone on the list whose case had been frozen for months or years, the government magically unfroze that case. I'd tried to capture the State Department's attention by delivering my list quietly in February, but it wasn't until articles started appearing in major papers that Iraqis began to receive interviews at our embassies in the region. I kept a revolving short list of Iraqis willing to talk with the media, and notified the Refugee Bureau whenever someone would be the subject of an upcoming profile.

"Americans aren't going to give one stinking damn about Iraqi refugees on their own!" An audio technician from *ABC World News* with thick fingers was clipping a microphone to my shirt and snaking the wire under my shirt and down my chest. With a furrowed brow, I warded off someone approaching me with a powder kit in hand. Another crew member adjusted an off-camera lamp. The TV producer continued: "That's why we need you for the piece. The fact that you're a young white guy from the Midwest makes it much easier for them to plug in to this whole thing!" I shifted in my seat as the lamps turned on and the camera started filming.

And so I sat in front of cameras in air-conditioned studios, talking about people that had been raped or tortured by power drill because they worked for the United States. I was glad that the American public might finally learn about the largest refugee crisis in the world, a direct result of our botched occupation. But I was growing uneasy with the tidiness of the stories: several articles referred to me as the Schindler of the Iraqis.

Americans don't like to be presented with intractable problems or morally confounding situations. We like to think of our bombs falling on only the right homes, our bullets bending around good guys in search of bad flesh, our torturers as rare bad apples. And so overzealous members of the media were already anointing me as a hero when I hadn't helped a single person to safety. All I had done was double-click on Microsoft Excel and make a list. I didn't want Americans to hear about millions of refugees and think that everything was fine because of my meager effort.

Despite my misgivings, I was mindful that media interest was fleeting. I figured the State Department was hoping to weather a little negative publicity over the refugee crisis with the hope for a speedy return of the clear skies of American apathy. It could wheel out a new interagency group and promise to "ramp up," and enough people would be satisfied. I treated each interview as though it would be my last, using the media to advance as many cases on the list as possible before it all evaporated.

In June *ABC World News*, the first television program to profile the list, asked to tag along on my next trip to Washington, my first time back since Packer's *New Yorker* piece. I had just settled into a burgundy armchair in the high-ceilinged waiting room of office 317 in the Russell Senate Office Building when the double doors burst open, and Edward Kennedy barreled through with a bellow: "Where's Kirk Johnson?!"

In my surprise, I half expected someone else in the room to stand up and announce himself as me. I leaped up and felt my hand disappear into his firm grip.

"C'mon inside. Let's have a talk."

I followed him, tugged by an orbital force as he ambled swiftly through a second room of staffers into his main office. He pulled forward a chair for me and sat down so our knees were touching. I completely forgot about the cameras filming the meeting.

As he answered some quick questions from nearby aides, I managed to pry my eyes loose from his face and glance at the mantle over his left shoulder. Two busts stared down at the sitting area: one of JFK, the other of RFK. He patted my knee and brought me back into his orbit.

"So, tell me, when were you in Iraq? You were with AID, no?"

I couldn't tell at first if he was just making small talk for the camera, but when I responded, he leaned forward slightly and listened to me, furrowing his brow at points, nodding at others. Over the next thirty minutes, he asked precise questions about my experience with the Iraqi staff and shot instructive glances at his staffers, who took notes as we spoke.

He had quickly emerged as the leader in Congress on the issue, having called the first Senate hearings a few months earlier in January 2007; but by the scope and depth of his questions, it was clear to me that he had more in mind. I tried to keep up with his questions about the process, about which stages were proving the most problematic for the Iraqis on my list, and how many Iraqis I thought might be affected by the stigma of collaborating with us.

I was halfway through responding to a question when the doors opened, and his Portuguese water poodles raced in and jostled around our legs.

"She wants to play," Kennedy said, handing me a tennis ball damp with canine saliva.

I rolled the ball along the floor and tried to remember the question I was answering, but the dog returned, nudging the ball against my thigh until I plucked it out and tossed it again.

Eventually I yielded my seat to the ABC correspondent, who interviewed the senator about the list. I sat on a couch and looked around the room in bewilderment as they spoke. Every square inch of wall space was filled with photographs with leaders, Kennedys, letters from schoolchildren, clippings of articles.

I snapped to attention when Kennedy bellowed, "We *know* who these people are! They aren't terrorists! They helped us over there, and now there's a target on their backs."

His outrage was invigorating, a clamorous and fearsome arrival of reinforcements, an entire regiment in one man. I allowed for a little optimism: the Iraqis on the list were not alone anymore.

When the ABC profile ran in July 2007, about five months after I first brought the list to the State Department, it included a damning interview with Assistant Secretary of State Ellen Sauerbrey, who strongly disputed my claim that the White House was loathe to resettle Iraqi refugees because doing so would be an admission of failure in Iraq. "I really reject that. There has been no constraint placed on us by the administration. The administration has been fully supportive." Emboldened, she said, "People like to compare this period to the fall of Vietnam. . . . At that time, we did not have the security process that has been put in place after 9/11. It's a different world that we live in today."

The correspondent asked a simple question: "Why haven't any of the Iraqis on Kirk's list been given visas yet?"

> Sauerbrey: If Kirk Johnson has a list, I wish he'd give it to us.
> Correspondent: He says he has.
> Sauerbrey [startled]: If we have a list, if we have any such list, I've not seen it.
> Correspondent: You're saying that Kirk's list, that's gotten all this publicity—that you don't have it?
> Sauerbrey: I don't have Kirk's list.

ABC closed its piece by reporting that the State Department called shortly after the interview to say that it did, in fact, have my list, but that Secretary Sauerbrey had not been properly briefed. Not long after, another TV producer hoping to do a profile on the list was told, "If Kirk Johnson is part of your piece, Assistant Secretary Sauerbrey won't sit with you."

If Packer's article had opened the spigots for other reporters, the ABC profile unleashed the hydrant of the American viewing public. Within minutes, my in-box began to vibrate with messages of support and condemnation. I was amused by the hate mail but at a loss to respond to the hundreds of strangers who wanted to help. A World War II veteran asked where he could send a check. A yoga instructor wrote to say she wanted to donate. Several computer programmers volunteered to make a website for me. A family in Ohio wrote to say they would host any Iraqi on my list if they made it to America. A woman volunteered to marry an Iraqi on the list if it would help him get to safety.

Others wrote, usually from anonymous accounts, to register their venom. Subject line: "Why don't you take your dumb ass back to Iraq! Why don't you spend your time telling Iraqi people to fight for their own country instead of whining?" Subject line: "You pervert what it means to be American, shame on you! You must admire Benedict Arnold!" Others told me that I was naïve: Muslims could not be trusted with a visa to our country.

Although Iraqis emailed me with excited updates about upcoming visa interviews, I was unsettled by the knowledge that there simply weren't enough journalists to write about every Iraqi on the list. Flying by the seat of my pants, I had managed to use the media to advance a number of cases, but if Yaghdan and Ziad and others were to navigate the straits of the US refugee bureaucracies, I needed to find an organization powerful enough to help those on my list in a more official, systematic way. I developed a new plan to steer all of the donors and people offering to volunteer to a proper nonprofit, one that would know far better than I ever could how to solve the crisis.

15.

The List Project

I had a crippling pain in my head that I suspected was a migraine. I fell asleep each night with my laptop open next to me, the screen a jumble of half-written emails. I had no health insurance, and the headache was getting worse; any time I glanced to the left or right, a jolt of pain burrowed into my brain.

My mom mentioned my self-diagnosed migraine to her gynecologist, who wrote a prescription. She dropped the pills in the mail to me, and I sat with anticipation on the front porch, waiting for the mailman. The snow was melting in Brighton, disinterring a winter's worth of cigarette butts, frozen leaves, and dog shit. After three days, the pills arrived, but they did nothing to ease the pain.

I was worried that whatever caused my accident was surfacing again, that something had given way in my brain. I walked over to St. Elizabeth's Hospital and sat down in the emergency room. I filled out an application form for MassHealth, Massachusetts's health care for low-income residents, sheepishly entering "0" for annual income. I stared at the check boxes on the paper, an impromptu evaluation of my life. Twenty-six. Broke. Uninsured. No job prospects. Sleeping fitfully in an unfinished basement. Relying on my mom's gynecologist for prescriptions. My dating life was still in a yearlong slumber, as I spent most nights entering names of Iraqi refugees into Excel.

After a CT scan, an IV dripped heavenly morphine into my forearm, relieving me of the headache for the first time in weeks. I stared anxiously at the drops lolling down the tube, fearful that the cost of the visit would exceed what remained of my credit card limit. I was stubbornly refusing all offers of financial help from my worried parents. The last thing I wanted after a miserable year of setbacks was to become financially dependent on Mom and Dad once again.

The attending ER doctor came in with my CT scan results and asked in an excited tone, "So what *hap*pened to you, Mr. Johnson?"

I smiled, and explained my accident.

"Are you a little stressed right now?" he asked.

"Yeah. I guess I am."

"What do you do?"

What did I do?

"It's kinda hard to explain. I've got a list of refugees . . ."

The morphine was making me drowsy, but I was aware of how incoherent I was sounding.

"Okay, well we're going to keep you in here for another couple hours to rest and then send you home with some medicine to help you out. Try to control your stress levels, though, okay? We don't want to see you back in here again with the same problem."

That afternoon, I checked out with an acute tension headache and walked from the hospital into downtown Brighton. I sat at a café, charged a two-dollar cup of tea to my credit card, and stared distractedly into the glass. More than three hundred Iraqis, widows and fathers, infants and elderly, were depending on me. My thoughts, once again, seesawed toward quitting. For my own sanity, I told myself, I should just write to everyone to announce that I'd run out of money and energy and could no longer help.

While I was in the hospital, another fifteen emails had arrived. It seemed as though many had only heard my name over the phone from other Iraqis, addressing me as "Mr. Kirk" and referencing the friend who had referred them.

I found an email from someone at the State Department requesting a call. The painkiller administered by the hospital was still working its way through me, but I dialed and stared out the window as the bureaucrat complained about a quote of mine from a recent article. Someone across the street was stapling a sheet of paper to a telephone pole. Intrigued, I wandered over, half listening to the USGspeak tumbling into my right ear—". . . will require interagency resources that may or not be available . . ."—and found a picture of a black-and-white cat under the heading "Lost." A $50 reward was posted. My eyes bulged. I set out in search of the cat and then tuned back into the call. ". . . If they don't answer their phone, you know, we can't really help them."

"I don't understand; have you tried calling them?" I snapped. "They all tell me they're desperate to hear from you."

"I can't speak about the particulars of any case, as you know, but I know that sometimes refugees don't answer the phone."

"Okay. Well, I'll make sure they pick up the call."

I wandered up a steep side street in Brighton as we talked, peering into front yards and around trash cans.

"You know, there are some of us here who think you're not being entirely fair about what State can and can't do in this situation."

"Uh-huh," I said, my voice slightly winded from the uphill climb.

She was growing bolder: "I don't think you realize that we have had to rent office space in the region! We've had to fill those offices with staffers and get all kinds of equipment!"

At this, I paused in my search for the cat.

"Okay, so what am I supposed to say to that? Do you want me to tell these Iraqis to stop being so impatient because the State Department needs to rent office space and buy printer toner?"

I felt a twinge of guilt. This was not a political appointee capable of steering policy but a career foreign service officer doing some time in the PRM Bureau. But she had been the one to start this debate, and she parried: "We are not the only actor in the resettlement process! The Department of Homeland Security is also responsible! So is UNHCR! So is the International Organization for Migration!"

"But I don't understand. Is this a budgetary and logistics problem for State? Or is the problem at DHS? Explain it to me so that I'm not being unfair."

She reined herself back in, and the portcullis of USGspeak dropped on the conversation:

"We have committed to doing what we can, as one actor in a multi-actor refugee resettlement program, to help the Iraqis on your list."

As the conversation ended, I realized I was a thirty-minute walk from home and decided that the cat couldn't have strayed so far. I made my way back and transcribed as much of the conversation as I could before deciding to heed the ER doctor's advice and take the rest of the day off.

I needed help. I called several of the established refugee advocacy organizations and asked if they would take over my list, but was politely rebuffed. Even though I depended heavily on their expertise and reports from the field, I was soon disabused of the notion that I could simply dump my list on another refugee nonprofit. Some organizations receive funds to help refugees in the field; others work to help refugees who have been resettled in the United States. But I didn't need an organization to pass out short-term relief to those on my list in Syria or Jordan. I didn't need a stateside-focused organization, because nobody on my list had made it to America yet. I needed to find a group that acted as the bridge, to shepherd a refugee through that vast and dark space of the US Refugee Admissions Program.

So when Sharon Waxman and Janice Kaguyutan, senior advisors to Senator Kennedy, suggested that I get in touch with an attorney friend of theirs who had worked on Iraqi asylum cases, I leaped at the idea.

Chris Nugent, at the law firm of Holland and Knight, was clearly in a trench of his own. Over the course of a ten-minute call, paralegals and attorneys kept walking into his office to ask questions, his keyboard never seemed to stop clacking, and an unanswered cell phone rang persistently. He had read George Packer's piece and knew about my list, he said, before walking me through a number of Iraqi asylum cases he had successfully represented. Chris had a stellar foundation in asylum and immigration law and knew far more than most people in DC about what was happening in Iraq, as a result of interacting with his clients.

Before we hung up, I asked him if I could call him occasionally for advice. Soon I was peppering him with several calls a day. What would happen if Yaghdan and Haifa were deported back to Iraq? If we could somehow get them into Europe, would that speed the process along?

Were there any laws against wiring money to him in Syria? Chris started to help Yaghdan and other colleagues of mine, giving concrete guidance about the refugee resettlement process. There was never any discussion of payment.

On Valentine's Day 2007, a former Iraqi colleague of mine was murdered. His name was Nouri, and he had helped to maintain the vehicles in the motor pool that shuttled Americans to and from meetings in the Green Zone. One day, when he reached into his pocket to pay for a haircut, he inadvertently dropped his USAID badge on the floor. He was assassinated within two days. USAID management issued a condolence note and took up a small collection for Nouri's wife; Iraqi staffers were demoralized to find out that the Valentine's Day bash scheduled for that night would go on. I received the news immediately from grieving Iraqi friends.

As angry as I was about USAID, it had no role in the refugee resettlement process. If I spent all of my energy fighting the agency, the Iraqis on my list would get nowhere. Besides, USAID carried little political weight in Washington anymore: even if it had been a vociferous supporter of protecting US-affiliated Iraqis, it was hard to imagine much benefit.

A week after Nouri's assassination, I received a frantic phone call from Tona and Amina, my two former colleagues from USAID who had been photographed by a man in Iraqi police uniform as they walked out of the Green Zone. Since then, Tona had claimed asylum while on a skills-training course in Washington administered by USAID in late 2006. Amina, who had just arrived on a similar course, was desperate to do the same.

By this point, several Iraqis working for the State Department and USAID had "defected" during these training missions. The agency was embarrassed by the defections, since the US Citizenship and Immigration Services would now need to adjudicate whether its Iraqi employees had knowingly intended to claim asylum on a short-term visitor's visa, thus committing visa fraud. The US government spends a lot of money each year bringing in Fulbright scholars, officers in foreign militaries, professors, and many others through exchange programs intended to strengthen bonds with other countries. If everyone abused these programs as a way to emigrate to America, there would be no exchange, and the programs would be rendered pointless.

I had no idea that Amina was coming to the United States. In a quivering voice, she told me about the man with the gun at the Qadisiyya checkpoint who had been imprisoned after Amina had alerted a nearby American soldier. Her family had called her during her training in Washington to tell her that the gunman had just been released from detention. They told her not to come home.

"I don't know what to do. I promised USAID that I wouldn't stay here, but I'm scared. They will be so angry with me if I stay. And I don't know if—"

When I realized this young woman was still putting the wishes of a bureaucracy before her own safety, I cut her off midsentence and told her to forget about USAID. I walked her through the basic process of claiming asylum, and connected her with Chris Nugent that same night. She went to the law firm of Holland and Knight the following morning, where Chris began to draft her application for asylum.

When she wrote to her boss at USAID to inform her about the new threat and submit a resignation letter, the executive officer back in Baghdad was furious. Amina received a scathing reply, blaming her for the negative impact her decision would have on the rest of the FSNs, USGspeak for foreign service nationals, or the Iraqis who worked for the agency:

From: _____ (IRAQ/EXO) [mailto:*********@usaid.gov]
Sent: Tuesday, February 27, 2007 1:33 AM
To: Amina
Subject: RE: Resignation

Amina, given the talk I had with you last Tuesday night, I am surprised and disappointed. I thought I had made it very clear that we were placing enormous faith in you by sending you to the US and that if you failed to return it would have serious negative repercussions on the rest of the FSN staff.

I can only hope that you do not intend to remain illegally in the US. You should know that if you do and are caught you will be deported back to Iraq as an illegal alien and turned over to the authorities.

I wish you no ill but can not condone your deceit. May God protect you!

Amina called me within minutes of receiving the email, past one in the morning. She was in hysterics, terrified that police would show up at her door to deport her back to Iraq. The executive officer's reference to handing her over to the authorities suggested the new Iraqi Ministry of the Interior, which had already earned a heinous reputation for its torture rooms.

I told her to store my number in her quick dial and that she should call anytime she was feeling scared. I was getting used to making promises I wasn't sure I could keep, but I knew enough about asylum law to be confident that she would succeed in her application. I adopted a daily routine of checking in with her, trying to buoy her spirits.

Once Chris had filed her asylum petition, Amina's fears of being deported in the middle of the night subsided, leaving her with the more profound realization that she had just filed paperwork that would sever her from her homeland.

I was angry about the way that USAID treated her, but I knew by now the pointlessness of attacking a bureaucratic hydra. People came and went, but the titles and positions and attitudes remained. The woman who sent the nasty email to her would leave Iraq in a couple months, dispatched to another part of the world to keep the locals in line there. Whoever replaced her would send the same warnings to other Iraqi employees of the agency. Until the positions—not the people holding them—received new policy instructions from on high, nothing would change.

A plan was emerging from my calls with Chris. I had spent so much time looking for a refugee organization to take over my list; it had never occurred to me that a law firm might help. If I could somehow find funding to defray the costs of a paralegal, Chris was optimistic that

Holland and Knight would take on my list as a formal pro bono initiative. He could then train other attorneys at the firm, allowing even more Iraqis on the list to benefit from direct legal counsel. I was soon introduced to another gifted attorney named Eric Blinderman, who had worked with the Justice Department in Iraq on the trial of Saddam Hussein. Since his return to work as a litigation lawyer with the firm Proskauer Rose, he had tenaciously orchestrated the resettlement of several former Iraqi colleagues to America. He thought that Proskauer Rose might also commit to the project.

I was at another crossroads—my biggest since drafting the op-ed that had set everything in motion six months earlier. I'd received an embarrassing number of rejection letters from law schools but had been offered a spot at the University of Michigan. My health was starting to flag as a result of the high stress of handling hundreds of refugees' petitions. My credit card debt continued to mount. I'd been unable to find a refugee organization that could help the list in any real way.

Still, I felt the tug to finish what I had started. If I quit, I was certain that Yaghdan wouldn't make it to the United States. What would have been the point of all this work if I bailed on him now? I was meeting fascinating people, helping to raise awareness about a humanitarian crisis, and generally happy when I woke up each morning, despite the stress.

I also had a pair of blue-chip law firms offering to help. Why couldn't I just create my own organization to do what the others couldn't?

Though a small army of people had pledged to donate money in the wake of the media coverage, it wasn't enough to cover the salary of a staffer. With little sense of what I was doing, I drafted a grant application and sent it off to the Tides Foundation in California. Within a few days, I was on the phone with its founder, Drummond Pike, who listened patiently as I laid out my plan to work with the lawyers. I asked him for help.

A few weeks later, I got it. Drummond called to inform me that I would receive $175,000 from the foundation. This was on top of an additional pledge of $125,000 from an anonymous donor. I had never worked in the nonprofit world, but I knew a groundswell when I felt it.

Before I could use any funds, though, I'd need to obtain nonprofit

501(c)(3) status. Drummond said that Tides wanted to help. Rather than wading through the slow-moving process of incorporating a nonprofit, setting up accounting and payroll systems, and all of the administrative demands necessary for any NGO, Tides functions as an incubator for people who need to get to work immediately. In exchange for a fee, all of its support and administrative services would be made available instantly. My project would receive its nonprofit status in the process, and I could maintain my focus on the list.

I called the University of Michigan and deferred my spot in the law school for one year.

I then called the State Department to inform it that I was mobilizing law firms to help the Iraqis on my list. The official on the other end of the line paused and said, "Kirk, this is over the top. Refugees don't need lawyers."

On June 20, 2007, World Refugee Day, the List Project to Resettle Iraqi Allies was launched. Nearly one hundred attorneys gathered to receive training on handling Iraqi refugee cases in a constellation of conference rooms in the Washington office of Holland and Knight. In a gesture of cooperation, I invited officials from the Departments of State and Homeland Security to make a presentation to the group. In my first step as director, I hired Tona and Amina to help manage the burgeoning caseload.

16.

Pod 23

Kids

In the Hassaniyah neighborhood of the southern Iraqi city of Basrah, a father is digging a well in his backyard. He is too old for the task, made more difficult by a hip shattered long ago by a shell from an earlier war. In the front yard run rows of roses, tomatoes, and other vegetables. He knows the healthy grass carpeting the rest of the yard will soon parch and fade. Two palms and a pomegranate tree stand guard by the front gate. He curses the name of Saddam Hussein as he shovels, because there is no water in the pipes, and the Americans are coming to bomb. Inside play his two little girls, Zina and Tara, nine and ten, giddy that school has been canceled. It is 1991.

Eyeing the dwindling supply of food in the pantry, the girls' mother hopes that the war will be brief. She was of an earlier, more liberal era in Iraq, and had worn miniskirts in college. It was customary then for women to become teachers or nurses, but she wanted to be an accountant. Her father, of Saudi descent, wouldn't let her move outside the province to study, so she became a teacher and waited, hoping that a university would open inside the province and offer accounting. When one finally did, she went to night school, becoming one of the first female accountants in Basrah. She made sure that Zina and Tara went to one of the best elementary schools in the province, an Armenian school in the Jaza'ir neighborhood.

In high school, Zina had had trouble fitting in. She scored highly on her examinations and placed into a good school, but although she had friends, she never felt comfortable. She thought she was the ugliest girl in her class, and the boys teased her because her skin was darker than that of the other girls, and her hair curled where theirs was straight. While other kids played outside, she played inside with Tara, read magazines from the 1970s, and watched American movies, their room wallpapered with posters of the Backstreet Boys, Britney Spears, and Christina Aguilera. The 1984 teen flick *Footloose* looped relentlessly.

Under Saddam, kids learned early how to disappear into the crowd, but Zina was stubborn. She questioned everything, so when people told her that Islam was the greatest, she asked why. As one of the only Sunni families in an overwhelmingly Shi'a community, her mom urged caution, but Zina didn't worry about what people thought of her and sometimes went out of her way to demonstrate as much, clomping to school in platform shoes like the kind worn by the Spice Girls. Her classmates could judge all they wanted.

When the regime started appropriating Islamic symbols and speech, Zina noticed more of her classmates and neighbors wearing the hijab, but to her, the headscarf felt like a prison. She grew annoyed when some of her friends said the hijab freed them from boys' gawking eyes. Why should she have to change? She was smarter than the boys in her school but wasn't free to do half the things they could, like go jogging or ride her bike through the street. When she looked at the pictures of her miniskirted mom when she was her age, Zina felt as though she'd been born into the wrong decade.

College

She scored well enough on the university admissions test to be placed on the sciences track, specializing in biology, but her mom had always said she was smart enough to be a doctor or an engineer. To shift her degree to engineering, Zina started going to night school, just like her mother had. She enrolled at the Basrah Engineering College in September 2001. Like all Iraqi students, she lived at home and commuted to school. Zina didn't like to think about what she would do when she graduated, because the future seemed grim. As a Sunni in Basrah, she would not have the connections to find a good job like her Shi'a classmates. She didn't know if she would ever be an engineer, but she looked at her admission to the Engineering College as proof that she was just as smart as the men who dominated the profession.

Eighteen months later, Zina was halfway through her sophomore year, and the Americans were once again loading their weapons across the border in Kuwait. The regime issued a warning that the Americans would use chemical and biological weapons during the land invasion, so Zina and her family and everyone else on the street taped plastic over their windows and waited.

She figured it would be another short war, maybe a month of bombing before the Americans left. Even if they knocked out Saddam, he would regroup and take over again. They all slept on the floor the night of the invasion. When it came, it turned the floor into an ocean, the blasts sending tides and waves beneath her. Her mom screamed at them to stand with their backs against the wall, but Zina was so scared that her knees started to sag. She tried to recite the verse from the Quran that one says right before dying, but she couldn't remember the words.

There was silence for a few hours. Then more attacks. Then silence.

Within a year, Muqtada al-Sadr's Mahdi Army had taken over her campus, setting up a checkpoint at the university's gate, where they searched the cars and backpacks of every student. Zina flipped through an outdated Academy Awards issue of *People* magazine while waiting in line at the checkpoint one morning. When a militiaman saw the glossy pages of red carpet gowns and tuxedos, he yanked it from her in a rage and dragged her to his supervisor. "She's reading a magazine with naked infidels!" he shrieked. "She has crossed the line so badly that she should be kidnapped!" Shaken, Zina was allowed to enter her campus with a warning.

The thrill of learning faded for Zina as the social pressures grew more caustic. Another militia member stopped her in a hallway because he felt her clothing was too tight. He cursed at her, called her things in front of passing students that nobody had ever called her, insulting her parents for raising her poorly. He demanded to know if she was Sunni or Shi'a.

She stopped going to campus unless it was absolutely essential. All she wanted was the piece of paper conferring a degree so that she could get out of Iraq. She filled her free time by frequenting a nearby Internet café called the Farahidi Institute, which offered classes in computer programming and Photoshop.

Marriage

One afternoon at the Internet café, Zina received a chat invitation from a stranger through her Hotmail account. His name was Wael, he told her, and he was a foreigner working in Basrah. He was Jordanian by nationality, but his bloodline hailed from the Caucasus. "By the way," he said, "I'm just a few computers down from you, in booth nine." Zina walked over, slipped past the booth's privacy curtain, and found a handsome man with gaunt, almost Germanic features. She had seen him before in the café, she realized, as he grinned through a wreath of cigarette smoke. Two walkie-talkies, a cell phone, and a pistol rested next to the computer.

They started dating, but their meetings were confined to the Internet café. Zina did not want people to talk and didn't want to make any mistakes. Wael worked for the British, managing a security firm that guarded the ports of Basrah. His British boss was too frightened to come to Iraq, so Wael was promoted. His deputy, a young and armed Iraqi, followed him like a shadow and waited outside the café while he talked with Zina.

He was ten years older, thirty-one, and madly in love with her. She arranged for him to meet her mother for coffee. Zina loved Wael but acknowledged that marriage would be a way out of Iraq. All of her relatives came over to the house to celebrate their engagement on the first Friday in April 2004.

In the evenings after the engagement, Wael came over to sit in the garden with his new fiancée. When it was time for him to return to his room at the Rasheed Hotel, Zina would walk with him past the pomegranate tree to the gate, where his deputy stood guard. After a week, though, his mood darkened. He was much quieter than usual. After seeing a black cat wander past, he groaned, "Oh God, we're going to hear some really bad news." Zina laughed, but she didn't understand what was weighing on her fiancé.

Ten nights after their engagement party, Zina and Wael had a fight. She wanted to know why he was so distant. He wanted her to be more affectionate with him. Though she pushed against other social pressures, she was still nervous about others speaking ill of her or her family. At the end of the evening, he begged her to let him spend the night on the couch in their home, but she said no, knowing that the neighbors would surely notice. When she began to walk with him as usual toward the front gate, he told her not to walk with him all the way, so she turned back to the front door with bruised feelings.

She didn't call him the next day. She was hoping for him to take the first step after their fight, but after two days, he still hadn't called. She called the hotel and asked to be patched through to his room.

"Who are you?" demanded the receptionist.

"I'm his fiancée. I call over here all the time."

"Are you sure you're his fiancée? How do you not know?!" he asked.

"What do you mean?"

"Wael was taken."

She thought the man might have been joking, but this frail hope was soon dismantled as he continued. A group of seven men in Iraqi police uniforms had entered the hotel at eleven o'clock three nights earlier, the night of Zina and Wael's fight. They disconnected all the phones from the receptionist's desk, raised their rifles, and asked, "Do you have any foreigners staying here?" He gave them the number of Wael's room. They dragged him out through the lobby of the hotel without saying another word.

Zina and her family raced over to the hotel, but there was nothing to be found. British forces conducted a cursory investigation. They went to the morgue. Zina's mom told her to wait in the car while she went inside. She examined each face but did not find her daughter's fiancé.

Zina hoped that someone had just kidnapped Wael for the ransom payment. Most of those people were released after a few days, unharmed. Every time she heard a car pass the house, she thought it might be him. She answered her phone calls on the first ring, desperate to hear his voice.

Unknown Iraqis began to call, peddling a service that had emerged alongside the booming kidnapping industry: in exchange for thousands of dollars, they would find him or his body. Wael's family in Jordan gave $20,000 to a man who promised to deliver their son. The man vanished.

Two weeks after the abduction, Zina's uncle saw Wael on the al-'Alam television channel. The station ran a video supplied by the Abu Abbas Islamic Group, a Shi'a militia in Basrah, in which Wael and twelve other hostages stood before the camera. A member of the militia declared that these men were British spies and would all be killed if British forces did not withdraw from Basrah. But Zina had missed the broadcast, and nobody at the television station ever responded to her requests to see the clip.

After three months, the thread holding her together unraveled. She felt remorse for not having let him stay over that night. He must have known about the danger he was in and was asking her for help, but she had refused because of what her neighbors might have thought. Zina was furious with her fellow Iraqis for all the kidnapping and ransoming and killing that burned away in her country. She was mad at God, mad at Iraq. She worried that her family might now be at risk. After all, they had accepted Wael as a husband for their daughter: what did that say about them in the eyes of the men who abducted her fiancé?

Zina turned inward. She stopped answering her phone. Her social circle contracted until she spent all of her time alone in her room.

After a summer of searching for Wael, she returned to her final year at Basrah Engineering College. The Mahdi Army was now in full control of the campus, and Zina tried to make herself invisible. Though she despised them, she also feared them; her confrontational spirit had fallen silent.

Work

Zina received her degree in June 2005. As she expected, her Shi'a class-mates used their connections to find jobs, but Zina's network didn't extend much beyond her sister, mother, and father. When she heard that the telecommunications company Asiacell had hired many of her class-mates, she went down to its headquarters to ask for an interview but could not even make it past the security guard in the lobby. She waited for hours, hoping to recognize someone who might put in a good word for her, but eventually she gave up.

She went back to the café where she had met Wael and searched online for jobs. She found several openings with the Halliburton sub-sidiary KBR. In August she and her sister Tara walked through the Iraqi checkpoint at the outer edge of the sprawling compound of US and Western companies flanking the Basrah airport. They walked for one hundred yards until they reached the British-manned checkpoint, where a bomb dog sniffed at them for explosives. They cleared the KBR checkpoint and were hired within an hour.

The girls did not tell their father where they worked, but they kept no secrets from their mother, whose worry consumed the hours of each day until her daughters returned home safely. She sat by the window over-looking the front yard and the gate, which still bore the scars of Iranian mortars decades earlier. Through the largest opening, she could see parts of passing cars, the waists and chests of passersby.

Even though it was only a cluster of trailers in the desert, Zina loved the compound. Everything about it felt good to her: the cool air-conditioned rooms, the new computers, even the smell. Once she cleared the final checkpoint each morning, she sensed that she had stepped into a different country. Zina was assigned to the quality con-trol office, where she worked closely with engineers who were fixing oil refineries throughout Iraq.

But after six months, the excitement of working at KBR faded and the logistics of entering the compound became increasingly perilous. Zina began wearing a hijab and a loose-fitting *abaya* over her clothes to placate the militants who idled in a pickup truck outside the checkpoint. She came to feel that her work was only helping people in Texas get richer, which didn't seem to warrant the risks. The pros and cons were thrown into a bleaker contrast when two other young women working in the compound were assassinated. Zina and her sister decided to quit.

There was a problem, though. Even if she managed to find an opening in an Iraqi company, Zina knew that her work history would come up in the very first interview. Unless she took the risk of revealing her prior American employer, her work with KBR had locked her within the constellation of American contractors and agencies.

Tara had a friend who worked in Baghdad for the American company Titan, one of the largest contractors employing Iraqis as interpreters for the US military. If they were hired into Titan's pool of interpreters, they would live inside a military base, relieving them of the danger of clearing checkpoints each day. The sisters drove to the capital, where they sat in a row of school desks with twenty other young Iraqis applying for work. When the Titan recruiter posted the results at the end of the examination, Tara ranked first and Zina second. They were hired immediately, pending a background check.

They returned to Basrah to pack and to spend time with their parents. After a couple weeks, their clearance arrived along with a pair of plane tickets to Baghdad. They would be assigned to Camp Taji, a US military base twenty miles north of the capital.

At the airport, Zina and Tara stood on the other side of the security checkpoint, cheeks streaked with tears. Their mother walked a few steps, and then stopped and turned back to look at them. She couldn't bring herself to leave. A security guard at the airport came over and said, "Hey, auntie, are you okay? Why are you crying?" but she didn't answer. She took a few more steps and looked back at her sobbing daughters, and then left.

Her family wasn't rich, but Zina could have stayed at home and lived off their dad's salary. She could have become a schoolteacher like her cousin, but she wanted a job where she could be herself. She didn't want to rely on some well-placed cousin for promotions. The only place she thought she could excel through hard work alone was with the Americans.

That was how she felt on optimistic days, at least. During darker days, she knew that she was trying to escape her hometown and Wael's disappearance. She felt like an outcast, miserable and yet unable to adapt her personality or opinions enough to fit in with her fellow Basrawis. With the Americans, she hoped to be more accepted and better understood.

Pod 23 was a run-down compound surrounded by barbed wire in a corner of Camp Taji, a military base constructed by Saddam Hussein. There was only one way in and out of the Pod, through a checkpoint manned by American soldiers. Like the other interpreters sent to live there, Zina and Tara were not permitted to leave its suffocating confines without an American escort, and yet there was no cafeteria in the Pod. The only food was on the other side of barbed wire.

Inside the Pod, there were a few rows of trailers for housing—six interpreters in each, sharing one bathroom—a larger trailer with showers and toilets, and a dilapidated one-story building that served as a common area for the interpreters, who were called "terps" by the soldiers. When Zina and Tara were deposited in their trailer the first night, they found bed frames with no mattresses. They were embarrassed to have to ask for them. Their experience with the Americans in KBR had been much more professional; they'd had their own desks and computers. They tried not to cry the first night in their strange new home.

Each morning, the Iraqi interpreters of Camp Taji would kill time in the common area until an army unit dropped by the Pod on its way out of the base. The room had sagging, stained couches, old magazines, and a TV. Some watched the television; others sat on a cot in the shade of the large tree outside, smoking.

A unit would announce that it needed one or two or three interpreters, and the sergeant in charge of the Pod would come into the common area and select Iraqis for the mission. As she stood there, waiting to be picked, Zina felt subhuman, on display like a slab of meat for sale at the butcher shop, the pride of her recently received university diploma deflated. This was the first time she had ever lived away from home, and it wasn't starting well.

On her very first mission, Zina rode with a convoy into town to attend a meeting of the provincial council, where tribal leaders, Iraqi government officials, and high-ranking military officers discussed municipal affairs. The captain sat in the back row of the room, leaned over to Zina, and said, "Okay, tell me what's going on." She listened to the conversation, which was loaded with the acronyms and technical terms of local governance, and had no idea what was happening. She didn't know what some of the words were in Arabic, much less in English. She started to cry and looked over at the captain, who did little to mask his frustration with her. She went back to Pod 23 and between sobs wondered if she was good enough for the job. The other Iraqis consoled her, telling her she'd get better, and taught her the most commonly used phrases of the provincial council.

In time Zina and Tara found their stride and became the most sought-after interpreters in the Pod. Tara rode in different convoys on different missions, but the sisters spent evenings together. Whenever possible, they called their worried mom in Basrah. They were assigned to the civil affairs team, which led small-scale reconstruction projects throughout the province. The area receiving the most attention, Tarmiyah, was also the most violent.

Zina began to work with the major of the civil affairs team, an indefatigable leader who devoted meticulous attention to the projects under his command. He assigned Zina a desk in his office and placed a small mountain of forms in front of her. Each sheet was a complaint submitted by an Iraqi requesting reimbursement for damages incurred during military operations. After soldiers kicked in the door of a suspected insurgent, a request for $500 was submitted, parts and labor included. When a firefight on the edge of a farm resulted in a dead cow, a request for $5,000 appeared. Zina translated the forms and appended a summary opinion on each. When the major griped about the difficulty of tracking all of the disbursements, she spent days constructing an Excel worksheet that reflected each tiny change in his substantial budget. He was so ecstatic that he ran over and hugged her.

Zina and the major went everywhere together. His Humvee was easily identified by the 001 stenciled in black over the front doors. In the beginning, she wore sunglasses and a handkerchief over her mouth to disguise her identity but eventually stopped bothering. She was proud of the work they were doing, trusted the major, and didn't want to hide.

Several weeks into her assignment, an Iraqi called the major's cell phone and asked to speak with Zina. He didn't give his name but said that he had met Zina and the major during one of their many trips into Tarmiyah. There was something about her that he trusted. He told her that insurgents had laid five IEDs along the road emerging from Camp Taji. When the explosive ordnance disposal team was dispatched, it found five bombs. Zina called the informant, who told her that he would speak only to her from that point forward.

She nurtured the relationship with the man, who she believed was motivated partly by conscience and partly by self-interest: the informant needed surgery that Iraqi doctors were ill equipped to perform, and he wanted to know if the army might help him in exchange for his tips. The major told Zina to say yes, even though they both knew that the army was not likely to help. The intelligence continued to trickle in, and the major told her that her work was saving lives, both American and Iraqi.

The job was exciting, despite the risks, and Zina had figured out how to excel at it. Whenever she stood between an Iraqi and the major, she changed her posture to a slight slouch, making her appear less feminine; she wanted the men to forget that she was a woman so that they could focus on the discussion at hand.

A couple months into the job, during a site visit to one of the major's problematic projects in Mushahada—one of Tarmiyah's rougher neighborhoods—she translated the major's unhappiness with the quality of work. The Iraqi contractor angrily turned to her and called her a traitor and other slurs. Zina remained silent, choosing not to interpret his words, but the major sensed the tension.

"What did he say, Zina?"

"Nothing. What else would you like me to translate?"

"I want you to tell me what he said."

Zina reluctantly voiced the offensive words in English, at which point the major grabbed the Iraqi by the throat and shoved him against a nearby wall. She felt happy that her boss was standing up for her, but she knew that his response had been an escalation and could easily come back to harm him or the reputation of the civil affairs team.

Bombs

One day two IEDs went off, one after another, narrowly missing her convoy.

Another day, as the civil affairs team was returning from handing out reimbursements to the residents of Tarmiyah, Tara was riding in the same convoy, a vehicle ahead of her sister. Zina was sitting behind the major in the rear right seat of the Humvee. As the convoy proceeded through sparsely populated farmland, the radio went dead. The driver, busy shaking the handset, took his foot off the accelerator just as a massive bomb erupted beneath the engine.

Zina was drilled back against her seat by the blast. The gunner, standing up through the opening of the Humvee's turret, was injured and medevaced to Germany but survived. Tara whirled around at the sound of the explosion but couldn't see if her little sister was okay.

Had the bomb exploded a second later, they wouldn't have survived, but Zina and the major were fine. They scrambled out of the smoldering Humvee and raced from the area. An investigation later determined that insurgents had spent days loading a drainage pipe running beneath the road with 1,400 pounds of explosives.

Tarmiyah erupted in the weeks that followed. While Zina sat with the major during a meeting in a small conference room downtown, a sniper's bullet pierced the window and thudded into a nearby wall. Not long after that, another bullet whizzed past her and grazed the major's arm.

She asked a straightforward question: "If they keep attacking us, why are we going there?"

He gave the reply of a believer: that no matter how many insurgents operated in Tarmiyah, there was at least one kid that would benefit from a repaired school or extended segment of water pipe.

On October 17, 2006, Zina's convoy eased to a halt in front of the building where the provincial council met. Before Zina and the major had even dismounted from their Humvee, an Iraqi sniper hidden in a nearby building shot a soldier in the mouth. While he was being loaded into a medevac chopper, the major called off the meeting with the council and ordered a return to base.

The convoy turned onto a road where a captain had been killed by an IED the night before. As the convoy slowly passed, Zina noticed the dark sinkhole of the crater left by the blast.

Zina sat in the third Humvee. She saw the first IED flash, missing the lead vehicle. She saw the next bomb explode directly beneath the second vehicle, blasting open its doors. Two men leaped from their right side of the Humvee, which coasted forward until it collided with a transformer pole. The men were on fire, flames leaping from their shoulders and heads.

A firefight broke out as insurgents closed in, hoping to kill any survivors. White smoke billowed from the second Humvee. Zina remembered a recent tip from the informant: militants had stolen a large amount of chlorine from the nearby water treatment plant. She sat in the backseat of her Humvee, screaming at the soldier in the turret who unloaded gunfire upon the encroaching insurgents, begging him not to leave her alone. Even if she survived the attack, she worried that the chlorine gas would burn her lungs away.

Eva was a young Iraqi Christian from a poor family. She was gorgeous, with shiny black locks. She had taken a job as an interpreter out of financial desperation, hoping to support her family. The Christian community in Iraq had been devastated, sinking from a prewar population of 1.5 million in 2003 to several hundred thousand within years. Eva had become close friends with Zina and Tara. The three would stay up late together back at the Pod, talking about their families. On the afternoon of the sixteenth, before the attack, the sisters had brought Eva a care package from the major's family, filled with notepads and pencils and school supplies for her younger siblings. Later that night, Eva came over and said she couldn't fall asleep, so the sisters gave her issues of *Oprah* magazine to take back to her room.

Eva, twenty-two when the chlorine bomb went off, died instantly.

Another interpreter, a handsome young Iraqi nicknamed Snake, burned to death. The major tried to extract the gunner from the turret of the second Humvee, but his body was scalding. After the firefight, Zina opened her door and walked toward the wreckage. The major told her not to look, so she turned away, but not before seeing one of the gunner's arms burning on the hood of the Humvee.

As she rode back to Camp Taji, the pendulum of each second swung like a wrecking ball. The vehicle, the road, the air—it could all explode in an instant. She looked out the small window of the Humvee's door and saw a bomb behind everything, inside everything, and said, "This is the end!"

Flight

She could no longer go on any missions. Nobody told her she had to leave, but when she stayed behind in Pod 23 while the others went out each day, she felt useless. Eva's few belongings and the major's care package still lay in her room in the adjacent trailer.

It was over. Zina and Tara called their mom in Basrah and told her they needed to leave Iraq for good. For several weeks, they struggled to find someone who could purchase their airplane tickets, since they were not permitted to leave the Pod without an escort. When the day finally came, the major arranged for a meeting with a ministry official down in Baghdad. As he loaded the sisters' bags into the Humvee, the other interpreters and soldiers from the civil affairs team gathered around to hug them good-bye. When he dropped them off at the airport on his way to the ministry building, she saw the major cry for the first time. On November 15, 2006, they boarded a plane for Egypt and became refugees.

Their father stayed behind in Basrah. Their mother probably would have been safe had she stayed in Iraq, but she could not bear the thought of being away from her daughters, so she left everything behind and became a refugee. They rented a small apartment in the Sixth of October City on the outskirts of Cairo. For tables, they flipped cardboard boxes and draped sheets over them. The trauma of their final weeks in Iraq—the chlorine bomb, Eva's death, the inability to say good-bye to their dad—was the uninvited fourth guest.

Zina applied for jobs as soon as they had arrived, unaware of the work restrictions preventing refugees from taking jobs in Egypt. She was thrilled when she was called in for an interview in the Cairo branch of her old employer, KBR, but the excitement unraveled as soon as they realized that she was Iraqi and would therefore be unable to receive a work permit. The message to refugees from governments throughout the region was very clear: "feel free to burn through your life savings, but don't get too comfortable here."

The line for refugee registrations outside the UNHCR building was long. Zina had never thought of herself as a refugee before: when she thought of the word, she pictured poor and uneducated Africans. As the line inched forward, though, she saw mostly Iraqis. By mid-2007, well over one hundred thousand Iraqis had fled to Egypt, making it the third-largest host of refugees from the civil war, behind Syria and Jordan.

Farther up the line, an Iraqi man started shouting as an American woman who worked at the UNHCR walked past. He cursed, telling her that her invasion destroyed his country, and now he had nothing. She apologized, saying she was not a politician and had nothing to do with the war. She was there to help them, she said, but the man was not placated. When the woman continued down the line, Tara whispered to her, "We know it wasn't your fault." The American woman smiled and asked them to follow her back to her office.

As she registered their names, they told her about everything they had been through and the different army units under which they had worked. The American woman told them about an organization helping US-affiliated Iraqis, and wrote my name and email address on a slip of paper.

17.

Waiting

From: Zina
Sent: Saturday, June 30, 2007 10:18 AM
To: The List Project
Subject: hello

Hello,

I have been checking your website and I thought to send you asking for any kind of help you can offer.

I'm 25 years iraqi female, I worked for KBR in Iraq in 2005 and for the Coalition Forces- US army in camp Taji north of Baghdad in 2006 as interpreter, I was assigned to the Civil Affairs unit. You all know what kind of difficulties we (as interpreters) face at present and because of my affiliation with the army I and my family (my sister who worked with me for the army and my mother) were threatened and we had no option but quit the army and leave Iraq. I live now in Egypt which I don't considar as a safe place for me. I registered in the UNHCR as refugee and I had 3 interviews with them but still nothing about the resettlement. I was threatened in Iraq for 5 times so going back is impossible for me, I have been in Egypt for 7 months now, running out of time and money and despertly need help to get to a safe place. I tried to contact many people and many embassies here asking for asylum but no help. I have people in the states ready to help me but they don't know where to go.

I hope you take few minutes of your time to read this email because I despertly need help. I will be so thankful f you can offer any help or just tell me where to go. I will send you all the douments I have from the army if you can help me.

Thank you so much.

I received Zina's email ten days after the birth of the List Project, in June 2007.

To my astonishment, within seven months of Yaghdan's first email to me, I had a staff, a budget of several hundred thousand dollars, and a small army of lawyers clocking thousands of hours of pro bono counsel to help those on my list.

After a wealthy donor read about my efforts, I was able to leave behind the mattress in the Brighton basement. In addition to writing a sizeable check to the List Project, the donor opened up a free apartment for me on Central Park South in New York. The blinds had their own remote controls. The door to the refrigerator was clear glass: you could see emerald San Pellegrino bottles inside without opening the door. I would no longer need to steal Wi-Fi.

And although I had never imagined running a nonprofit, I was excited to hire Iraqis like Tona and Amina and Basma, brilliant Iraqi women who had worked with me back in Baghdad. The law firms provided them with free office space, and they became the List Project's front line, handling the torrent of applicants to the list, assigning cases to lawyers, and sitting in on phone calls between the lawyers and refugees, translating words and cultural cues.

Armed with my own organization, I was growing increasingly confident. Until now, it had been a lonely fight on behalf of a few Iraqi friends against a bureaucracy. The articles I'd written had helped to force its hand, but that wasn't enough. With the arrival of the law firms, though, I had brilliant lawyers to battle the bureaucracy case by case. I was sure that the US government would never be able to withstand the shrewd persistence of the List Project's attorneys. Inquiries were coming in from other firms around the country, and I was already in talks with Marcia Maack, the pro bono coordinator at Mayer Brown, to bring them on as our third firm.

The first attorney at Holland and Knight to respond to a firm-wide appeal for help with my list was a litigation attorney in Miami named Dana Choi. Before becoming a lawyer, Dana had worked in a then-

classified US Navy program training dolphins to attack potential sabo-
teurs swimming near our naval fleet. When I laughed, incredulous, she
forwarded me a series of articles about the use of dolphins for national
security, dating all the way back to Tuffy the bottlenose dolphin in
1965. Dana used to dive off the coast of Florida in the dead of night,
floating in blackness until the navy trainers sicced their dolphins to rain
bottlenose blows upon her. Now she specialized in white-collar crime.

Dana seemed an unlikely candidate for refugee work, but as it turns
out, lawyers like her are perfect for it. They know how to work with
emotional clients. They know how to quickly absorb complicated regulations. Because they haven't spent a career in the realm of refugee advocacy, they aren't jaded and don't stand to lose anything professionally if
they push the US government.

While Tona and Amina prioritized and assigned cases to our growing
group of attorneys, the firms had produced a broad-ranging question-
naire that approximated the questions most frequently asked by Department of Homeland Security officials when they conducted the final
interviews of refugee applicants. Each Iraqi on the list had to answer
a confidential list of questions, some 150 in total, so that we could
gather basic chronological data and supplemental evidence and anticipate problematic areas such as the "material support bar": a post-9/11
contrivance that ended up banning Iraqis who had paid ransom to free
their kidnapped children, since this was viewed by the US government
as providing aid to terrorist organizations.

The extensive set of questions might have seemed like drudge work to
those on the list, but the resulting chronologies were invaluable. If an Iraqi
was unable to state the exact date of the event that caused him or her to
flee, for example, his or her petition might be viewed with less credibility
by the American adjudicator. Those who quickly and consistently supplied
precise details over several interviews would be viewed more favorably.

When Dana asked for her first case from the List Project, she was
assigned Zina's file. Soon the refugees whose names I'd spent months
collecting began to receive phone calls from attorneys at the nation's
highest-rated law firms.

———————

For all of the apparent progress, not everyone was optimistic. By mid-July 2007, only a month after the launch of the List Project, Yaghdan had nearly given up. Over the course of the previous six months, he had gone through several UNHCR interviews, at which he was asked the same set of questions over and over and then told to wait for another interview. He was losing faith in the process and in my ability to help. From my perspective, each new interview was a coup bringing him one step closer to resettlement, but had grown to see them as little more than bureaucratic theatrics. By the time the US Embassy in Damascus called to request that he come in for an interview with the Department of Homeland Security, his nerves were frayed. He wrote to me and said, "I am done with this. It doesn't make sense to do these interviews anymore. Haifa and I are tired."

Although not a single Iraqi on the list had made it to America yet, I pleaded for his trust. He was the entire reason that the List Project had come into existence, and now he was on the brink of giving up: it was hard to imagine a more crushing defeat. I begged him to go to the interview, which I knew was one of the final steps in the process. After a few days of silence, he wrote back to say that he would go. I breathed a sigh of relief. Chris Nugent at Holland and Knight called him immediately to prepare him.

"Homeboy" Hayder was also in a state of anxiety. The $21,000 he won in a settlement from AIG in 2005 had seemed like a lot of money, but six months had passed, and there was still no sign of movement with his application for refugee status in America. Amman was prohibitively expensive, and his wife, Dina, had already sold off her jewelry. There was no plan other than to wait for the US government to help.

When he first applied, in 2004, Hayder's family and friends were shocked that he was not granted a visa immediately. As the months of waiting became years, their disbelief hardened into derision. "You said they were going to protect you. Look at what you did for them, and now they dumped you!" Hayder's instinct was to defend the United States, but they would cut him off as soon as he would start. "You want to defend them? Those idiots?!"

Each day turned on him like a vise, 2005 bleeding into 2006, and then 2007. The family moved to smaller and smaller apartments, each shabbier than the last, each neighborhood rougher. As an Iraqi, he was not permitted to work in Jordan. He asked his relatives for money, each "loan" another puncture through which his pride drained. Ali was getting older, growing up as an illegal immigrant, unable to go to school. Hayder's relationship with Dina was strained. He needed therapy for his leg—his prosthetic needed constant adjustments that he could no longer afford—and for his mind, which tormented him with nightmares.

Hayder kept calling the embassy, but its answers were noncommittal. The staff's tone reminded him of the unsatisfying answers he got whenever he had asked US soldiers in Baghdad when the electricity might come back: "Please be patient. Your application is being processed."

In time Dina's frustration turned to fury. More than four hundred thousand other Iraqi refugees had fled to Jordan by the middle of 2007. She saw only folly in his hope for a visa to America. They argued constantly. One night she told him she had given up: "We need to go back and face our destiny inside Iraq!" Hayder repeated what he always said to her, asking for just a little more time, and she erupted. "I don't give a shit anymore! Fuck America! All these lies. You're in the desert, Hayder, running after a mirage! We're not going to America." Ali cried at the sound of his parents fighting.

In late 2007 Hayder got an email from Ronald Dwight, the former advisor to Paul Bremer who had tried to help him after he lost his leg. "There's an American guy defending you inside the US," Dwight told him. "This guy is shouting through a big trumpet, and people are starting to listen to him, and you need to get your name on his list." At the end of his note, Dwight gave Hayder my email address, and a note soon appeared in my in-box:

From: Hayder
Sent: Monday, October 15, 2007 9:56 PM
To: The List Project
Subject: seeking help

Hello Sir,

I would like to introduce my self. my name is Hayder. I'm an Iraqi
Citizen living in Jordan-Amman I used to work with the US forces
Back in Iraq 2003 during my work I got ambushed on the night of 6th
August 2003 with my unit the 82nd Airborne C/C 325 and a cause
of the ambush I was shot & injured my injuries cased to amputate my
right leg & a bullet to my left leg I can't feel my foot. I had a very hard
life after the accident because I had PTSD & it has effected on my life
hardly I'm trying all my best to pass it but it isn't easy

Today I live in Jordan with my beautiful son & wife without no
home or work or any kind of income most of all I don't have a feeling
that I have a homeland because I can't go back to live in Iraq because
of threats I have received of getting killed because I served in the
American Army & afraid that my wife or kid gets kidnapped & many
be killed later on. I've been Registered in the UNHCR Amman

many Iraqis have run away from Iraq searching for safe places to
live but please I don't deserve all what I've through and I heard many
people have already left to USA

Once you create something, you have to feed it. Before long, instead
of contacting Iraqis, I was calling donors. In the beginning, I didn't have
any employees to help me with fund-raising, so I did my best to keep
up in writing thank-you notes, donor updates, and returning phone
calls from small donors myself. I assembled a small advisory board,
chaired by a brilliant problem solver named Julie Schlosser, who worked
patiently to iron out my rougher edges, edit grant proposals, and map
out budgets.

Behind this flurry of activity lay a fundamental tension: I did not
want the List Project to exist a day longer than necessary. It seemed to
me that too many organizations, founded to confront one problem,
eventually outlive the original problem and go searching for new problems. Before long, they're devoting a sizeable amount of funds they raise
to activities that raise more funds. As stimulating as the work was, I
wasn't looking for a career in refugee work or prognosticating on Iraq. In
letters to donors, I predicted that the List Project would likely conclude
its mission by the end of 2008. I wanted to get the list to safety and
move on with my life.

One by one, the names came, and out they went to the lawyers, the machine humming like a drill into the steel wall of a State Department safe. I was certain it could work and that visas were in there—a massive hunch that vibrated between certainty and delusion, redirecting my life with an intensity rivaling that December night in the Dominican Republic. Here was Iraq again, but rather than repressing a sense of failure, I felt that this effort might actually succeed.

I kept the machine oiled, traveling the country to give speeches, recruiting students and law firms and anyone who might join the cause. I felt healthier and collapsed into a deep sleep at the end of each day. Among the many benefits of having a staff was that I could start to shield myself from the daily carnage coming into my in-box: I no longer had to see dead or wounded bodies.

This all felt like momentum, but the numbers couldn't lie. Assistant Secretary of State Sauerbrey was doing a poor job. The month after I delivered the first list, eight Iraqis were admitted. In April, when she said, "We could resettle up to twenty-five thousand Iraqi refugees this year," *one* Iraqi was admitted. In May, one Iraqi. For all the ink and outrage spilled since my op-ed over a half year earlier, only fifty-three Iraqi refugees had been granted visas, and none from the list, which now approached five hundred names. While members of the Bush administration, such as Undersecretary of State Paula Dobriansky and Secretary of Homeland Security Michael Chertoff, made lofty statements about US-affiliated Iraqis, the White House and President Bush remained silent.

After the embarrassing ABC piece, when Sauerbrey claimed to have no knowledge of my list, her days as a recess appointee of the Bush administration were numbered. In the fall of 2007, the White House did not reappoint her, so Ellen retired to Maryland, where she later started a short-lived blog about the Tea Party.

Of the promised 7,000 visas in fiscal year 2007, only 1,608 had been issued, predominantly to Iraqis that had fled long before the war in Iraq had even started and whose cases were therefore already "queued up." In the face of withering criticism, the White House appointed two "czars" at the Departments of State and Homeland Security to lead "interagency efforts" to improve the process. (The media had already forgotten about Undersecretary of State Paula Dobriansky's interagency task force, announced only six months earlier with the same mandate in the same USGspeak.) In fiscal year 2008, 12,000 visas were promised.

As 2007 drew to a close, despite the efforts of the List Project's attorneys, Hayder, Dina, and little Ali had been languishing for nearly four years in Amman. In Cairo, Zina and Tara were beginning their second year of waiting. They had all advanced through interviews but had no way to know if they were at the beginning, middle, or end of the labyrinthine process. Only Yaghdan seemed close, but the message of this lethargic program was unmistakably clear: the US government did not actually wish to help US-affiliated Iraqis in any swift manner. Each time we believed that our drill had punctured through the State Department's safe, it issued a new policy requiring a new sheet of paper to be signed or a new interview to be scheduled.

I looked at the growth curve of the size of the list versus the rate of admissions and figured that I would need another sixty years to get the rest of the Iraqis to safety. Unless the president or Congress was brought into the debate, the List Project was doomed. I couldn't afford to waste time debating low-level officials in the Refugees Bureau; I needed to aim for their bosses and their bosses' boss.

18.

Politicians

Assistant Secretary of State for Population, Refugees, and Migration
Ellen Sauerbrey testifies before the House Committee on Foreign Affairs
on March 26, 2007. George Packer is over her right shoulder;
the author is over her left.

EXCERPT FROM:

Iraqi Volunteers, Iraqi Refugees: What Is America's Obligation?

Hearing Before the Subcommittee on the Middle East and South
Asia of the Committee on Foreign Affairs, House of Representatives,
One Hundred Tenth Congress

Mr. Gary Ackerman, D-NY: You anticipate the number of Iraqis
who have worked for the United States or our coalition is in excess
of 100,000?

Ms. Ellen Sauerbrey, Assistant Secretary of State: We do not really
have that number. We have been talking to contractors trying to get
a better understanding. . . . However, I have to point out that because

of the security measures that were put in place with the changes to the INA following 9/11, getting Iraqis into the country today is very time consuming; there are multiple security checks that slow down the process. It is not like it was in the days of the fall of Vietnam when we were able to bring in huge numbers of people without any security measures.

Mr. Ackerman: Is it because in Vietnam despite the fact we were at war with them we decided that not everybody in Vietnam was a security risk or an evil person?

Ms. Sauerbrey: We did not have the measures in place at that time that were put in place by the Congress and by the Department of Homeland Security following 9/11.

Mr. Ackerman: And how many people do we have doing the processing?

Ms. Sauerbrey: We have ramped up. In the last several months, we have ramped up the capacity of our overseas processing entities so that we are now getting a stream of referrals from UNHCR.

Mr. Ackerman: I find it very frustrating when we are dealing with an administration that is supposed to be part of a unified government, and we are talking to the people who are responsible for refugees, and everything depends on somebody else, and numbers are not available, and that it is hard to understand why the department responsible for helping people resettle in the United States, you know, does not have these numbers at their command. I would think that is what you would do.

It sounds like a lot of foot dragging. Well, let me say this. There are many people who believe that if we started in earnest bringing in the people who so many of us in a nonpartisan fashion believe deserve to be rescued because of what they did to help us and trusted us, that if we began doing that it would be admitting a failure in the war, which, for some reason, some people do not want to come to terms with, and, therefore, they will put every roadblock possible in the way of bringing these refugees over here.

President Ford did not have to wrestle very long. He said, "Get this done," and it got done. I think we have met the enemy, and they are us.

The Great Do-Over

As kids, whenever my brother Derek beat me in a game of one-on-one, I'd snatch the basketball and declare, "C'mon, best two out of three!" If he won the next game, I'd pant, "Best three out of five!" He usually cut me off when I begged for best four out of seven.

In 2007 the war was in its fourth year. In each of those years, the Bush administration and war planners had tried to locate victory with every manner of strategy short of quitting. They toppled Saddam, hoping that the Iraqis would figure things out on their own. They trained Iraqi troops to take over their own security—troops who soon turned their weapons on us or each other. They tried to repair power plants, but contractors pocketed most of the funds and then asked for more. They flew in new rulers, who were rejected. They rushed elections and unwittingly herded Iraqis into voting along sectarian lines. Hoping to change the narrative that the war was a fiasco, the White House relentlessly introduced catchy phrases to roll out new strategies: "As they stand up, we'll stand down." "Oil spots." "Clear, hold, and build." "Operation Together Forward." "The New Way Forward." Some elements of the strategy were named by the media, such as the "Baghdad Wall," where we emplaced miles of concrete around hot spots to keep insurgents in or out.

When these failed to stanch the bleeding or to convince the American public that Iraq had not become a "lost war" like Vietnam, the war planners and think-tank sages teed up a ternary set of options for President Bush, following the bruising results of the 2006 midterm elections:

+1, or "Go big," in which tens of thousands of additional troops could be sent in a last-ditch "surge" to somehow change the course of the war;

0, or "Go long," in which the status quo is maintained, but for a period so dispiritingly long that the insurgency peters out; or

-1, or "Go home," in which the president acknowledges the overwhelming domestic dissatisfaction with the war and initiates a withdrawal.

For President Bush and many of the neoconservatives who led the charge into Iraq, the "Go big" option of a surge presented a tantalizing opportunity. It was a do-over, a best-four-out-of-seven attempt to break the narrative that the war had become one of the greatest blunders in American history. By the time that the president announced the surge in January 2007, one estimate counted 93,964 Iraqis who had already died and nearly 2 million refugees. More than 3,000 US troops were dead and approximately 23,400 wounded.

But no matter. There was still a chance to *win*. Columnists and pundits and experts and hosts and congressmen picked their side of the debate like Little Leaguers choosing teams. With only a year left in office, the president needed the surge to succeed, or to at least look as though it were succeeding, and the executive branch agencies under his control needed to operate as though it were succeeding. The decision to surge soon worked its way through the arteries and intestines of the federal bureaucracies.

The president sent a charismatic, Princeton-educated general named David Petraeus. He would herald a new type of war, the papers whispered excitedly, in which the concept of protecting civilians was more important than body counts. After years in the wilderness, America finally had a strategy figured out, and apparently it only needed another thirty thousand troops.

Less reported, though, was the seismic shift that had occurred in Anbar Province known as the *Sahwa*, or "Awakening," in which more than one hundred thousand Sunnis—many of them former insurgents—abandoned the anti-American insurgency in order to take up arms against Al-Qaeda in Iraq and other foreign fighters that had overplayed their hand by instituting their version of sharia law in a number of Iraqi towns. They effectively joined our side, getting placed on the Pentagon's payroll, in order to help rid Iraq of what had become a common enemy. The trend lines of US casualties soon dropped, along with the media's and public's concern with the war.

As I made the rounds in Washington, the parlor game of the surge debate had hardened into a new narrative: America was *winning*. In a tense meeting on the fifth floor of the State Department with Deputy Secretary John Negroponte, a small group of refugee organization directors criticized the department's languorous pace of resettling Iraqi refugees. At one point, when I was describing a spate of death threats and assassination attempts that the List Project had documented in the previous weeks, Negroponte cut me off and said, "Look, I don't know if you've noticed, but we're winning! The surge has worked. I've been in Fallujah when nobody lived there, and now people are moving back!"

John Bolton, Bush's ambassador to the United Nations, spoke for the Darwinian id of the White House: "Our obligation was to give them new institutions and provide security. We have fulfilled that obligation. I don't think we have an obligation to compensate for the hardships of war. . . . Helping the refugees flies in the face of received logic. You don't want to encourage the refugees to stay. You want them to go home."

Since the new narrative meant that things were getting better, why didn't everyone just go back home? They were needed by their countrymen. Besides, if the US government brought too many educated Iraqis to safety, numerous officials lectured me, Iraq might suffer a brain drain, depriving the country of its best and brightest when they were needed most. "What about an Iraqi who isn't working for the US anymore and who is being hunted by a militia?" I'd ask of deaf ears. "What about those who did try to work for the government of Iraq and received death threats when their prior work with the Americans became known? Could helping a few hundred people on my list really trigger a brain drain?"

But there were other, more primal forces at work against the mission of the List Project.

The Gorilla in the Bureaucracy

"You know, Kirk, not everyone agrees with you that the best thing for this country is the resettlement of large numbers of Muslims," an exasperated senior official in the State Department's Refugees Bureau snapped at me after I'd called to check in on the list. It was nice to finally hear someone speak so candidly. Of the various arguments against swiftly helping US-affiliated Iraqis, this was the shortest answer I could relay whenever someone asked me why it was so difficult and time-consuming to get an Iraqi a visa: nobody wanted his or her signature to be on the visa papers of the next 9/11 hijacker.

For years, the American public had been instructed that Iraqis were part of an "axis of evil." In speech after speech, President Bush told us that we needed to invade Iraq to rid it of terrorists. When the public's support of the war began to dwindle, our president told us that we needed to stay there to save it from sinking into a failed state that harbored terrorists, inveighing against anyone who suggested withdrawing. "However they put it," Bush said, "the Democrat approach in Iraq comes down to this: the terrorists win and America loses."

NBC's David Gregory once asked George W. Bush why he was still a credible messenger on the stakes of the war. The president's response was feisty:

> I'm going to keep talking about it. That's my job as the president, is to tell people the threats we face and what we're doing about it. They're dangerous, and I can't put it any more plainly to the American people, and to them, we will stay on the offense. It's better to fight them there than here.
>
> And this concept about, well, maybe, you know, let's just kind of just leave them alone and maybe they'll be all right is naïve. These people attacked us before we were in Iraq. They viciously attacked us before we were in Iraq, and they've been attacking ever since.
>
> They are a threat to your children, David. And whoever is in that Oval Office better understand it and take measures necessary to protect the American people.

After years of being told by our president that we fight them "there" so that we wouldn't have to fight them "here," it made sense that an official in the refugee bureaucracy would do whatever he or she could to keep anyone who looked or sounded like "them" from coming over here.

This wasn't pleasant to relay to Iraqis on the list, but it made it easier to explain the many nonsensical dimensions of the "enhanced" screening measures for Iraqis, such as the requirement that they must obtain a slip of paper from the local police station clearing them of any crimes, even though many of them had fled the civil war into neighboring countries illegally.

It was painfully apparent that President Bush's unwillingness to lead, much less utter a syllable about tens of thousands of imperiled US-affiliated Iraqis, meant that his executive branch agencies—the Departments of State and Homeland Security—would never step in front of him by taking any bold or urgent action.

If there was to be a breakthrough, it would have to come from the Congress.

Congressman Earl Blumenauer of Oregon's Third District was the first to sponsor a bill in the House dealing with the refugee crisis. The genteel, bow-tied Democrat rode his bike to the Capitol Building each morning. When we met, he spoke quietly but eloquently about our moral obligation to protect US-affiliated Iraqis. I was eager to recruit support for the bill. Dennis Hastert was no longer in Congress, but Peter Roskam, an old family friend and former colleague of my dad's in the Illinois State Legislature, had just been elected to the US House. To boot, his chief of staff had some experience in Iraq working for a USAID grantee. I sent Roskam and his chief a note urging him to sign on to the Blumenauer legislation, which would create a special preference for those who had served alongside the United States as well as for Iraqi Christians, whose ranks had been decimated during the civil war.

A few days passed before his chief of staff called to notify me that Roskam would not be signing on to the legislation. As it turns out, the bill would have also protected gay Iraqis, whom militants were killing in shocking numbers. As the war worsened, the most common method of murdering gay Iraqis was to crush their skulls with cinder blocks. On principle, the representative would not sign on to anything that created "preferential treatment" for gay people.

A few months later, after the Blumenauer legislation failed to pass, his chief of staff sent me an email with the name of an Iraqi that he wanted added to my list.

————————

After the collapse of Representative Blumenauer's legislation, progress was fitful until Senator Kennedy took up the cause. He drafted a new bill that utilized a little-known program called the Special Immigrant Visa, which had been created in 2005 at the urging of the marines. The original SIV program had opened fifty slots for interpreters each year, but as soon as it had passed, there was a decadelong backlog of applications. So in late 2007 Kennedy led a bipartisan coalition of senators, including Republicans Richard Lugar, Sam Brownback, and Gordon Smith, and Democrats Barack Obama and Hillary Clinton, in an effort to expand the SIV program to five thousand visas per year for five years. These twenty-five thousand visas were designated exclusively for Iraqis who had worked alongside the United States. The Refugee Crisis in Iraq Act also established in-country processing, meaning that Iraqis would no longer have to flee to Syria or Jordan in order to apply for resettlement; they could go directly to the embassy in Baghdad.

The morning the legislation passed the Senate, Kennedy's staff arranged a phone call with several refugee organizations that had played a role in crafting the legislation. "This is a big one!" he exclaimed from a cell phone on the floor of the Senate.

After the call, I flopped down onto the couch and laughed. My list was approaching a thousand names. Even if every one of them took a Special Immigrant Visa, there would be tens of thousands of slots remaining for Iraqis that weren't on the list. My optimism bubbled up wildly: it had been less than a year, and a solution for tens of thousands of US-affiliated Iraqis was already in sight. We had beaten the bureaucracies. The List Project's attorneys would help everyone apply, and within a year, at most, I could shut down the nonprofit and get on with my life.

Iraqis in West Chicago

In August 2007, two months after I begged Yaghdan not to give up, I received a phone call from a Voluntary Agency in Chicago. Voluntary Agencies, or VOLAGs, are organizations that receive federal funds from the Department of Health and Human Services to provide assistance for incoming refugees. They were calling to see if I could come sign a form acknowledging my sponsorship of Yaghdan. "They're approved?!" I shouted into the phone.

"We don't know their travel date, but yes, they will be resettled to West Chicago. You still live there, correct?"

I had half-jokingly volunteered my parents earlier in the year, saying that they could be the first to open their doors to Iraqis on the list. "Absolutely!" they said.

It wasn't the first time they had made such a commitment. In my first weeks in Fallujah, Hurricane Katrina ripped through New Orleans. (I watched the coverage with a shocked marine lieutenant colonel from Biloxi, Mississippi, which was also battered.) A Palestinian-American buddy from college and his family had been displaced by the flood, so I called home to ask my dad if they could host them. He chuckled and said that he and my mom had just talked about finding a way to help someone displaced by the hurricane. A week later, my friend and his family, seven in all, piled into a van and drove up to West Chicago. They stayed with my parents for a couple months, at which point they moved into a house that my parents' church rented for the family.

The first call I made after hearing Yaghdan's news was my dad.

"We'll be ready for them!" he said.

While he waited for a travel date from the embassy in Damascus, Yaghdan sent me questions about life in America:

Q1. What is the best salary to have a decent life in the US in general and in Chicago?

Q3. Can I buy a car? How much does it cost to buy a nineties model Japanese car?

Q4. Are there any Arabic people in Chicago?

Q6. My wife covers her head with scarves. Is there any problem with that?

Q10. I have books like the Quran and two other books for prayer. Is it ok to bring them or is it forbidden?

In late August, in the midst of replying to one of his notes, my cell buzzed with a voice mail alert. Yaghdan's voice warbled through as though from another dimension, from a pay phone on Hadara Street in the Syrian city of Homs, where he and Haifa had been holed up in order to avoid Muqtada al-Sadr's Mahdi Army representatives in Damascus. "Hello, Kirk! We got a travel date. We are flying in two days. We will see you in Chicago."

I flew back to West Chicago to help my parents prepare for their arrival. Though ten months had passed and a thousand names had been added to the list since my op-ed in the *Los Angeles Times,* the entire reason that I had become involved in the first place was about to arrive in my hometown. I was proud of this moment. I had stumbled my way to this point, but Yaghdan's arrival was a sudden illumination: it *was* possible. As slow moving and complicated as the refugee resettlement process was, I had my first win.

My folks had readied the small cottage in the backyard that had played host to Jewish refugees from the Ukraine in the 1990s and my Palestinian friends just a few years earlier. My mom had printed out a Google map of mosques in the western suburbs, along with halal grocers and butchers. The night before Yaghdan arrived, my dad and I sat on the front porch, talking about the events of the past year. He rocked in his chair, wisps of pipe smoke overhead, and ribbed me: "I think you owe the State Department a whole lot of thanks, now that Yaghdan's here, don't you?" I knew he was joking, but I couldn't constrain my annoyance at the idea of thanking the government.

The morning of August 29, 2007, I drove from West Chicago to O'Hare International Airport to meet Yaghdan and Haifa. It had been nearly two years, and the only image of him I'd seen since I left was his smiling face in the picture I snapped of the USAID staff, several of whom were now dead. And there he was, twenty yards away and grinning as he walked past the luggage carousels, at least six inches taller than the twenty Iraqi refugees who had also made the flight with him out of Syria through Jordan, settling at last in Chicago. My grin was uncontrollable, as I held my arms up and opened hands in a "How did this happen?" state of delight.

Yaghdan saw me and laughed. He advanced ahead of the group and gave me a strong hug.

When I saw Haifa, I wanted to ignore Muslim convention and give her a hug but instead smiled and welcomed her. The exciting strangeness of the moment was amplified by the fact that although I had never met her, our lives had been wildly redirected by each other's. Within an hour, they would be living in our house.

Their arrival was made bittersweet when we learned that the airline had lost two of their three bags—two-thirds of their earthly possessions that Haifa had packed frantically while Yaghdan went to the USAID compound to ask for help the day of the death threat.

As I drove them out to the suburbs, my mom and dad sat in the kitchen, practicing their welcome phrase, *as-salaamu 'alaikum*. When we arrived, they were waiting in the driveway with their Arabic greeting and balloons.

After a tour of their new home, my dad told Yaghdan that he wanted to take him on a tour of West Chicago. I sat in the back seat of the Buick as we sailed down Route 59 past the Taco Bell, where I had positioned imaginary tanks during the bleak winter of 2006. My dad pointed out the landmarks to Yaghdan, who laughed and said, "It's amazing that everyone obeys the lines on the roads! Not in the Middle East . . ."

I hadn't prepared Yaghdan for how to win over my dad, but singing the virtues of American rule of law was a surefire bet.

"Everyone here seems so peaceful," he reflected, as we turned past the high school and junior high.

"Yeah, you know, it's true, Yaghdan. I think you'll find we really are a peaceful country." My dad tapped the dottle from his pipe into the ashtray as he spoke.

From the backseat, I mustered a "Yep."

When I flew back to West Chicago a few months later to celebrate the holidays, Yaghdan and Haifa were already full-fledged family members. He had taken to signing his emails to me as "the fourth Johnson brother" and was settling into suburban life surprisingly smoothly. He found a job in the intake center at the emergency room of the Good Samaritan Hospital, taking every possible shift. When the hospital gave him a Christmas ham, he politely accepted it and dropped off the pork at the Johnson clan's kitchen.

On December 29, my brothers and I poured a few glasses of whiskey and toasted the two-year anniversary of my survival in the Dominican Republic. It was hard to remember feeling so elated at any other point in my life. I had somehow managed to ride a flood of events that culminated in Yaghdan and Haifa's arrival, and Senator Kennedy's creation of twenty-five thousand visa slots for US-affiliated Iraqis, which would effectively solve the crisis, I believed. The glasses clinked and the new year came.

19.

George W. Bush

Journalist Bob Woodward: How do you think history
will judge your Iraq war?

President George W. Bush: History. We won't know.
We'll all be dead.

As a flood spreads wider and wider
the water becomes shallower and dirtier.
The revolution evaporates,
and leaves behind only the slime of a new bureaucracy.
The chains of tormented mankind
are made out of red tape.

   —Franz Kafka

E very American high school student learns that Congress makes the laws and the president executes them. But it seems that the intent of Congress is often misinterpreted by the executive branch.

I had my attorneys, but the Bush administration had its own, who skimmed through the Refugee Crisis in Iraq Act and decided that it did not need to be implemented, at least not yet. Despite the use of the word *crisis* in the name of the act, the White House and State Department attorneys claimed that they were uncertain as to whether Congress had intended the legislation to be enforced immediately or at the start of the following fiscal year, which was a full six months away. Unless Congress amended the act, there would be no new Special Immigrant Visas (SIVs) issued yet.

Let it never be said that bureaucracies are unimaginative. All the MFAs in the country couldn't outmatch the creativity demonstrated by the Departments of State and Homeland Security when instructed by Congress to do something they didn't want to do. Wherever an opportunity to narrow the impact of the Kennedy legislation existed, the Bush administration's lawyers seemed to find it. Beyond delaying the start date of the bill, the Department of State's attorneys produced a consular interpretation that limited eligibility for the SIV. Hoping to cast a wide net of eligibility, the Kennedy legislation indicated that Iraqis who had worked directly for the US government (the State Department, USAID, and the military) or for a government contractor (Bechtel, KBR) could apply for the SIV. But when the List Project's attorneys submitted the applications of scores of Iraqis who had worked for groups such as the International Republican Institute or the National Democratic Institute, we were swiftly informed that they were ineligible because IRI and NDI were grantees. A grant from the US government differs from a contract in terms of reporting requirements, but no militia or member of Al-Qaeda in Iraq knew or cared about the subtle differences in federal funding mechanisms. Even Iraqis working for the US Institute of Peace, which is funded directly by Congress and is required by law to have the sitting Secretaries of State and Defense on its board, were deemed ineligible.

And so the SIV program was euthanized in its infancy. Of the 5,000 slots allocated in the first year, only 438 visas were granted, an 8 percent success rate during a year of civil war, extrajudicial killings, and flight. Only a handful of those were granted to Iraqis on my list. Once jubilant, they soon saw the program as a myth—a lot of words with no truth behind them. They returned to submitting their applications through the traditional US Refugee Admissions Program, where they waited in line with tens of thousands of Iraqis who did not work for America.

I was losing. I traveled frantically to raise awareness and find enough funding to avert the shuttering of the List Project, but my fatigue overwhelmed me one miserable evening a few weeks before the 2008 election. After eighteen straight days of talks and meetings on the road, I flew back to New York a few hours before a fund-raiser in midtown. In my opening remarks, where I thanked the various donors and law firms in attendance, my weary eyes skipped over the names of the donors who had provided the apartment I'd been living in. Before I'd even finished, they had stormed out of the event. I raced down to find them donning their coats in the lobby, and apologized for the mistake, asking them to come back up so I could correct it. One screamed, "You ingrate! I want you out of the building!" while the other called for a cab. I was mortified: it had been an error, not any deliberate snub, but I couldn't get through to them.

When I walked back to the building later that evening, the doorman informed me that I had twenty-four hours to vacate the apartment. I sprinted to Hertz in my suit and rented an SUV, which my girlfriend and I packed up until three in the morning. I left an apology letter on the kitchen table.

"I'm sorry I got us kicked out," I said wearily to my teary-eyed girlfriend as the confused goldfish flitted around in a Ziploc bag on her lap, New York sliding out of view behind us as we drove north to Boston.

A child wailed in the next room. I reclined in the chair and stared up at the ceiling while my dentist wiggled her hands into rubber gloves.

A large, dopey cartoon of Goofy grinned back down at me. I wasn't sure why, but my insurance company had authorized only one dental provider, a kids clinic called Kool Smiles. Someone put goggles over my eyes before the dentist took a sander to my front teeth. I'd been grinding down my molars during sleep to such an extent that my front teeth were colliding, another unfortunate result of my mounting fatigue. The dentist decided to sand some length off the front to keep up with the loss in the back. "God, it's nice to work in an adult mouth!" she said. "So much more room!" I blinked politely.

Things were falling apart. The Kennedy momentum was dissipating rapidly. By the fall of 2008, the war in Iraq was a wisp in the exhaust hanging over the campaign trail. In the year and a half since President Bush knighted General Petraeus and his counterinsurgency campaign, the American casualty rate had dropped substantially, but Iraq was still in turmoil. To those willing to look beyond the cult of Petraeus-as-savior narrative, a core factor behind the drop in anti-US attacks was the Awakening movement. For the cost of roughly $370 million, the insurgency was "rented," creating a period of quiet during 2008 and thus removing the war as an election year issue.

The surge gave America psychological license to leave with the belief that it had somehow won. The White House negotiated a status-of-forces agreement (SOFA) with Nouri al-Maliki's government, establishing a timeline for withdrawal—a concept that only a year earlier had been considered traitorous by the Republican Party.

By November, the Bush administration and the Pentagon had grown so confident of the surge's success that an order came down through the war bureaucracy: Iraqi interpreters could no longer wear balaclavas to conceal their identity while on patrol with US forces. "We are a professional army, and professional units don't conceal their identity by wearing masks," bleated Lieutenant Colonel Steven Stover, army spokesman. Those who refused to remove their masks could "seek alternative employment." The policy was dropped after much criticism by the List Project and others, but it signaled a bleaker truth: in addition to opening up the possibility of leaving, the surge's "success" gave us permission to forget about Iraq. With imploding stock and housing markets, failing banks, and the specter of economic collapse, there was no longer any interest in following what was happening in a war that we'd "won." The major media outlets began to shutter their Baghdad bureaus, and the country's attention turned inward.

Unsurprisingly, this also meant that big-budget items such as funding the Sahwa members fell along the wayside. Al-Maliki's Shi'a-dominated government in Iraq turned its sights on the Sunni Awakening movement, which had lost its American patron. Many were killed, others arrested, and even more fled the country. By the end of 2008, I was receiving appeals to take on Sahwa cases, an idea that I rejected at once, knowing the history of many of these former insurgents. When I mentioned this to Yaghdan, he chuckled and told me that the group had set half his home on fire with a rocket-propelled grenade and then occupied it once the flames subsided.

The American public couldn't be bothered with the minutiae of the status-of-forces agreement, but the Iraqis on the list paid close attention to the negotiations. They looked on in terror when America agreed to dismantle the bases as a condition of the SOFA. When the surge had intensified, many US-affiliated Iraqis could no longer afford to risk traveling past the *alassas* into military bases and the Green Zone each day, so large numbers of interpreters simply moved into the security of our bases. Applications flooded into the project from desperate interpreters whose confidence in the US government had been shaken by the mask ban and the SOFA. They wanted to know if they would be left behind when we withdrew. Unless the newly elected Democratic president acted swiftly, it was hard to imagine any other outcome.

20.

Barack H. Obama

EXCERPT FROM:

"Turning the Page in Iraq"

A speech.

We must also keep faith with Iraqis who kept faith with us.

One tragic outcome of this war is that the Iraqis who stood with America—the interpreters, embassy workers, and subcontractors—are being targeted for assassination.

An Iraqi named Laith who worked for an American organization told a journalist, "Sometimes I feel like we're standing in line for a ticket, waiting to die." And yet our doors are shut. In April, we admitted exactly one Iraqi refugee—just one!

That is not how we treat our friends. That is not how we take responsibility for our own actions. That is not who we are as Americans. It's time to at least fill the seven thousand slots we pledged to Iraqi refugees and to be open to accepting even more Iraqis at risk.

Keeping this moral obligation is a key part of how we turn the page in Iraq. Because what's at stake is bigger than this war—it's our global leadership.

Now is a time to be bold. We must not stay the course or take the conventional path because the other course is unknown.

To quote Dr. Brzezinski: we must not allow ourselves to become "prisoners of uncertainty."

—Candidate Barack Obama

September 12, 2007
Clinton, Iowa

In January 2009, two weeks before Barack Obama's inauguration, the Kennedy Center for the Performing Arts in Washington, DC, hosted a performance of George Packer's award-winning play about the abandonment of US-affiliated Iraqis. *Betrayed*, which had won critical acclaim off-Broadway, drew heavily from his *New Yorker* piece. There was even a character named Prescott, an American who compiles a list of his former Iraqi colleagues after a freak accident ended his service.

My guest for the evening was Samantha Power, the "rock star" humanitarian who'd written a history of America's response to genocide. Three years earlier, as soon as the casts were sawn from my arms in West Chicago, I'd driven to Boston with the flighty notion that I'd work as her research assistant. When Obama had been elected to the US Senate in 2004, she served as his principal foreign policy advisor and was now set to take a senior role in the upcoming administration.

Power was an obvious ally. In 2007 she wrote a magazine piece for *Time* in which she assailed the Bush White House for its meager results in resettling Iraqi refugees. An ex-girlfriend of mine taking Power's course at Harvard University's John F. Kennedy School of Government emailed me in surprise to say that she had been assigned my op-eds for that night's reading.

Her influence on Obama was clear. In the fall of 2007, when no other candidates in either party had uttered a word about the fastest-growing refugee crisis in the world, Obama gave a major campaign speech about how he would address Iraq if elected president, devoting several paragraphs to the plight of our interpreters.

The significance of Obama's election was debated in the loftiest terms, but in my wearied state, I was simply relieved. No more of the ideological timidity demonstrated by the Bush White House and its executive branch agencies, which never failed to generate a 9/11-rooted justification for the torpid pace of granting visas to Iraqis on the list. No more of the "The surge worked!" mantra, which might finally allow for honest appraisals of the situation on the ground in Iraq. No more political appointments for money bundlers in posts that required experience and competence. No more hostile interpretations of congressional intent by administration lawyers. No more silence from the White House.

We would have a pragmatist in charge. A man who was not burdened by a political need for Iraq to look a certain way on account of decisions he'd made but who could address it on its own terms. A man who had spoken eloquently about the need for bold solutions to protect the Iraqis who had kept the faith with America. A man whose key advisor had written forcefully about the issue and who knew about my list.

In a fever of hope, I reasoned that the remaining names on my list, now some two thousand long, could be resettled within a year of Inauguration Day.

After the curtains dropped on Packer's play, I was seated at a dinner next to Power and Ben Rhodes, Obama's talented speechwriter who'd penned the "Turning the Page in Iraq" speech. For nearly two hours, we discussed the minutiae of the Bush administration's Iraqi refugee policy and the bureaucratic pitfalls that had riddled the process.

I laid out my concern, which was simple: the refugee resettlement bureaucracy they were about to inherit from the Republicans would not work quickly enough to keep pace with the withdrawal. Unless they made some serious changes and initiated some contingency planning, the United States would abandon thousands of its Iraqi employees, and it would be bloody.

Although Obama had campaigned on withdrawing from Iraq, the timetable and framework for withdrawal had already been established for him in December 2008 by the outgoing Bush administration. Within six months of Obama's inauguration, US forces would withdraw from the archipelago of forward operating bases and outposts throughout Iraq's cities, consolidating into a number of large bases in more remote parts of the country. Following that, twenty thousand troops would be reassigned to logistics, implementing the largest movement of soldiers and matériel since World War II. "Hannibal trying to move over the Alps had a tremendous logistics burden, but it was nothing like the complexity we are dealing with now," crowed Lieutenant General William G. Webster. The effort was so advanced that logistics teams had the capacity to track a coffeepot from a dismantled forward operating base in Baghdad all the way along its journey back to America.

For all of this advance planning, though, nobody in government seemed to be considering what would happen to the thousands of Iraqis still living and working for our troops in those bases. In early 2009, when it was clear that the withdrawal was under way, many of the Iraqis on the list were told they'd need to wait an entire year for just their initial interview, and much longer for a travel date, if they were lucky. I suggested to Power that there would be an increase in applications for visas as more interpreters were laid off, placing greater strain on an overstrained system.

The implications were far from hypothetical. As we ate, I went through each of the recent examples set by our coalition partners. The previous year, British forces beat a hasty withdrawal from southern Iraq without any contingency plans to protect their own interpreters. A ghastly campaign of targeted assassinations commenced with the public execution of seventeen British-affiliated Iraqis. Their bodies were dumped throughout the streets of Basrah as a warning.

Only after a public outcry in the United Kingdom did the newly elected prime minister, Gordon Brown, commit to reversing the policy bequeathed to him by Tony Blair. The British Royal Air Force subsequently airlifted its Iraqi interpreters directly to a military base in Oxfordshire, England, where they were screened and granted refugee status.

Denmark quietly airlifted hundreds of its Iraqi interpreters in a single night. Poland and Australia did the same. None of our allies had contrived a convoluted process that condemned Iraqi employees to a year or longer of hiding and survival as they waited for an interview with a lumbering bureaucracy. Our coalition partners simply loaded their endangered Iraqis onto planes, flew them back to controlled military bases, and screened their cases swiftly.

The United States had its own history of airlifts. In 1999 President Clinton airlifted twenty thousand Kosovar Albanians who had fled from Yugoslav president Slobodan Milošević's forces. The refugees were flown directly to Fort Dix in New Jersey, where they were granted refugee status under the Immigration and Nationality Act.

Just a few years earlier, after a 1996 uprising in the north of Iraq, Clinton ordered Operation Pacific Haven, in which nearly seven thousand Iraqi Kurds were evacuated in advance of an attack by Saddam Hussein's army. Clinton's administration understood that the traditional mechanisms for resettling refugees would never work quickly enough, so Eric Schwartz, then senior director for multilateral and humanitarian affairs at the National Security Council, worked with the US Army to fly thousands of Iraqis in a matter of days to Andersen Air Force Base in Guam, where the average processing time was ninety days. Major General John Dallegher, commander of the airlift, stated, "Our success will undoubtedly be a role model for future humanitarian efforts."

By the end of dinner, I had made my case for what we called "the Guam option" in the best way I knew. Tens of thousands of the Special Immigrant Visa slots created by the Kennedy legislation were sitting there for them to use, I said, urging Power not to get lost in the thickets of minor tweaks within the bureaucracy but to remember what the United States has been capable of when the president takes the lead in protecting refugees. She, of course, knew far more than I did about this history.

A few weeks later, Power was appointed to President Obama's National Security Council in the same position that Eric Schwartz had held under Clinton. Serendipitously, Schwartz was appointed to Ellen Sauerbrey's old post as assistant secretary of state for population, refugees, and migration.

Beyond the promising appointments, the Obama administration's first term began with a radically different approach: it granted us access. In April 2009 Power convened the first meeting between the National Security Council and leaders of organizations involved in confronting the Iraqi refugee crisis. While waiting for the NSC officials to arrive, two advocates next to me whispered excitedly to each other, "I can't believe we're about to meet Samantha Power!" There was a general atmosphere of catharsis: refugee organizations had for years tried to get through to the Bush administration. (At one low point, the Bush NSC had sent out an email soliciting the names of potential invitees for a discussion on the issue. But when the list of advocates desperate to finally speak with someone in power came back, the Bush White House decided that it was too long and simply canceled the meeting.) After a two-hour discussion of the broader refugee crisis, each organization deposited its most recent field reports in a stack before Power. I gave her a two-page letter that simply reiterated my recommendation of the Guam option for US-affiliated Iraqis.

Access to the Obama White House was a welcome change from the Bush years, but as 2009 wore on, I grew anxious about how Iraqis on my list were faring in the midst of the withdrawal. Thanks to the tenacity of the law firms, more than seven hundred Iraqis had made it through the gauntlet to safety in America since the launch of the List Project in 2007. But the list was well over two thousand names long and growing mercilessly. The first critical benchmark in the status-of-forces agreement, in which US forces were to pull back from their outposts and checkpoints throughout Iraq's cities, passed on July 1, 2009. Shortly thereafter, I decided it was time to return to Iraq. If I was going to be effective in advocating on their behalf throughout the withdrawal, sitting around in meetings in Washington wasn't going to help much. I needed to go back to see exactly how they were faring under the new administration's bureaucracy. I wasn't thrilled about returning but had convinced myself that it might help bring about "closure": after all, it had now been four years since I'd left Fallujah on what was supposed to have been a weeklong vacation.

This time, of course, I would not be going as a government official, protected by a ring of taxpayer-funded mercenaries. I inquired with a security firm about the cost of a week's worth of protection and found the gunslinging business alive and well in Iraq: one week would cost the List Project upward of $50,000, an impossible sum. I was left with two options: travel with a low profile with Iraqi friends in soft-skin cars, potentially increasing the risk to them in the process, or embed with the US military as a "journalist," thereby securing the protection of the military. I opted for the latter, traveling with Chris Nugent, the Holland and Knight attorney who had single-handedly helped scores of Iraqis on the list to safety in the years since the launch of the List Project.

My twenty-ninth birthday began on the outskirts of Kuwait City, surrounded by snoring grunts and contractors in tent P7 at the Logistics Support Area of Ali Al-Salem air base. After cajoling our way onto the next manifest into Baghdad, I threw on some body armor on loan from the military and led Chris up the ramp of the C-130.

Wind whipped in through the back of the transport plane as we hurtled north from Kuwait over Karbala' toward Camp Victory. On the red mesh bench next to me sat a heavyset KBR employee engrossed in a book called *Thong on Fire: An Urban Erotic Tale.* Across the way, Chris clicked away on his BlackBerry, responding to Iraqis on the list and bureaucrats back in Washington. In a fit of nostalgia, I queued up my old HELO playlist and leaned back as the Rolling Stones blasted over the din of the plane.

I soon found myself back at the same tent- and generator-clogged corner of Camp Victory that I had left years earlier, waiting for the same up-armored Rhino Runner bus to sneak me into the Green Zone in the dead of night. If I had hoped for a wave of closure upon my arrival, I was met instead with a prickly rash of unanswerable questions: What was I doing back here? Why was I still dealing with Iraq when all of my friends had long since moved on? Why did I think anything would happen as a result of this trip, when nobody in Washington cared about Iraq anymore? What in God's name was I going to tell all of these people who were emerging from hiding at great risk to meet with me? When would this all end?

I wandered restlessly around the base and noticed little had changed. There was Wi-Fi now, and the morale, welfare, and recreation tent was much busier than when I had left in 2005, but that was about it. Soldiers and contractors sprawled out on black pleather couches and stared sleepily at B movies flickering on a wrinkled movie screen. On the other side of the massive tent, several rows of carrels were filled with young men watching episode after episode of TV shows on DVDs that they checked out from an Indian man behind a nearby counter. A sign hung above each carrel: "Please limit usage to one season only." Others sat at folding tables with PSPs, squinting into the tiny screens as they played games. Everyone already seemed to know the war was over, two years before they were allowed to come home.

I slipped out of the tent and ambled past a grinding generator, which powered the lights illuminating the basketball courts. Taco Bell had made its way into the base, encased between rows of blast walls. A Nepalese employee wearing a Taco Bell Baghdad hat smiled as he handed me a Crunchwrap Supreme and nachos, both oozing orange sauce. The McDonald's now had a bright red bench upon which sat a human-sized Ronald McDonald statue, lounging in clown makeup with his arm over the back of the bench.

Who was going to pack up all of this shit?

Twenty minutes later, stomach churning from the toxic cheese sauce, I made my way back to the plywood and canvas tent that served as the waiting area for the Rhino Runner. I tilted a packet of purple Gatorade powder into a bottle of water and watched it disperse into the shape of a small inverted explosion. A couple grunts sat behind a desk littered with empty cans of Red Bull, zoned out in oppressive boredom, waiting for the nighttime run. A flat-screen TV suspended on a nearby plywood wall blared out Fox News. I took a long sip and shut my eyes.

My ears pricked up when someone on TV shouted "the Tides Foundation!" which had given a grant to the List Project and served as our fiscal agent. I had never heard Tides discussed in the media before. I opened my eyes to find a squat, comical man in Keds standing in front of a blackboard and flailing his arms.

Glenn Beck described the many projects of Tides as pushing a radical agenda, part of a left-wing conspiracy dedicated to destroying capitalism using a group of "all the people that hate America." I took off my armor and tried to steal an hour of sleep before the military transport arrived.

(A year later, a forty-five-year-old Beck devotee in Oakland named Byron Williams hopped into his mother's Toyota Tundra truck. Wearing a bulletproof vest, he headed to the Tides headquarters in San Francisco. On the passenger seat, he placed a 9 millimeter handgun, a shotgun, and a .308 caliber rifle, which he had loaded with armor-piercing bullets. En route, he was pulled over for erratic driving: he fired his weapons and injured two police officers before being shot himself. Later that night, in the hospital, he told investigators that he had been trying to "start a revolution" by killing "people of importance" at Tides.)

Many of the Iraqis had traveled for days to meet with me. My staff had sent texts and emails to Iraqis on the list giving them the dates of my arrival, and word soon spread throughout the community of US-affiliated Iraqis. They hid their badges in their shoes and brassieres and waited quietly in the lobby of the Rasheed Hotel, where I had rented several rooms overlooking an empty pool. The mattresses were thin and lumpy, the curtains pungent with years of gathered cigarette smoke. We rotated as many in as possible: while I met with someone in my room, Chris met with another in his, and a group waited in the third room. Over scores of hours, we triaged their cases, offering counsel and preparing the lucky few who had upcoming interviews.

The stories no longer shocked: our binders of cases had grown too numerous and grief-filled. I barely raised an eyebrow when I wrote "wife taken and raped" in my notebook. Another dropped his pants to show me the bullet wounds across his leg and torso. Another lifted his shirt to show me his scars. One man's wife was on a Fulbright scholarship to study medicine in Saint Louis, but his neighbors had found out and told him that he had seventy-two hours to leave. Kids abducted, ransomed, limbs mangled, family members missing, threat letters folded up alongside faded American certificates of appreciation.

When I asked a man to show me his US government badge, he looked at me remorsefully and told me he had eaten it. He had been thrown into the trunk of a Shi'a militiaman's car for being a Sunni in the wrong place. If they discovered that he was also an interpreter, there was no chance at survival or paying a bribe, so he feverishly broke the plastic badge into bits and swallowed them before they pulled him from the trunk. As he now struggled to make his way through the visa process, he'd have a harder time verifying his employment with the United States: "If you worked for us, where's your badge?"

Their children sat glumly on the mattress while we smoked and filled notebooks with the details of their bureaucratic limbo, took copies of their papers, the names of their friends, the names of their Iraqi colleagues who'd been assassinated, the names of their American bosses whom they needed to find in order to verify their employment, names, and more names. All of them had been waiting at least a year without seeing any real progress in their applications. They asked me if Obama would save them. I didn't know how to answer.

I took a break during lunch one day to visit a close friend in the USAID compound who had been posted back to Baghdad. She escorted me through the compound security gate, where guards wiped me down for the bomb residue detection machine. I walked past the familiar palm trees and piazza back into the mission, feeling like an intruder. In the years since I left, I had become involved in a proxy war with the agency, which had treated my former colleagues poorly and made unsubtle threats when pressuring me to keep quiet. I was worried that management would toss me out of the compound, but I wanted to see my old house and office.

She brought me into the twelve-thousand-square-foot Hammurabi Office Building, which had been under construction when I first arrived in January 2005. After clearing the bombproof ballistic security doors, I found myself staring into the unchanged forest of blue cubicles. My friend trailed me as I walked up and down each row, remembering where Yaghdan, Tona, Amina, Ziad, and my other friends had sat. Only one Iraqi from 2005 still worked there: the rest had fled, and thanks to the List Project, the majority now lived in the United States.

I poked my head into the panic room, where Yaghdan had been told three years earlier that the only support USAID could provide was a month's leave. I did not linger at my old cubicle, site of the manufactured *Iraq Daily Update*s.

I wandered over to my old house, its mortar-proof roof crumbling. As I walked into the cafeteria, my concerns about a scene with USAID management gave way to an embarrassing realization: nobody had a clue who I was. A couple years earlier, Iraqi colleagues informed me that they had been explicitly warned by their American bosses, "Kirk Johnson can't do anything for you; do not write to him." Since then, staff attrition had rinsed from the compound any recognition or hostility toward my efforts.

Before I left, my friend gave me a parting gift common among foreign service officers in the final phase of the war: a miniature blast wall, hewn from the real thing, with the seal of the Embassy of the United States in Baghdad. Its edges crumbled at the slightest touch.

That night, I stretched out on the Rasheed Hotel's pitiful mattress and listened to a small-arms skirmish crackle along the Tigris. A birthday cake, brought to me by one of my few Iraqi friends who was still stuck in Baghdad and would probably be left behind, decomposed on the hotel desk. The following day, we would work our way through the intestines of the occupation: long periods of waiting broken by peristaltic bursts of movement from Rhino Runner to tent to shuttle bus to C-130 to a whistling descent into the fiery haze of Kuwait. As far as I was concerned, this would be the last time I'd ever see Iraq.

The morning after I left, on August 19, a string of massive car bombs exploded across the Green Zone, damaging the Rasheed Hotel and the nearby Foreign Ministry. The attacks, which killed one hundred and wounded nearly six hundred, were the largest in over two years and were carried out by Al-Qaeda in Iraq. I had little left in the reservoir of my emotions to do more than send an all-clear email to my family. It barely registered in Western media outlets. Another explosion in Baghdad.

And as the Iraqis who'd met with us went back into hiding, we traveled onward to meet with others on the list in Syria and Jordan. Word had spread throughout the diaspora of US-affiliated Iraqis in Amman that I was coming. Although I hadn't told anyone where I was staying, a resourceful Iraqi who wanted his name added to the list cold-called hotels to ask whether anyone under my name was staying there. When I stepped out for breakfast the morning of my second day, I encountered a small group of Iraqis waiting by the hotel entrance. They hurried over to thrust copies of their badges and commendation letters at me and asked to be added to the list.

A few weeks after I returned from the Middle East, the roof of the USAID office building collapsed under its own bombproof weight.

When a friend asked me what I had learned from the trip, my mind raced through the questions that confronted me upon my arrival, but found no clear answers. The war was over. So long as Iraq didn't erupt into a new civil war, the Obama administration was fine with the strategy and policy bequeathed to it by the Bush White House. Pack up the Ronald McDonalds and Taco Bells and leave the refugee resettlement program as it is: a multiyear, understaffed, and underfunded embarrassment. The only people who still had any hope were the Iraqis we were about to abandon.

As 2010 approached, I felt as though I had reached the dead end. If the List Project had been the antigen that triggered a reaction in the refugee bureaucracy, it was depressingly clear that the antibodies had now formed and multiplied, numbing any sensation of urgency. Despite personnel changes at the top of the Obama administration's executive branch agencies, the timeline for getting a visa was growing increasingly protracted at a time when it needed to be accelerated. Every few months, refugee advocates met with the National Security Council to discuss the refugee crisis and remedies, but the meetings felt more and more like a ritual, each actor's role defined, nothing ever changing.

I had thrown everything I could think of against the problem, working with journalists and lawyers, testifying and pushing legislation, but I was running out of ideas. The List Project had helped nearly one thousand Iraqis make it to America, but there were thousands on the list still trapped in the system.

What else could be done? The media were uninterested: *the story's been written.* Congress was uninterested: *Iraq's finished; it's all about Afghanistan now.* The White House was uninterested: *this wasn't our war anyhow.* My law firms, ever steady, continued to prod the refugee bureaucracy, but everything had settled into a quiet stasis. The first, second, and nth laws governing this absence of motion were defined by terror—a state of terror so overpowering that the United States government regarded even its closest Iraqi friends as potential enemies. The bills passed by one branch were shredded by another, but no one really protested because we'd become brilliant at terrifying ourselves out of taking any risks in helping them: What if one of these visa programs, however well intentioned or just, let in someone bad? In one case, an endangered Iraqi Christian who worked as an interpreter had been granted a visa, pending the completion of his security check. Soon thereafter, his visa was revoked on the grounds that there was suspicion that he worked for Al-Qaeda in Iraq. When he and others appealed on grounds of common sense—that the terrorist organization wasn't in the business of recruiting Christians—an official said, "Yes, but wouldn't that be precisely the way they'd get someone in?"

We were in a spell of our own post-9/11 creation. When our government wanted to do something wrong, we accepted the exigencies of war and turned our backs on the moral choices of torture, extraordinary rendition, "black site" prisons, suspension of habeas corpus, unwarranted wiretapping, and unending drone warfare. We wanted there to be no constraints to do harm to other people if it might keep us safe. So the government swiftly cultivated a sophisticated ganglia of secret prisons throughout the world, contractors to assist in interrogations, a fleet of off-the-books airplanes to shuttle detainees to and from hostile countries.

But when we ask our government to do something right or just, we accept every possible constraint it summons as an excuse for inaction. We accept that it takes the same government years to put an Iraqi interpreter—whose retinal scans, fingerprints, and polygraph results are all within our records—on an airplane and fly him to safety.

"Your country put a man on the moon," an exasperated Iraqi told me in Baghdad, an expired interpreter badge in hand, his daughter on his lap. "Why is it so difficult for America to give me a visa?"

What could I tell him? That it is the government that owns the language of security and that it doesn't want anyone to meddle with it when it says it's keeping us safe? That it owns the language of the counterfactual, which it uses to tell us what awful things might have happened if it had done things any differently? That it owns the language of prediction, which it employs to tell us what terrors might come if we poke or prod it to do too much? That I'd been shouting at it for years about our moral obligation to Iraqis like him, and all they ever murmured in reply was *Tick, tick, tick, boom*?

I was sick of the narrowness of thought in post-9/11 Washington. Even the best humanitarians among us who put on nice suits and walked into federal buildings seemed unable to change the government's behavior.

There was really only one strategy left, and it was a real Hail Mary: if I could somehow reframe the debate by appealing to the lessons of history, arming leaders with the precedents established before *everything changed on 9/11*, the government might finally snap out of it and start acting with an urgency that the imminence of the withdrawal required.

After all, my list was not the first.

21.

Past Is Prologue

EXCERPT FROM:

Minutes of Washington Special Actions Group Meeting
Washington, April 2, 1975, 10:43–11:28 a.m.

Subject
Indochina

Summary of Conclusions

Secretary [Henry] Kissinger: We have spent millions of dollars over the past ten years so that the North Vietnamese could tear up South Vietnam. I think we owe—it's our duty—to get the people who believed in us out. Do we have a list of those South Vietnamese that we want to get out?

Mr. Philip Habib [US assistant secretary of state for Far Eastern and Pacific Affairs]: There is one, but it's limited.

Secretary Kissinger: Tell Graham Martin [US ambassador to South Vietnam] to give us a list of those South Vietnamese we need to get out of the country. Tell Graham that we must have the list by tomorrow.

Mr. Habib: The problem is that you have different categories of people. You have relatives of Americans, tens of thousands of people (Vietnamese) who worked for us. . . . One thing I would recommend is that the embassy destroy all personnel records when they leave.

Secretary Kissinger: The Communists will know who they are anyway. Let's get a look at the different categories of people who need to get out. There may be upwards of ten thousand people.

Mr. Habib: There are ninety-three thousand already on the list.

Secretary Kissinger: Well, get that list. We'll try for as many as we can.

Mr. William Stearman [member of the National Security Council]: It could reach a million people.

Secretary Kissinger: Well, that is one thing this Congress can't refuse—humanitarian aid to get people out.

Mr. Habib: It depends on the nature of the collapse.

Mr. Stearman: One possible solution to the evacuation problem is to move some of the people to those two islands offshore.

Secretary Kissinger: Yes, that's a possibility. Let's get that list of people who have to get out and some ideas on where we should move them. We may have to ask Congress for military force to help rescue these people. I can't see how they could refuse.

Secretary [of Defense James R.] Schlesinger: Yes, after a forty-five-day debate . . .

We shall not cease from exploration
And the end of all our exploring
Will be to arrive where we started
And know the place for the first time.

—T. S. Eliot

A Tamarind Tree in Saigon

It had been three years since the Bush appointee had yelled at me for "dragging the nation back to the rooftop of Saigon." Back then, when the list was only a few dozen names long, it had seemed comically over-wrought. But as 2010 began, when there were thousands of names and no measurable progress during President Obama's first year, I was desperate to revive the lessons of the final months of the Vietnam War.

I waded through hundreds of pages of declassified "memcons"—memoranda of White House conversations—from the final weeks of the war, kicking myself for not having studied them earlier and alarmed by what they portended.

In early April 1975, as intelligence reports flooded in that signaled the imminent invasion of the North Vietnamese into South Vietnam, President Gerald Ford convened daily meetings with advisors with the hope of forestalling disaster. A last-second request for $722 million of aid to prop up President Nguyen Van Thieu and the South Vietnamese government was rejected by Congress, all but guaranteeing its collapse.

Secretary of State and National Security Advisor Henry Kissinger instructed our ambassador in Saigon, Graham Martin, to supply him with the names of the South Vietnamese employees who would need to be evacuated. In discussions with the president, Kissinger estimated that there was an "irreducible list" of 174,000 South Vietnamese employees of the State Department, USAID, and the CIA, but he needed the embassy to produce an official list. In Saigon, the slow-moving Ambassador Martin appeared more concerned with the optics of openly conducting contingency planning than with the fate of our Vietnamese employees: creating a list would send a signal of distress. In the circular thinking of our ambassador, any planning would precipitate the very need for a plan.

Two young foreign service officers serving in Vietnam, Lionel Rosenblatt and Craig Johnstone, were furious about the lack of urgency in the embassy, so they struck out on their own and implemented an ad hoc operation to spirit Vietnamese employees out on departing military flights. When embassy officials discovered their efforts, they issued arrest warrants for both Rosenblatt and Johnstone, who had donned false identities as French businessmen. In the weeks before Saigon fell, the military ran an evacuation out of the nearby Tan Son Nhut air base, loading American civilians and thousands of South Vietnamese onto C-130s and C-141s, but there simply wasn't enough time or planning to get all of our Vietnamese employees out.

Ambassador Martin described those pushing him to prepare for an evacuation throughout April as "mattress mice," and in the final days, he denied a request to prepare an evacuation landing zone in the yard of the embassy compound; this would have required hacking down the massive tamarind tree that provided shade for his car, a step the ambassador refused because he thought it would create a sense of panic.

The contingency plan for the last Americans in Saigon was to listen for a code-phrase on Armed Forces Radio that signaled that final evacuation was under way at the embassy: "The temperature in Saigon is one hundred twelve degrees and rising," followed by Irving Berlin's "White Christmas."

When the code was delivered on April 29, the tamarind was hacked down as incinerators burned millions of dollars and classified documents. (They failed to destroy staffing lists of Vietnamese employees, though, which were soon snatched up by North Vietnamese forces.) Thousands of South Vietnamese realized that there wouldn't be room for them on the small number of helicopters approaching the embassy.

Such was the contingency plan that emerged in the final moments of a long war: a lucky few managed to force their way past the marine security guards or over the fifteen-foot barbed-wire walls and into one of the helicopters. An army captain named Stuart Herrington shouted, "We're not going to leave you! Don't worry about it!" through a megaphone at some four hundred panicked local employees, and then made his way to a helicopter on the embassy roof after telling them that he was going to use the bathroom.

After these early mishaps, though, the Ford administration took command of the situation. During a White House discussion about where Vietnamese refugees might be resettled, a congressman suggested the island of Borneo, prompting Ford to interject, "Let me comment where they would go: our tradition is to welcome the oppressed. I don't think these people should be treated any differently from any other people— the Hungarians, Cubans, Jews from the Soviet Union."

The American public was not enamored with the idea of resettling a great number of refugees from a war that had torn the country apart, however, and the US Immigration and Naturalization Service pushed back with legal rationale against any large-scale evacuation. So the president addressed the country, declaring that America bore a responsibility to these refugees, and that "to do less would have added moral shame to humiliation." Congress passed the Indochina Migration and Refugee Assistance Act a couple weeks later in May 1975, allocating an astonishing $600 million, and within a few months, more than 130,000 Vietnamese were airlifted by the military to our base in Guam, where they were processed before flying to the United States.

Within several years, nearly one million Vietnamese had been granted visas.

I was embarrassed. This wasn't ancient history, after all. In my trial-and-error approach to prodding the government into acting more swiftly, I had not thought to harness the wisdom of those who had worked on the 1975 evacuation. I asked Frank Wisner, a retired ambassador who had helped implement the massive airlift, to join the board of the List Project to counsel me on strategy. He soon introduced me to others who'd been involved in the efforts, including Judge Mark Wolf in Boston, who had represented the Office of the US Attorney General during the airlift.

Two lessons had emerged from my conversations about the fall of Saigon: one, wishful thinking and excessive concern about optics led many of our employees to be left behind, and two, once the president of the United States stepped in, the myriad excuses put forward by the various bureaucracies fell away and lives were saved.

Abandonment was coded into every war's end. No matter the continent, skin color, decade, or century, I found local collaborators facing post-withdrawal reprisals by their countrymen. The Hmong in Laos, trained by the CIA to fight against the Pathet Lao, were left behind when the Communists overran the country in 1975. The Harkis in Algeria, loyalists to the French colonial pieds-noir, who held the colony for 131 years, were strung up in the streets after a hasty withdrawal by their protectors in 1962; estimates approached one hundred thousand killed. A common tactic of vengeance upon these "traitors" was to force-feed them the medals bestowed upon them by the French.

For all of the facile comparisons made by journalists to Schindler and his list in articles about the List Project, I was utterly ignorant about our visa policies during World War II. I found my entry point in a *Foreign Affairs* article about bureaucrats who had defied orders during the Jewish refugee crisis. Its author, the legendary diplomat Richard Holbrooke, put forward a thought experiment:

> Imagine that you are a consular officer in the middle of a diplomatic career that you hope will lead to an ambassadorship. There are two rubber stamps on your desk. Using the one that says "Approved" would allow the desperate person sitting in front of you to travel to your country legally. Using the other stamp, which says "Rejected," could mean consigning that person to prison or death.
>
> It sounds like a simple choice, but there is a catch—a very big one. The person in front of you is Jewish, and your boss has told you to devise ways not to use the "Approved" stamp. Your government does not want these people—these people waiting outside your office, milling around in the street, hiding in their houses— in your country. Approve too many visas and your career will be in danger. Follow your instructions and people will probably die.

Intrigued, I bundled up and trudged to the bookstore down the street in search of a book referenced in Holbrooke's article, but soon stumbled upon *Refugees and Rescue*, a newly published collection of diaries and memoranda from the 1930s by a man I'd never heard of named James McDonald. I scurried back to my apartment and began to read.

McDonald, who chaired Franklin Delano Roosevelt's Advisory Committee on Refugees from 1928 until the end of World War II, dictated a diary entry to his secretary at the end of each day. Though the diaries were never intended for publication, McDonald's daughter brought them to the United States Holocaust Memorial Museum, which released the first of three volumes in 2007.

As I thumbed through the diaries, my heart sank. Though hundreds of thousands of Jewish refugees fled Eastern Europe in the late 1930s, the United States was wary of admitting them, turning ships filled with Jews away from our ports, often under the rationale that they posed a security risk to the homeland. President Roosevelt warned, "Now, of course, the refugee has got to be checked because, unfortunately, among the refugees there are some spies, as has been found in other countries. And not all of them are voluntary spies—it is rather a horrible story, but in some of the other countries that refugees out of Germany have gone to, especially Jewish refugees, they have found a number of definitely proven spies."

The president's warnings produced immediate and stalling effects in the State Department. McDonald's diary included a June 1940 memo to consular officers from Breckinridge Long, the assistant secretary of state overseeing the Refugees Bureau: "We can delay and effectively stop for a temporary period of indefinite length the number of immigrants into the United States. We could do this by simply advising our consuls to put every obstacle in the way and to require additional evidence and to resort to various administrative devices which would postpone and postpone and postpone the granting of the visas."

Long's cable effectively halted all immigration through bureaucratic tricks. I could have been reading from my own in-box when I found an exasperated letter from Rabbi Stephen Wise to McDonald a few months later, in September 1940: "With regard to political refugees, we are in the midst of the most difficult situation, an almost unmanageable quandary. On the one hand, the State Department makes all sorts of promises and takes our lists and then we hear that the Consuls do nothing. A few people slip through, but we are afraid, - this is strictest confidence, - that the Consuls have private instructions from the Department to do nothing, which would be infamous beyond words."

Not only were the tactics and language similar, the success rate was nearly identical. Shortly after receiving Rabbi Wise's letter, McDonald noted that 567 names had been given to the Department of State, but that after considerable time, only 15 visas had been issued. When McDonald passed along further documentation of visa delays to First Lady Eleanor Roosevelt, she wrote a note to FDR: "They handed 2,000 names to the State Department and the consuls abroad have not certified more than 50 to come to this country. . . . I am thinking about these poor people who may die at any time and who are asking only to come here on transit visas."

After Pearl Harbor, the prospects for Jewish refugees only worsened. In the conclusion of the McDonald diaries, the historian Richard Breitman remarked, "President Roosevelt moved away from humanitarian action. The war changed his views as to how much humanitarian spirit the United States could afford at a time of grave dangers abroad and perceived foreign dangers to national security. State Department officials, most of whom dragged their feet during earlier refugee initiatives, quickly found evidence and ways to reduce immigration. . . . The most restrictionist phase of American refugee policy—from mid-1941 to mid-1943—overlapped with the first two years of the Holocaust."

Tragedy on the Horizon

The historical parallels were at once infuriating and empowering. After years of struggling with government officials, I had burned myself out of ideas. But in every war I researched, I found people who struggled on behalf of their own lists, against many of the same officials in the same bureaucracies. The people who held those positions were dead, but their titles and tactics lived on.

All my reading of history would be worthless if it wasn't used to fuel one final campaign for the Guam option, the remedy I had proposed to Samantha Power on the eve of Obama's inauguration and in every meeting since. I recruited a brilliant group of students from Vanderbilt University's Law School who had started a List Project chapter to help Iraqis who had been resettled in the Nashville area, and we began to draft a historical, legal, and policy assessment of how a departing power's withdrawal affects those who collaborated with it. We examined how our allies had used airlifts to evacuate their Iraqis as they withdrew in the late 2000s, and how President Clinton had airlifted twenty thousand Kosovar Albanians to Fort Dix in 1999 and seven thousand imperiled Iraqis to Guam in 1996. We extracted the lessons of Vietnam, Laos, Algeria, and World War II, making it clear that unless the president took ownership of the issue, the bureaucracies would never take it upon themselves to act boldly.

Since they had ignored my calls for a Guam option, I shifted my tactics: rather than politely asking the White House to preempt a predictable tragedy upon our withdrawal, I would get Congress to force it to begin contingency planning.

The idea of placing so much hope in a report seemed foolish to some of my friends, but I clung to the only strategy left in the quiver. While there was still time to improve the refugee resettlement process before the withdrawal, the situation was grim. Beyond the average wait of over a year for an initial interview, the Special Immigrant Visa created by the Kennedy legislation to resettle 5,000 interpreters each year was a shambles, granting visas to only about 150 Iraqis each month. Maddeningly, nearly 20,000 Iraqis were admitted through the traditional Refugee Admissions Program in Obama's first year, but only 250 of them were from the list. Though they may have had legitimate persecution claims, the overwhelming majority of those who were granted visas had zero affiliations with the United States. And with a population of refugees in the millions, it was a given that only those in the most dire circumstances could be resettled to America. For every Iraqi on the list who made it in, though, there were fifty stuck in administrative purgatory. US government policy in the final phase of the war was Darwinian: survive your death threats for a year or two while you wait for an appointment for an interview, and we might consider granting you a visa.

Shortly before we released the report, I came across a strategic document issued by the Islamic State of Iraq, an umbrella organization that included Al-Qaeda in Iraq. The ISI and its member organizations were responsible for the assassination of hundreds of interpreters and other Iraqis. They prescribed "nine bullets for the traitors and one for the crusaders." The ISI closed with an exhortation: "This won't be an easy mission; we'll have to confront both social and security obstacles, but it is a worthy struggle . . . just because the goals are difficult doesn't mean we should abandon them." As I read the pragmatism and discipline undergirding the lethal ambitions of our enemy, I was embarrassed by the shabby excuses offered by my government for its own languid efforts to protect the Iraqis on the list.

On the thirty-fifth anniversary of the fall of Saigon, the List Project released *Tragedy on the Horizon: A History of Just and Unjust Withdrawal.* We urged Congress to instruct the executive branch to produce a contingency plan for a Guam option. We also pushed legislation requiring the first-ever government-run assessment of just how many Iraqis had worked for the United States, how many had applied for resettlement, and the status of those applications. For years, in hearing after hearing, nobody in the government had a sense of this basic number: with estimates ranging between 30,000 and 130,000, I knew that my list of several thousand names was far from exhaustive. I wanted the government to make its own list.

The response to the report was immediate. Within a week of its publication, Representative Alcee Hastings of Florida and Senator Ben Cardin of Maryland invited me to speak at congressional hearings that they called to discuss how the Obama administration's withdrawal would affect US-affiliated Iraqis. Hastings sponsored legislation requiring the executive branch agencies to produce a contingency plan and to determine the numbers of Iraqi allies at risk. While it didn't order an evacuation, the preparation of such a plan would present the president with a tool to draw on in the event that a campaign of violence unfolded in the wake of our withdrawal.

My dad flew in from West Chicago to watch my testimony. Assistant Secretary of State Eric Schwartz entered the hearing room followed by a claque of staffers from the Refugees Bureau—among them the woman to whom I had given the very first copy of the list nearly four years earlier. After the secretary's initial statements, Senator Cardin pressed him on the Guam option.

Schwartz leaned toward his microphone and let loose the dam of USGspeak:

> You don't have to remind me about the Guam program because I managed it at the National Security Council. . . . We take very seriously concerns expressed by many that there will be increased reprisals against Iraqis who have worked for us in Iraq. We currently have a range of robust resettlement and visa programs that benefit Iraqis, as you know. And I think we need to bolster them and strengthen them and increase contingent capacity in neighboring countries. We need to do all of that—think about ways that adapting these programs to changes in circumstances to enhance capacity to move people who are at imminent risk because our capacity to do that right now—we have capacity, but it's limited.

The assistant secretary closed with a classic yes/no flourish: "At the same time . . . so while we don't anticipate the kind of problems to which you allude and we're certainly—you know, our plans and our efforts are in the absolute opposite direction; reconciliation, reintegration, and normalcy—we do need to look at options for the kind of contingencies that your question addresses."

Put simply, the Obama administration did not foresee the kind of postwithdrawal bloodletting that I was predicting. Even though nearly every withdrawal throughout human history had been stained by reprisals, and even though at least a thousand Iraqi allies had already been assassinated, for some reason the White House thought things would be fine when we left.

I testified alongside Craig Johnstone, the former foreign service officer whose struggle to evacuate his Vietnamese employees during the fall of Saigon in 1975 was rewarded by the State Department with a warrant for his arrest. He recounted the lesson of Vietnam: "We stepped up to it too late in Vietnam in many respects, but we did step up to it, and we need to be sure that we are ready this time . . . and that we leave the situation honorably."

I implored the Obama administration not to repeat the mistakes of the Bush White House in Iraq by basing its plans upon wishful, best-case scenarios. While "reconciliation, reintegration, and normalcy" were nice goals, the stigma borne by those who worked for us would probably last a generation. Why not plan to use some of the twenty thousand unused Special Immigrant Visa slots to bring them back with us?

Alcee Hastings's legislation cleared the House within weeks of the release of *Tragedy on the Horizon* but stalled for nearly six months in the Senate due to the fight over the repeal of the military's "don't ask, don't tell" policy.

In January 2011, the Hastings legislation cleared the Senate as part of a major defense funding bill. I was exhausted from watching the little shrub of hope sprout and wither each year, but I approached the last year of the war in Iraq with guarded optimism. The challenge of raising funds for a cause related to a forgotten war had forced me to lay off half my team and halve the salaries of those that remained, but I knew that the List Project had to continue until the bitter end.

When Obama signed the bill, a 120-day deadline for the administration's preparation of the Guam option was set into motion.

22.

Game Over

And how can something so clear in retrospect become so muddled
at the time by rationalizations, institutional constraints, and
a lack of imagination? How can it be that those who fight on
behalf of these principles are the ones deemed unreasonable?

—Samantha Power, *A Problem from Hell: America and
the Age of Genocide*

In February 2011, I walked down the hallway of the Bureau of Population, Refugees, and Migration with another binder of five hundred
names to give to Assistant Secretary of State Eric Schwartz. Ellen Sauerbrey beamed bright white teeth at me from the row of official portraits
of previous bureau chiefs outside of Schwartz's office.

I had scored a legislative victory with the passage of the Hastings
amendment, which required the Obama administration to make contingency plans in order to protect US-affiliated Iraqis throughout the
withdrawal. The legislation had also instructed federal agencies to determine just how many Iraqis had worked for the government, how many
had applied for refugee resettlement, and the status of their applications. On the basis of this information, the Obama administration was
instructed by Congress to prepare a Guam option contingency to evacuate Iraqis as necessary.

In conversations with Lale Mamaux and Marlene Kaufmann, unflag-
ging aides to Representative Hastings and Senator Cardin, respectively, I
had suggested ninety days as a deadline for the congressionally mandated

report. In response, the administration had requested 120 days. I asked for a meeting with Assistant Secretary Schwartz to gauge its progress.

"Kirk, you don't need to be coming after me," the secretary said as he leaned forward for a sip from a can of diet soda. "I'm on your side. And the people who can make the decisions you're looking for are above me."

I looked around the room. The bureaucrats sitting off to one side of his office were unchanged from the Bush administration. I forced a smile in their direction, crossed my legs, and inadvertently bumped my boot into one of the coffee table legs, breaking it loose.

"Whoops!" I said. "Your furniture is falling apart here." I looked around his office, which had prison-cell-sized windows looking out onto another bureau's bank of prison-cell windows. It didn't seem as though they could be opened more than a couple inches, like suicide-proof windows in hotels. I continued.

"Well, you can understand, Secretary—"

"Eric. Just call me Eric."

"You can understand why I might be confused. You're the only person in the entire federal government with the word *refugee* in his official title." I paused. "Are you saying Samantha Power has the reins, or what?"

"I'm not going to get into specific names, but what you're looking for—*the Guam option*—that kind of thing wouldn't originate out of this bureau."

I pulled a slip of paper from my backpack and handed it to the secretary. It contained only a few paragraphs: Section 1233 of the National Defense Authorization Act of 2010, the Hastings Amendment. The NDAA was the vehicle through which our wars were funded, part of a screwy world of shadow budgeting in which the true costs of the war were kept from the annual books for the bulk of the war's duration.

"What am I looking at here, Kirk?"

I spoke as though I were just refreshing his memory, unwilling to contemplate the possibility that he truly didn't know. "That's in the current Defense Authorization requiring you and other agencies to survey the current population of Iraqi employees and to produce a contingency plan."

"I've never seen this before." He looked back up at me and asked, "This is the law of the land?"

"Yes. It has been for about fifty days so far. The deadline is about two months away."

Schwartz turned to his row of backbenchers. They all had L-shaped erect postures. "Guys, did you know about this?"

"Yes, Mr. Secretary," someone replied. "We are in interagency talks about it."

Contented, he turned back to me and said, "Yeah, so interagency discussions are under way, Kirk," and then set the paper on the broken table.

I handed him the latest binder of names on the list. He passed it to a staffer, who thumbed through it and said, "Kirk, we can't expedite five hundred names. Can you give us, say, the fifty most urgent cases in this binder?"

Annoyed, I said that they were all urgent, but I agreed to send them an email within twenty-four hours highlighting the fifty most critical cases in the binder.

In May 2010, the deadline of the Hastings Amendment, the FBI announced the arrest of two Iraqi refugees in Kentucky in a sting operation in which the men apparently tried to purchase missiles to send back to Iraq to use against American forces. A confidential informant, reportedly another Iraqi refugee, tipped off authorities after one of the men bragged about planting bombs back in Iraq. When the FBI looked into their backgrounds, they discovered that these two men had carried out hundreds of attacks against US forces in Iraq, and that their fingerprints were linked to a phone that had been used to detonate an IED and was now stored at the FBI's Terrorist Explosive Device Analytical Center in Quantico, Virginia. More than seventy thousand defused bombs from Iraq and Afghanistan were warehoused at the center, but analysts were six years behind in extracting intelligence from the IEDs.

These men had come in through the traditional Refugee Admissions Program. They never claimed any affiliation with the United States but somehow made it through the process that so many of my former colleagues were struggling to navigate.

Hearings were scheduled, during which freshman senator Rand Paul of Kentucky crowed, "There's no reason to continue this policy" of granting visas to Iraqi refugees. To the assembled officials from the Departments of State and Homeland Security, Paul continued, "I don't fault you for missing the needle in the haystack. . . . You've got to make the haystack smaller."

The response was as fierce as it was predictable. I'd lost track of the number of times over the years that the government announced "enhanced" screening measures for Iraqis, but there would be still more enhancement. The following month, the Iraqi refugee program sputtered to a near halt. The traditional Refugee Admissions Program, which had hit a monthly average of roughly 1,500 Iraqis, was back down to numbers not seen since the earliest days of the crisis: 111 in March, 184 in April. The Special Immigrant Visa program remained lifeless: each year, fewer than 20 percent of the 5,000 slots were filled. Iraqis on my list had all but given up.

The Kentucky arrests pushed the debate all the way back to the John Bolton days, when people asked why Iraqis should even receive refuge in the first place. There was a self-defeating and maddening circularity to it all: even though the government had slowed the process of granting visas to a glacial pace over the years, it still screwed up by admitting two men who clearly should have been denied. Its own failure then justified further measures to slow the program. With roughly a half year left in the war, the time frame for receiving a visa had stretched to an average of eighteen months.

The deadline for the Hastings Amendment was only a couple weeks away, but I knew from my meetings with Schwartz and sources inside Iraq that the Obama administration had ignored it entirely. No needs assessment had been conducted, and no contingency plan had been drafted.

I contacted Tim Arango, the Baghdad bureau chief for the *New York Times*. He wrote a front-page story about the disregarded Hastings Amendment, which included a dismissive quote from Secretary Schwartz: "We feel that we are prepared to deal with any variety of contingencies."

The negative publicity prompted an eleventh-hour report by the Pentagon, a juvenile effort consisting mostly of guesswork and useless charts that had been copied and pasted from other reports. "Preparation of this report cost the Department of Defense a total of approximately $5,001" was emblazoned across the cover page. In an angry op-ed for the *Washington Post*, I pointed out that by comparison, the Pentagon had spent $15 billion on air-conditioning the previous year.

They had won. Everything I threw at the bureaucrats in the State Department—op-eds, lists, journalists, lawyers, politicians, history, hearings—it was all deflected by a wall of USGspeak. When I thought I had finally contrived a way to force them into action through legislation, they simply ignored it.

On November 4, 2011, I participated alongside other refugee organizations in my last National Security Council meeting with Samantha Power, although I didn't know then that it would be my last. The tenor was quite different from earlier in the administration, when everyone had been so excited to meet her. The numbers were disastrously low, and refugee organizations were no longer impressed by her personal stature. At one point, a veteran refugee advocate asked Power why the United States even had a refugee program if the process was so tortuous and inefficient.

"We've undertaken a number of reforms," she said, "the first phase of which was completed this spring, but we're still at it." I thought back to the number of times over the past five years I had been told that the government was "ramping up" its efforts.

A State Department representative revealed that the backlog for in-country cases—those who had applied at the embassy in Baghdad—was thirty-five thousand names long. Given the current pace of processing, it would take years to clear.

A director of another refugee organization confronted Power with a case that he had just worked on in which a man with a mentally handicapped son and wheelchair-bound mother was denied a visa on security grounds. "How could this make sense?" he asked.

"We're operating with very highly classified material, and having been in your shoes for most of my career, I know how frustrating that is to hear." She replied that although she could not go into precise details of what causes a red flag to be raised, "the trend lines are the product of a stark fact: the system we had in place before wasn't recognizing the threat."

In a somewhat impolitic tone, I suggested that just because something has the word *Intelligence* on it doesn't make it smart. I said that these were the same excuses that the Bush administration used to rationalize its failure to do more to help our Iraqi allies.

She wasn't pleased. "I take issue with the suggestion that we're invoking security as a way to explain away the numbers. A huge amount has been achieved. I meet on this issue more than any other. I don't know what the Bush administration's explanations were, but we are not single-issue here, and we're not going to do anything that puts in danger the security of the United States."

I was being unreasonable, I suppose, for focusing on a single issue. Never mind that we had been invited in to discuss that issue. She addressed my call for the Guam option, saying that the Refugees Bureau at the State Department had developed the capacity to "get someone moved from Baghdad to Amman very quickly," but those of us working the issue had heard this unfounded claim for years.

I thought about the binder of five hundred names we'd given to Secretary Schwartz at the beginning of the year. In the nine months since we had flagged the fifty most urgent cases for his bureau, not one had been moved to Jordan. Only about ten had been granted visas.

The disregard for the Guam option was made more bitter by the fact that only a week earlier, the administration announced that the US Air Force had ordered scores of wounded Libyan rebels airlifted directly to Boston for medical treatment. Little was known about the rebels, but a C-17 medical evacuation aircraft staffed with doctors and nurses whisked them in. A few days before my last NSC meeting, a *Rolling Stone* magazine article about the war in Libya quoted a White House official close to Power as saying that she had grown frustrated with "doing rinky-dink do-gooder stuff" like advocating on behalf of Christians in Iraq.

But I perked up as a junior NSC staffer chimed in to announce two major "solutions" that the White House had placed on the table. The first was a "web tool" to help Iraqi interpreters locate former supervisors. The second was a waiver of the "original signature" for the Special Immigrant Visa: Iraqis could now email the application rather than bring it to an Iraqi post office. I stared down at the notes I had just taken and suppressed a laugh. Of the thousands of Iraqis on the list, not a single one had ever complained about having to mail in the application that might save his or her life. And the overwhelming majority had little difficulty finding their US supervisors—in fact, many had been referred by their American bosses.

The problem wasn't in the application phase, it was the fraught period of waiting after the application was submitted. All they got were form replies from the US government saying, "Your application is pending."

After the meeting, an NSC staffer approached Marcia Maack, the pro bono coordinator at Mayer Brown who had handled hundreds of List Project cases, and said, "We know the Iraqis on your list have a *subjective* fear, but there's no *objective* basis for them to be afraid after we leave."

On December 14, 2011, the president flew to Fort Bragg, home of Hayder's former unit in the Eighty-Second Airborne, to announce the end of the war in Iraq. He promised to provide adequate benefits to the many wounded warriors: "Part of ending a war responsibly is standing by those who fought it. It's not enough to honor you with words. Words are cheap. We must do it with deeds. You stood up for America; America needs to stand up for you."

The next day, five years to the day after I first wrote about Yaghdan, the *New York Times* ran an op-ed in which I excoriated the Obama administration for its failure to protect US-affiliated Iraqis as we withdrew from Iraq: "The sorry truth is that we don't need them anymore now that we're leaving, and resettling refugees is not a winning campaign issue. For over a year, I have been calling on members of the Obama administration to make sure the final act of this war is not marred by betrayal. They have not listened, instead adopting a policy of wishful thinking, hoping that everything turns out for the best.

"For the first time in five years," I wrote, "I'm telling Iraqis who write to me for help that they shouldn't count on America anymore. Moral timidity and a hapless bureaucracy have wedged our doors tightly shut, and the Iraqis who remained loyal to us are weeks away from learning how little America's word means."

In the final month of the war, 153 Iraqis were admitted to America, the lowest since the early months of the Bush administration's feckless response to the crisis. The List Project received more and more pleas for help, but I could ask my part-time staff to take on only so much.

A few weeks later, in January 2012, a journalist called to ask about the most recent NSC meeting on Iraqi refugees, and I realized that I was no longer on the White House's invite list.

23.

Subjective Fear

From: Omar in Kirkuk
To: The State Department
Date: Tuesday, June 28, 2011. 12:38 p.m.
Subject: Immigration application

تحياتي الى العاملين في مجال الهجرة المواطنيين الى الامريكا ارجو
من سيادتكم التفضل بقبول طلبي هذا وهو اجاد حل سريع ومناسب
في وظعي الامني الممتلء بالتهديدات المستمر وخوفي ان ياتي
لحظة وينفذون الغرضهم معي وهي قتلي كوني عملت مع الجيش
الامريكي وارجو من سيادتكم الموافقة على اجراءت سفري الى
الامريكا//// وهذا بعض الشهادات ومستندات الذي حصلت عليها
اثناء عملي مع الجيش الامريكي واشكركم واشكر جهودكم

Greetings to those of you working in the immigration office. I ask your
help in considering my request. . . . I need a speedy solution to my situ-
ation, which is filled with persistent threats. My fear is that they'll be
carried out: people want to kill me because I worked with the U.S. Army.
Please help me come to America. Attached are some of the certificates and
records of my work. Gratefully . . .

Omar's Certificate of Recognition from the 15th Brigade
Support Battalion, US Army.

Omar's Certificate of Appreciation from the 501st Brigade
Support Battalion, US Army.

From: The State Department
To: Omar
Date: Sunday, October 9, 2011. 8:29 a.m.

Dear Applicant,

Please be informed that your application is in process but we still need a VALID official email address for a supervisor or HR officer who can identify you and verify your employment and a copy of the CONTRACT between your company of employment and the U.S. Government so that we continue processing with your application normally. Please note that we need this to prove that your employment was funded by U.S. Government through an official contract or agreement.

If you could not provide us with required contract number <u>please print and read the attached form carefully and then fill it, sign it, scan it and finally send it back to us</u>, so that we be able to help by trying to contact your former employer for the information.

Please reply directly to this email and do NOT change the subject line.

Thank you.

Shortly after they arrived in my in-box, I spread Omar's documents and emails out across my kitchen table, trying to arrange them in chronological order. When I ran out of space, I used the chairs, then the floor, and then the walls.

A picture of the man was emerging. Omar had driven a forklift for the US Army in Forward Operating Base Warrior, where he helped to load and unload shipments of food, vehicle parts, medical equipment, and other materials for our troops. His support letters glowed with praise: "Your dedicated service to the U.S. is appreciated and will not be forgotten," and "Your commitment, dedication, and efforts to ensuring all missions were accomplished to the highest of standards in support of the American warfighter."

In one email, I found a scan of his passport, which he obtained a couple months after first applying for refuge in America. He was my brother Derek's age and kept his hair cropped short for his passport picture. There is a very faint sense of a smile.

But after I located his initial application—submitted six months before the end of the war—and the first response he received from the State Department, I knew at once that something was terribly wrong. Although he had submitted six letters of commendation from Americans in his first email, I wondered why State was asking a forklift operator who did not speak English to locate a copy of the federal contract under which he worked.

I searched through the stack of pages for the next round of correspondence, which occurred two weeks after President Obama announced the end of the Iraq War:

From: Omar
To: The State Department
Date: Saturday, December 31, 2011. 9:46 a.m.

Peace and respect for everyone who works in your office. My brothers, I wonder if there's any news that you might share with me? What is the latest with my case? With great thanks.

From: The State Department
To: Omar
Date: Wednesday, January 4, 2012. 3:50 p.m.

Dear Sir/Ma'am,

Thank you for your email.

We have checked your case and found that it's in processing pending verifying your employment.

Please note that once you are scheduled for an interview he will be contacted.

Your patience does assist us in accelerating the process.

Six months had already passed since he applied, and although the State Department had apparently stopped asking for a copy of the federal contract number, it was now requesting contact information for someone who could verify Omar's employment history. This was despite the fact that his original application included the names of ten American supervisors, seven of which were active soldiers in the US Army.

The State Department wouldn't do anything with his case until it received yet another email address, for some reason, but Omar was struggling with a deteriorating sense of his security in Kirkuk. He drafted his next letter in bright red, as if to underscore the urgency of his situation:

From: Omar
To: The State Department
Date: Thursday, February 16, 2012. 5:23 a.m.

Peace and respect to you all. I'd like to explain some of the critical developments that have happened to me in Kirkuk. I feel that I'm in a very critical situation. My security situation isn't good, and I'm seeking your guidance.

I fear for my life and the life of my family, and I'm asking for you to help me by transferring my case to a neighboring country. If you were able to transfer my file to Turkey, then my family and I will go to finish the visa process there.

I await your speedy reply, God Willing.

From: The State Department
To: Omar
Date: Tuesday, February 21, 2012. 2:38 p.m.

Dear Sir,

Thank you for your email.

As per our phone conversation and as you were counseled regarding your wish to transfer your case to turkey, Please be informed that this program (Direct Access) is only run in Iraq, Jordan and Egypt. If you were in United Arab Emirates or Lebanon, please check with info@icmcturkey.org

Please note that you have to provide us with different contact info (Official Email address) for a supervisor or HR officer who can identify you and verify your employment.

Once we receive this, we will proceed with your case.

Kind Regards,

State soon sent another email to say that even if Omar fled, there were no guarantees that his application would be processed. They also pasted in the same form language, requesting "different contact info" for a supervisor or HR officer who could verify his employment.

A few days later, Omar sent the name of his cousin in America, who was sponsoring his application for resettlement.

The response was becoming distressingly familiar:

From: The State Department
To: Omar
Date: Sunday, March 11, 2012. 10:13 a.m.

Dear Sir/ Ma'am,

Thank you for your email.

Kindly be advised that your case is still missing please note that you have to provide us with different contact info (Official Email address) for a supervisor or HR officer who can identify you and verify your employment. (The email address must be an official one—not yahoo, Gmail, MSN, hotmail, etc.)

Once we receive this, we will proceed with your case.

Kindly be informed that we checked your case and found that it is in processing pending verifying your employment documents. Once it is completed we will move forward with your case.

Your patience does assist us in accelerating the process.

I wondered who came up with the final line, which was used in nearly every email exchange with Omar. If I had learned anything in five years of engaging with the State Department, it was that patience is not an accelerant within the engines of bureaucracy.

The day after Omar was told to be patient, the Lightning Brigade of the Ansar al-Sunnah Army—a known Al-Qaeda affiliate in Iraq—delivered a letter to him.

جيش أنصار السنة في العراق

كتائب صواعق

بسم الله الرحمن الرحيم

يَا أَيُّهَا الَّذِينَ آمَنُوا لاَ تَتَّخِذُوا آبَاءَكُمْ وَإِخْوَانَكُمْ أَوْلِيَاءَ إِنِ اسْتَحَبُّوا الْكُفْرَ عَلَى الإِيمَانِ وَمَن يَتَوَلَّهُم مِّنكُمْ فَأُوْلَئِكَ هُمُ الظَّالِمُونَ قُلْ إِن كَانَ آبَاؤُكُمْ وَأَبْنَاؤُكُمْ وَإِخْوَانُكُمْ وَأَزْوَاجُكُمْ وَعَشِيرَتُكُمْ وَأَمْوَالٌ اقْتَرَفْتُمُوهَا وَتِجَارَةٌ تَخْشَوْنَ كَسَادَهَا وَمَسَاكِنُ تَرْضَوْنَهَا أَحَبَّ إِلَيْكُم مِّنَ اللّهِ وَرَسُولِهِ وَجِهَادٍ فِي سَبِيلِهِ فَتَرَبَّصُوا حَتَّى يَأْتِيَ اللّهُ بِأَمْرِهِ وَاللّهُ لاَ يَهْدِي الْقَوْمَ الْفَاسِقِينَ

إنذار

إلى العميل الملحـ █████ بما انك لم تلبي أوامر المجاهدين بترك العمل لصالح القوات الأمريكي وهو عمل كالجاسوس لديهم المخزية لشرف البلاد الإسلامية في وادي الرافدين وأصبحتم مثل خادمين لقوات الاحتلال الصليبية الكافرة وقد حذرناك اكثر من مرة بترك هذا العمل ولكنك لم تهتم ولم ترجع الى الطريق القويم والثبات لذا قررنا نحن جيش انصار السنة في العراق أنزال عقوبة الإعدام بحقك ان لم تترك العمل .

فان كنت على غفلة فأفق فوالله انك لعلى خطر عظيم وشدة ايما وبيننا وبينك ليالي ووقائع تشيب من هولها الولدان .

واعلم انه لن يمنعنا عن قتلك من قتلك او فرد او حزب او احد الا أذن الله تعالى ثم توبتكم ووالله أنا لقادرون على أنفاذ وعيدنا عاجلا غير اجل ولكنا أردنا ان نعذر فيك فتبصر بحالك واعلم انك تحت قبضتنا وفي الختام نقول توبوا وافق من غفلتك واعلم ان أسود الإسلام ساهرة لإقامة عقوبة الله عليك وعلى كل من ارتد او أعان المرتدين فاغتنم هذه الفرصة للتوبة . وقد اعذر من انذر

والله أكبر وعزة للإسلام

٢٠١٢/٣/١٢

Omar's death-threat letter from Ansar al-Sunnah.

Omar had already stopped working for the Americans; the war was over and they were gone, but the Ansar al-Sunnah militia was untroubled by such distinctions:

To the atheist agent Omar,

You are warned that if you do not accept the orders of the mujahideen by leaving your work with the American forces, your work as a spy . . . we have warned you many times before, but you did not heed them, nor did you return to the correct path, so we, the army of Ansar al-Sunnah in Iraq, have decided to carry out the punishment of execution if you do not leave your work. . . .

I taped the death threat to my kitchen wall and sifted anxiously through the remaining pages of correspondence. These were the desperate pleas of a hunted man, and I struggled against the direction in which these emails were headed. In one letter, Omar wrote to say that he'd fled to Turkey the day after receiving the threat, hoping to find work and an apartment in which his family could stay while his application was processed. After a few weeks, though, he realized that he would be forbidden from working in Turkey, so he returned to Kirkuk. He began to move his wife and five-year-old son from house to house, hiding from the Ansar al-Sunnah.

In every letter he'd received from the State Department until this point, he'd been asked for the contact information of a "different" American supervisor. In late March, his cousin in America finally located the email address of one of Omar's first bosses, a materials manager for Parsons, one of the major US reconstruction contractors. Omar excitedly sent the contact info to the State Department.

A few days later, on April 5, the State Department's Iraqi Employment Verification Unit wrote to the Parsons supervisor, asking him to confirm Omar's work. His supervisor responded with a confirmation letter exactly twenty-five minutes later.

It seemed, as I read the next exchange, that the impasse had finally been broken:

From: The State Department
To: Omar
Date: Monday, April 9, 2012. 8:09 a.m.

Dear Sir/Ma'am,

Thank you for your email.

We have received the POC below in your email and it has been added to your case file.

You will be contacted in the future for any further updates.

Kind Regards.

From: Omar
To: The State Department
Date: Monday, April 9, 2012. 5:45 p.m.

Peace and greetings, my brothers. Now that you have the official email address, I'm wondering whether my file might be transferred to Jordan. Are there any steps left that I need to do?

I need resolution: the time is passing here. I don't own anything. I don't work. I'm moving from house to house, from here to there. I beg you to find a solution. Please call me.

I could hardly believe the State Department's subsequent reply. Less than ten days after informing Omar that it had received the employment verification letter from his Parsons supervisor, the following poorly written email was sent:

From: The State Department
To: Omar
Date: Tuesday, April 17, 2012. 1:41 p.m.

Dear Sir,

Thank you for your for your email.

We have checked your case and found that it's in processing your employment verification.

Please understand that the process is lengthy and might need a long period of time.

Your patience does assist us in accelerating the process.

> Since your employment has been verified yet you aren't advised
> to transfer your case to Jordan.
>   Kind Regards

All I could think of was Assistant Secretary of State Breckinridge Long's 1940 cable, in which he ordered his consuls to "put every obstacle in the way and to require additional evidence and to resort to various administrative devices which would postpone and postpone and postpone the granting of the visas." After all, Omar had submitted far more documentation than the State Department requires from refugees of any other country on the planet, but they kept asking him for more. And each time he gave them what they asked for, they asked for something else.

On May 22, seven weeks after it had received a letter from one of Omar's many American bosses that verified his employment, the State Department—as if all record of that letter had suddenly vanished—once again sent an email to Omar requesting "different contact info" for a supervisor. "We will proceed with your case once you provide us with the official email address of someone who can verify your employment," it promised.

On June 9, 2012, 338 days after submitting his application for refuge in America, Omar's cell phone rang. It had been seven years since he took his first job with the Americans. He had just finished dinner with his wife and young son in one of the many temporary safe houses he was shuttling his family through.

Omar took the call in another room, speaking for approximately two minutes. He returned to tell his wife that he needed to step outside but would come home soon.

Her worry mounted as she waited. She called his cell phone several times, but Omar did not pick up.

Shortly after ten o'clock, the local Kirkuk news channel ran a headline in the news ticker along the bottom of the screen announcing that the decapitated body of a young man had been found in her neighborhood.

Omar's wife called his brother in a panic, begging him to go to the police station to see if it might be Omar.

The police confirmed the headless body's identity by the ID card found in Omar's pocket.

At the funeral, Omar's brother received a text message from an unknown number, telling him that he would be next if he didn't flee.

After the funeral, Omar's wife received a warning that her son would be kidnapped if she did not leave Iraq.

Using Omar's email account, his brother wrote to the State Department:

From: Omar's Brother
To: The State Department
Date: Sunday, June 17, 2012. 10:47 a.m.

I am Omar's brother. Because of the numerous and continuing threats against him, he had asked you to expedite or transfer his case to Amman or Turkey.

But because of your delays, he was murdered a week ago at the hands of an unknown group.

From: The State Department
To: Omar's Brother
Date: Monday, June 21, 2012. 2:25 p.m.

Dear Sir/Madam,
Thank you for your email.
Please provide us with your brother's death certificate.
Kind Regards

Even in death, a requirement for additional information. I found a letter from State to Omar's widow, in which it said, "We would like to send you our sincere condolences for your husband's passing away. We are really sorry for your loss. May his soul rest in peace. Kind regards."

Omar's brother was having a difficult time obtaining the death certificate from the coroner, but he was under the impression that the State Department would not do anything to help them until he sent over a copy. He finally emailed a scan of Omar's death certificate on July 5. In the section requesting an explanation for the death, the coroner had two options: "1) a sickness or condition that led to death, or 2) other important factors that led to death not owing to any sickness." The coroner had left this section blank but scrawled "hemorrhaging from the neck due to the tearing of veins and arteries caused by a sharp implement" in the corner.

On July 18 Omar's brother sent State a copy of a death threat he received from a militia called the Army of the Men of the Naqshbandiya Order, composed principally of former Ba'athist militants: "You were with the agent Omar, who was a dog, acting as the eyes of the Americans." Omar's brother was now asking the State Department to evacuate the surviving members of the family from Iraq.

This was the response the family received:

From: The State Department
To: Omar's Widow
Date: Thursday, July 19, 2012. 2:55 p.m.

Dear Ma'am,
    Thank your email.
    As per our phone conversation, please provide us with the following:
    1. Your husband's death certificate
    2. different contact info (Official Email address) for a supervisor or HR officer who can identify your husband and verify his employment.
    Once we receive this, we will proceed with your case.
    Kind Regards.

Such were the "enhanced" procedures that the US government devised in order to assess the potential danger in Iraqis who risked their lives to help us: a mindless and insatiable demand for more information.

I sat on the floor of my kitchen, angrily leafing through the remaining pages, in which the State Department repeatedly requested information it had already received. Omar's supervisor at Parsons was sent the same email from State's Iraqi Employment Verification Unit several times over the summer of 2012: each time it came in, he responded with the same letter on official letterhead. Some period of silence would pass before the same request from State came back.

Each time Omar's widow and brother wrote to the State Department, they received the same auto reply asking for "different contact info" for a supervisor. "Your patience does assist us in accelerating the process."

As I studied Omar's increasingly panicked messages in the weeks and months before his assassination, I couldn't understand why the State Department was having such a problem with his case. If, for some reason, the letter from the Parsons supervisor was insufficient, couldn't it have reached out to one of the many US Army officers whose names and signatures emblazoned each of his many commendation letters?

It took me ninety seconds on Google to locate the official military email address of one of Omar's bosses in the warehouse at Camp Warrior in Kirkuk. I wrote to ask if she remembered Omar and received a response within forty-eight hours:

> When I arrived to Kirkuk there were about 10 workers to include Mr. Omar that were already working in the Class I warehouse and they became our continuity. Mr. Omar was very helpful in the changeover between my unit and the outgoing unit. He taught several of my Soldiers how to operate the forklift and helped to familiarize them with the warehouse. This was important and instrumental in our ability to hit the ground running without a break or delay in class I resupply; our Soldiers have got to eat! I am very sorry to hear this, he was a very hard worker and just wanted to provide for his family and be happy.

The List Project is now trying to get Omar's widow, son, and brother's family resettled to America, on a dead man's application. When we informed the State Department that we were taking on the case, the problem of verifying his employment suddenly disappeared.

As of July 2013, Omar's family is still in hiding in Kirkuk. State informed us that "if a case is not expedited, our estimate has been that it will take approximately two years from first enrollment in the program until the first interview. This is the unfortunate result of the popularity of the program and the security and logistical constraints that affect the capacity of our processing program.

"We have taken advantage of the departure of the military to expand that capacity (moving into a bigger building, hiring more people now that we have room for them), but ramping things up takes time.

"Unfortunately," the message from the embassy concluded, "patience will still be required."

Epilogue

◆•◆

But the Lord came down to see the city
and the tower the people were building.
The Lord said,
"If as one people speaking the same language
they have begun to do this,
then nothing they plan to do will be impossible for them.
Come, let us go down and confuse their language
so they will not understand each other."

    —Genesis 11:5–7

When I was little, a singsong Sunday school teacher taught me the Old Testament wrath of God. I followed along in my illustrated children's Bible, poring over brightly colored pages of flood and fire and destruction. The men of Nebuchadnezzar's Babylon once hatched a plan to build a tower tall enough to climb into heaven and verify the existence of the Lord, who was so threatened by the project that He brought their tower down, first by fire and then by earthquake. Anyone who laid eyes on the ruins went mute. God was exasperated: He had destroyed His creation only a few generations earlier with a great flood, but here they were, still rebellious and ambitious, collaborating with one another on a tower of doubt. So He smashed apart their ability to speak in one language, turning them against one another for eternity.

And *that's* why people speak different languages, cooed the Sunday school teacher.

Only a few chapters later, the Lord was planning new ruin, this time upon the sinful cities of Sodom and Gomorrah. But Abraham pleaded with God for their salvation: If He found fifty righteous people there, would He spare the cities? When God accepted, Abraham asked if the cities might be saved for forty-five righteous souls. Down and down he haggled with the Lord, until they settled: if ten righteous souls could be found, the cities would be saved.

The illustration in my Bible of the destruction that ensued terrified my young eyes: a rain of burning sulfur, immolating bodies and burning vegetation, ruin rising from the land like smoke from a furnace. Had the Lord found only nine righteous souls, I wondered?

After the Blackwater mercenaries were burned in Fallujah, I remember reading outraged bloggers calling upon American leaders to lay waste to the city as though it were Sodom or Gomorrah. As I rode through its ruins, there was little I could say to the kids other than to stay away from our Humvee; seven years of Arabic studies, and all I could do was to stare silently at them with the nervous hope that they weren't hiding grenades.

I still wonder whether Abraham might have talked God into sparing the cities to save just one or two righteous souls. The number that they agreed on, ten, reflects a legal maxim that is better known as Blackstone's formulation: it is better that ten guilty persons escape than one innocent suffer. Maimonides called it the 290th Negative Commandment, saying, "It is better and more satisfactory to acquit a thousand guilty persons than to put a single innocent man to death once in a way." During the Salem witch trials, Increase Mather declared, "It were better that ten suspected Witches should escape, than one innocent Person be Condemned."

Benjamin Franklin so fervently believed in the principle that he set the ratio at a hundred to one. The Supreme Court has repeatedly invoked Blackstone to support its interpretation that the due process clause of the Constitution requires prosecutors to prove guilt beyond a reasonable doubt.

That we should not reduce our principles to rubble as we size up evil in the world is a notion as old as the Bible. Shortly after 9/11, though, legal theorist Alan Dershowitz suggested that America found itself in a new, unprecedented era. To him and many others, the advent of terrorism meant "the calculus may have changed."

As I cleared the fateful correspondence between Omar and the State Department from my kitchen table, it occurred to me that the calculus of Blackstone has not simply changed, it has been inverted: the US government would rather leave behind one hundred innocent people like Omar to face assassination than to admit one potentially guilty man. An Iraqi interpreter must prove himself innocent beyond all bureaucratic doubt, however reasonable or unreasonable it may be.

I imagine that theorists like Dershowitz would argue that Blackstone's formulation wouldn't apply, since Omar wasn't an American citizen. But Omar was beheaded for aiding the United States. Skeptics might also suggest that his death was an anomaly, but it is painfully evident that many more have been killed. While no comprehensive list exists of slain and injured US-affiliated Iraqis, a partial account was leaked to me in 2008 by a sympathetic employee of Titan, the contractor that employed Hayder and Zina and thousands of interpreters under a $4.6 billion contract with the Defense Department. Over 679 rows, the database—meant to track potential insurance obligations—tracks the fate of hundreds of Iraqi interpreters:

- Death caused by multiple injuries sustained during torture
- Death due to booby-trapped house
- Gunshot wound jaw
- Gun shot wounds to the face and hip
- Shrapnel in the eye and lost a couple of teeth
- Kidnapped and death
- 1 round in Rt Thigh, 1 Round in the upper Rt thigh, 1 Round in the Scrotum
- Shockwave caused collapsed lung
- Extreme damage to the RLQ of abdomen and right thigh with apparent exsanguination (total loss of blood in the body)
- Loss of right leg above the knee and 3 fingers missing on the left hand. Possible loss of remaining leg.

The Titan database records 280 deaths over just the first few years of the war, but tens of thousands of Iraqis worked for other American contractors, so the true number is likely an order of magnitude greater. I have yet to meet an Iraqi interpreter who can't rattle off the names of several slain colleagues. If George Bush or Barack Obama had been willing to exercise leadership, many of them would have been saved, but instead the bureaucracies under each president's control continue to regard these friends as potential enemies. They do this, they say, to protect us against terrorists, who hate us for our values.

In 2007, soon after the founding of the List Project, I flew to Geneva to attend the first UN summit on the Iraqi refugee crisis. After checking into a small hotel in the village of Chambesy, on the outskirts of the city, I logged into my email to find an urgent message from a state.gov address. Its sender was a foreign service officer who said that he needed to meet with me that night. I brushed him off, giving him my phone number but declining a meeting.

My phone rang immediately. He was insistent that we meet, saying that he couldn't communicate what he needed to over the phone. "I served in Iraq," he said, as if to give me a clue. He asked where I was staying.

"Okay, listen, if you walk toward the train station which heads into Geneva, there's a footbridge. Do you know which one I'm talking about?"

"Uh, yeah," I mumbled.

"Okay, I'm gonna head out now. Go over to that bridge and wait beneath it. I'll be driving a dark sedan."

"How will I know you?" I asked flatly.

"Oh, look for the sedan with a license plate ending in a nine."

I waited by the bridge in the quiet still of early evening, studying license plates, wonder what could possibly require such cloak-and-dagger measures. I wondered why I had agreed to meet. The sedan finally approached. As I walked toward it, the passenger-side window slid down and club music pumped out into the sleepy lanes of Chambesy. "Kirk! Hop in!"

He drove us away from Geneva, making small talk but not yet explaining why he needed to meet me so urgently. After about a half hour, the sedan eased into the parking lot of a Chinese restaurant. I got out of the car warily and followed him inside.

We were ushered to a table, but as soon as I sat down, he wandered off. I watched as he worked his way around the restaurant, looking at the faces of the other diners. When he returned, I snapped at him.

"C'mon, what's the point of all this?"

He sat across the table from me, leaned in, and said, "I was just checking to make sure there wasn't anyone I recognized."

"Why?"

"You kidding? My bosses aren't very happy with you right now." He removed a folded slip of paper from his pocket and, adding to my exasperation over the faux-spy antics, placed it on the Lazy Susan in the middle of our table and rotated it toward me. I unfolded the paper and read the names of two Iraqis working for the embassy, both of whom had already been referred to me by another worried foreign service officer.

"They're already on the list," I said impatiently. "Can we go back now?" I didn't have much of an appetite.

"Oh, thank God," he sighed. "Are they going to be okay?"

A good man, going to absurd lengths to conceal an impulse to do the right thing.

This was not an isolated experience. It came in many shapes but was instantly recognizable, in the dingy Irish pubs in Washington with bureaucrats who were nervous to be spotted with me, in the worried emails from dummy accounts, in the knowing glances from the backbench during meetings with front-bench officials: insiders aware that the United States of America wasn't doing enough but patrolling the volume of their outrage nonetheless. Had I still been working for USAID, had I not fallen from the window, I imagine I might have done the same. Instead, in the government's new formulation of what constitutes a danger, I was one.

Seven years ago, a militant in Baghdad severed the head of a dog and lobbed it into Yaghdan's yard, the first link in an endless chain of events. In the years that have passed since I wrote that op-ed in the *Los Angeles Times*, the end of the List Project has become unknowable. Throughout each of those years, I tried to break the chain, writing pieces, testifying, recruiting lawyers, lugging binders to the State Department. But the Iraqis kept writing, and the bureaucracy kept stalling.

The eight firms and hundreds of attorneys representing those on my list constitute, to my knowledge, the single largest pro bono effort on behalf of refugees in US history. In 2012, Chris Nugent, the attorney at Holland and Knight whose relentless advocacy saved hundreds of Iraqis, including Yaghdan, was stricken with multiple sclerosis. He can no longer practice law, but the results of his work continue to be felt. My Iraqi team—Tona, Amina, and Basma—still burn the phone lines each day to guide others through the process. Marcia Maack, the pro bono coordinator at Mayer Brown, continues to train new lawyers and wrestle against the government, managing scores of cases for the List Project. Since Yaghdan and Haifa's arrival in August 2007, more than 1,500 Iraqis on the list have made it through the gauntlet of the resettlement bureaucracy and now live in America.

While the List Project achieved far more than I ever imagined, I seem capable of focusing only on the Iraqis we left behind. The List Project continues to receive a steady stream of applications from those who remain in great danger in the new Iraq. A few weeks after the end of the war, a young man on my list received a jar of sulfuric acid from a militia, which ordered him to leave before he was bathed in acid. An Iraqi in Ramadi received a knock on his door and found a policeman who told him he had forty-eight hours to flee or else he would be assassinated. Others have been abducted and killed.

But my prediction of a Basrah-style public execution of our Iraqi allies was incorrect. Instead, the number of assassinations climbs in tiny increments—a decapitated man here and there—with never enough of a "signature" to summon outrage in Washington or the attention of the few remaining journalists in Iraq.

The Special Immigrant Visa program established by Senator Kennedy's Refugee Crisis in Iraq Act is scheduled to expire in 2013. Nearly eighteen thousand slots remain unused. In February 2013, toward the

end of a lengthy discussion with a recently retired senior Obama administration official who was involved in refugee affairs, I laid out the sta-
tistics and asked how he felt history would judge the United States on
this dimension of the war. He sighed before saying, "Look, what do you
want me to say? In terms of protecting Iraqis who stepped forward to
help us, I think we did a crappy job. You'd have to put your head in the
sand to say otherwise."

Afghan interpreters, many of whom have written to me for help,
appear even worse off than the Iraqis. Although 1,500 Special Immigrant Visas were designated for Afghans each year, the State Department took nearly two years to "ramp up" its program. No sooner had it
become operational than Karl Eikenberry, our ambassador in Kabul at
the time, sent a February 2010 cable asking the State Department to kill
the program: "This act could drain this country of our very best civilian
and military partners: our Afghan employees . . . if we are not careful,
the SIV program will have a significant deleterious impact on staffing
and morale . . . local staff are not easily replenished in a society at 28
percent literacy." He proposed tightening the language of the legislation so that visas were issued only "in those rare instances where there
is clear and convincing evidence of a serious threat." The impact of the
cable was immediate and lasting: with our withdrawal from Afghanistan
looming, the average number of Afghan interpreters receiving visas each
month is four. The Afghan Allies Protection Act of 2009 is also set to
expire with thousands of unused slots.

As the List Project struggled with successive administrations, it was
impossible for me to evaluate our progress without considering the success of another organization that was launched around the same time.
Operation Baghdad Pups, an initiative of the Society for the Preven-
tion of Cruelty to Animals, was founded to resettle Iraqi dogs that had
befriended our troops. Their website had a flashy banner proclaiming
"No Buddy Gets Left Behind! . . . Abandoning Charlie in the war-
ravaged country would have meant certain death for him." In exchange
for a $1,000 donation, the group would cut through the US govern-
ment's red tape in order to bring these pets to "freedom" in less than six

months. Airlines donated free travel for the dogs. Crowds gathered at the airport, crying with joy when the animals arrived.

Mouayyad, Hayder's best friend, who drove only American cars and dreamed of one day coming to America, was still struggling to make it through the visa application process as 2013 arrived. After years of waiting, he read an article in the *Army Times* about "Smoke," a cigarette-eating Iraqi donkey from Anbar Province that had befriended the marines during their deployment. Marine colonel John Folsom told the reporter, "It didn't seem right that Smoke was left behind," so he and Operation Baghdad Pups raised $40,000 over thirty-seven days to evacuate the donkey to Omaha, Nebraska. In July 2012 CNN reported that nearly all of the $27 million donated by Americans to help Iraqi dogs (nearly fourteen times the amount the List Project was able to raise over the years) was used on direct-mail campaigns to raise more funds.

On January 2, 2013, President Obama signed the 2013 National Defense Authorization Act, which included an amendment to grant dogs working for the US military the status of "Canine Members of the Armed Forces." Animal rights groups and major media outlets ran a series of articles describing a troubling situation: these dogs were suffering from post-traumatic stress disorder and were struggling to get treatment.

When I heard a woman call into a radio program on PTSD to declare that she had developed it after watching too many episodes of *CSI: Crime Scene Investigation* on television, I realized that the stigma surrounding the disorder had evaporated. If dogs were now susceptible, why not the TV-viewing public? In 2011, senior Pentagon officials even launched a campaign to drop the *D* for *disorder* from the diagnosis, rendering it simply post-traumatic stress. "This is a normal reaction to a very serious set of events in their life," said Lieutenant General Eric Schoomaker, the army's surgeon general.

The nightmares that patrolled my sleep in the year after the fall have departed, but my flesh and bones offer up daily reminders of the accident. My left wrist makes a snapping sound when I twist it, and I sometimes nick my chin when shaving because the nerve endings around the scars are dead. Whenever I bite into an apple, I wonder if my front teeth—cracked little tombstones that grow duskier each year—will finally break.

But although the accident and the ensuing trauma have become memories, I have given up on the tidy idea of "closure" and the expectation that the Iraq chapter of my life will one day close. A full quarter of my life has been tossed into the abyss of that war, and even though it's over, I don't know how to keep that quarter from becoming a third. When I go to dinner parties, I try my best not to say the words *Iraq* or *refugees* but usually fail, and feel embarrassed later for what seems like my impoliteness. When I get home, I find more emails from refugees throughout the world, pleading for visas. Those who have made it to America write and call every few days with new requests: a cousin just received a death threat, a brother is looking for work, a daughter is applying to college, a family needs money for rent. Could I help?

The time may come when all the tiny cracks in what remains of my idealism will combine to shatter it to bits. I'll stop telling myself that next year will be the year the administration finally wakes up. Or that the same story won't repeat itself as we withdraw from Afghanistan. I'll stop believing in the power of a perfectly worded op-ed or that legislation and the intent of Congress still mean something. Or that bureaucracies shouldn't be allowed to wield the moral compass of the nation.

I'll leave the State Department alone. I'll get a steady job and stop responding to Iraqis. I'll sleep through the night and stop grinding down my teeth. I'll stop talking about wars nobody remembers. I'll click and post and retweet my outrage and feel content.

But until then, I'll wonder: Is it too much to hope that the government creates an assistant secretary of state for protecting local allies, with equivalent secretaryships at Defense and Homeland Security? Is it so far-fetched to imagine appointing someone to start building a list on the first morning of the next war? Is it too naïve to propose that all future war authorizations be coupled with a minimum number of visa slots for those who step forward to help? Ten thousand per year?

Until then, the List Project will carry on. In the spring of 2013, I initiated talks with an Afghan woman to join the organization on a part-time basis to begin compiling a list of US-affiliated Afghans. Maybe the president will help them before it's too late.

Americans

On the seventh anniversary of the invasion of Iraq, Yaghdan and Haifa had their first child, a boy named Ali. Their son arrived two months premature and weighed less than four pounds, but he was born a citizen of the United States. For the first eight weeks of his life, Haifa and Yaghdan could only visit him in the intensive care ward of the Good Samaritan Hospital in Downers Grove, Illinois, where a tiny feeding tube ran into his right nostril. I flew home and stood over his little hospital bed with his parents, who told me that Ali never would have lived had he been born in Baghdad so prematurely.

But Ali survived the challenges of his first weeks of life and grew quickly. A year later, Yaghdan graduated from DeVry University's Keller School of Management with a degree in accounting. We all gathered at the UIC Pavilion in Chicago to attend the fourth Johnson brother's commencement, crying and roaring with applause as he strode across the stage.

On October 19, 2012, almost six years to the day after receiving the death threat, Yaghdan and Haifa swore the oath of allegiance and became citizens of the United States of America. Ali looked on with large black eyes.

Zina, Tara, and their mother are thriving in Virginia. The sisters both work as translators for the State Department, interpreting for visiting dignitaries from the Middle East. Their father died in December 2012, but they were unable to return to Basrah for the burial.

Hayder, Dina, and Ali moved to Roanoke, Virginia, where Hayder took a job in a carpet factory. Then he found a job as a food prep at Isaac's Mediterranean Restaurant on Memorial Avenue. His boss used to bring over other employees and say, "Look, he works harder than you, and he's only got one leg!" Before long, he was put on the cook line, where his coworkers asked him questions such as "Why did America go over to Iraq again?" "What was it like getting shot?"

By the end of 2012, many Iraqis who had been resettled through the List Project began calling me to excitedly announce their new citizenship as Americans. Zina, Tara, Hayder, Dina, Ali, and hundreds more will take the oath in 2013."

Homeboy in Roanoke

Was this whole war in Iraq worth it? Me and you will say no, but the politicians will say it was worth it.

I always look back at that first day, when the 101st rolled into Baghdad. I ask myself why they didn't do this. Or if they did this, maybe that wouldn't have happened. Or why did I step forward? I ask myself these questions, but I always get the same answer: somebody had to do it.

Look, when I jumped in that day, I didn't look at him as a soldier or as an American, I looked at him as a human. And if I saw an accident on the street over here, I would do the same thing, I wouldn't hesitate. Although they tell me over here, I shouldn't because maybe he'd file a lawsuit against me. But I don't care, I'm gonna help, no matter what the law says.

To be honest with you, sometimes I drink at night to get over this stuff. I drink. Sometimes I remember, like flashbacks. And you know, these memories, although they hurt, they give me hope for the future. Because after they took my leg, a second part of my life began. "I have to reach America. I have to get out of Iraq and start my life all over again." Doesn't matter with one leg, with two legs.

Look, I love Iraq to death. I love America to death. If something happened here, I would stand up to help just as I did over there. But if I was born in America, I wouldn't have the feelings I have today.

My son sounds like a Turk when he speaks Arabic. It's funny! He is still too young to understand what happened to us. He sometimes doesn't even know that he's an Iraqi. Once, my neighbor asked him where he was born, and he said Jordan. I said, "No, you're not a Jordanian, you're Iraqi!" In school they asked him where Iraq is, and he said California. I asked him why he thought it was there, and he said, "Well, I heard all the Iraqis live there." In the future, he'll learn a few words of Arabic. But he'll maintain an American life more than an Iraqi life. Dina and I try a lot, but we can't change his life. I don't mind if he marries a white girl. We know Ali, though, he's gonna be a player for a long time! It's in the genes.

I don't make enough money to afford health care yet. I need a new leg, but you know how much they cost? Forty thousand dollars! I need a new silicone sleeve that helps connect my flesh to the leg, too. You're supposed to get a new one every six months, but they're eighteen hundred dollars, so I've just been wearing the same one for three years. It has some holes in it, and it's a little painful sometimes, but it's okay. These aren't real problems.

I'm not looking for great wealth. I just wanted to show that all Iraqis are not terrorists. Muslim people are not terrorists. Most people think the same way when you talk to them. I am a human being. I have the right to live on this earth. I have the right to work. I like to try to fix what is wrong.

But there are some issues that are out of our hands, because they're in the hands of people more powerful than we are. I'm just a little person, sitting in Roanoke, thinking about my future for me and my family.

Author's Note

——— •◆• ———

As of the summer of 2013, Iraq remains a profoundly dangerous place for Iraqis who once worked for the United States of America. Those who remain do so in hiding, fearful of the lethal stigma of "traitor" that continues to hound them. Those who have made it to America also tend to keep a low profile, worried that their new lives here may endanger extended family back in Iraq. (Many Iraqis have received death threats for the simple reason that a family member has lived or studied in America.)

For this reason, many of the names of the Iraqis in this book have been changed. After months of interviews with the primary characters, whom I have known for many years, I gave each of them the opportunity to change his or her name to protect their security. Some were adamant about telling their stories under their true names. Others opted to use a different name, most often providing the names they used while working for the Americans in their previous lives (many were given Western names or nicknames by young soldiers and marines who struggled with Arabic pronunciation).

For a story that covers such lengths of time, I had to rely on nearly a decade's worth of emails, notebooks, and memos written during and immediately after key meetings and moments. (I often emerged from meetings with government officials and raced to a café in order to write down as many of the key comments and quotes as possible before they became muddled by memory.) Emails referenced within the book come either from my in-box or from the Iraqis themselves.

Where the dialogue is in quotation marks, it comes from the speaker, someone who was present when the remark was made, or from notes. Where dialogue is not in quotes, it is paraphrased due to a lack of certainty about the exact wording of the statement—but the nature of the comment remains unchanged.

Finally, I have changed the names but not the actions of low- and medium-level US government officials. Over eight years of sparring, I have come to realize that policies rest in the position, not in the individual holding that position. I did not want the reader to think that results would have been dramatically different if not for one particular midlevel bureaucrat sticking to the letter of his or her orders. For that reason, I have left unchanged the names of people at the top of the bureaucracies, for they surely could have done more.

Acknowledgments

———⋅——

The shelves sag with books on Iraq, good and bad, triumphant and beleaguered. I set out to write a book about Iraqis, who care little about the legacy of David Petraeus or the surge or whether Bremer was the right man. Their lives have been rubbled by our war, which America is well on its way to forgetting. I hope I have done something small to illuminate their story.

Acknowledgment is far too frail a word to thank all the people who have helped this book along its way, too feeble to thank the thousands of Americans who have supported the List Project over the past seven years. I must say up front that there is simply not enough space here to thank everyone who played a part in this story, and I beg their forgiveness if I've neglected their names.

My agent, Katherine Flynn, cleared away the low-hanging clouds over this project the first afternoon I met her. She believed in the story at a time when nobody wanted to hear the word *Iraq*.

Paul Whitlatch calmly managed my first-book neuroses, shepherding an unwieldy herd of pages into the Scribner pen. I am indebted to him for his patient guidance and enthusiasm for this project.

I worried that by the time I finally wrote this book I would be too numbed by the daily stream of tragedy in my in-box to care about these stories. There never would have been a List Project without Yaghdan. He pulled me from my cave of self-pity and never gave up on me. My brothers and I are lucky to call him the fourth Johnson brother. Hayder reminded me why I was so motivated to help in the first place. He is the better human we all wish to find in ourselves and others. My special thanks to Zina and Tara and all the others who shared their incredible experiences with me.

The hundred Iraqis who risked their lives to work alongside me at USAID have never received a just reward. Those who died never will.

The founding law firms of Mayer Brown, Holland and Knight, and Proskauer Rose deserve unending praise. Weil, Gotshal & Manges, Dechert, Crowell & Moring, Kaye Scholer, and Steptoe & Johnson joined the List Project at a critical moment. Marcia Maack and Chris Nugent were indispensible, tireless, and above all, friends. Special thanks to Eric Blinderman, too. There is no happiness in this story without the contribution of these lawyers, whose groundbreaking work saved the lives of more than 1,500 Iraqis on the list. My list will not be the last, and I hope that their efforts can serve as a model for confronting future crises.

My Iraqi sisters and colleagues: Tona Rashad, Basma Zaiber, Ban Hameed, and "E"—the guardians of the list—deserve sainthood in any and every religion. I never imagined when I met them during my first days at USAID in Baghdad that they would wade into the tragic trenches of the crisis every morning for more than half a decade, for meager pay and insufficient recognition. They know the truth of what they accomplished. The rest of us are all bystanders.

Julie Schlosser absorbed the daily mania involved in running an organization and steered the List Project through many rocky straits as the chair of its board, and never let me know if I was overburdening her. Whenever my spirits sank, she was there with encouragement and brilliant counsel. I doubt that I'll ever be able to thank her adequately, but I'll keep on trying.

Special thanks to Ann McKittrick Horn and Matt Walleser for putting up with me as a long-distance boss and for keeping the List Project humming throughout it all.

Board members Paul Rieckhoff, Gahl Burt, Meena Ahamed, Frank Wisner, Gina Bianchini, George Packer, and Chris Nugent have each helped the List Project in enduring ways.

My deepest thanks to the anonymous donor whose generosity sustained the List Project for years. I hope I get the opportunity to say that to you in person one day.

Judge Mark Wolf, Marc Kadish, Tim Disney, Steve Hanlon, Whitney Tilson, Rena Shulsky, Sami David, Tom and Jan Thomas, Barb Toney, Drummond Pike, Jane Levikow, Yvette Diaz, Lorin Silverman, Dana and Sky Choi, Harlan Loeb, Peggy Nelson, and many others have been unfailingly generous over the years. There are far too many others to name here, but I hope they recognize the ownership they have in the List Project's successes.

Gratitude to the tireless Beth Murphy, Kevin Belli, Sean Flynn, and the Principle Pictures team, who spent years filming a documentary on the plight of our Iraqi allies and the List Project's work.

I am continually inspired by the passionate activism of Netrooters Liz Henry, Maddy Marx, Janice Kelsey, Phil Sweeney, and so many others who opened their homes and lives to newly resettled Iraqis.

I have also learned greatly from Michel Gabaudan, the late Ken Bacon, and the rest of the wonderful team at Refugees International.

Senator Kennedy, rest in peace. Lale Mamaux and Marlene Kaufmann remain a fearless presence on Capitol Hill, working with Representative Alcee Hastings and Senator Ben Cardin. Janice Kaguyutan and Sharon Waxman, thank you. Representatives Gary Ackerman, Earl Blumenauer, and many others in Congress understood what was at stake, and tried to do something.

I am immensely grateful to the institutions that permitted me to work and learn from the company of far greater writers. Special thanks to Gary Smith and the lovely staff of the American Academy in Berlin, Michael Knight at the Wurlitzer Foundation, and the Corporation of Yaddo.

Since we first communicated nearly a decade ago, my friend George Packer has never failed to teach and encourage me. It is one of my greatest honors to have fought the good fight alongside him.

John Wray, T. Christian Miller, Anne Hull, James Wood, Rajiv Chandrasekaran, David Finkel, Dexter Filkins, Azar Nafisi, and Nancy Updike have all been part of a council of elders, bucking my flagging spirits at various points over the years I spent thinking about the book.

Thanks to the doctors, surgeons, and emergency room staff at the Centro Medico in Bournigal. I'm sorry I was so nasty.

Tom Hadfield has been there, bottle opener at the ready, to brainstorm, support, cajole, nudge, distract, console, celebrate, and all the other things the greatest friends do. Along with Max Weiss, Shirley Feldman Weiss, Jesse Dailey, Tim Nelson, Eddie Patel, Justin Sadauskas, Zeba Khan, Christen Hadfield, Naila Ladha, Arie Toporovsky, Barbara Helfgott Hyett, Sherine Hamdy, Usman Khan, James Weatherill, and Deb VanDerMolen, I am lucky to have the friends that I do, and even luckier to realize that listing them all here would eliminate any remaining space. They have kept me sane in their own ways, bringing joy to my days, and I'm forever grateful that they endured years of talk about refugees and "moral imperatives." Thank you for opening your couches during the worst and best of it all.

Loubna El Amine put up with the many deadlines and moments of doubt, periodically abandoning the comforts of Princeton and Beirut to hike down mountain valleys in New Mexico and wade up trout-filled rivers in Montana with me, Xunzi in hand. In the peaks and troughs she set things straight and kept me happy, which is all I could hope for.

How was I fortunate enough to be born into the family I have? The small kingdom of oak and animals and foreign languages on our dead-end street in West Chicago allowed me to venture into the world filled with naïve hope for what it might be. My grammie opened the planet's doors to us. My mom, who forbade the word *boring* in our house, taught us to search for joy in life and to love others. My dad lived a life of service that made me proud to have the name I do. My brothers are my best friends, and life would have been unbearably gray without them. Soren taught me to love knowledge. Derek taught me to love friends and to read people. My sister-in-law, Carolyn, has been as close a friend as there is. Ever has brought much happiness to our family. I don't know if my nephews and nieces Vivian, Anders, Ever T, Owen, Berend, Virginia, and Charlie will ever be allowed to read this book, but I hope they learn one day what amazing parents and grandparents they have.

I have put them all through hell in my life, but somehow they still love me.

Glossary of USGspeak

People

CTO: Cognizant Technical Officer
EXO: Executive Officer (in a USAID mission, the third-ranking official)
FSN: Foreign Service National (Iraqi employee)
IDP: Internally Displaced Person
LES: Locally Engaged Staff (Iraqi employee)
MAM: Military Age Male (any male of fighting age)
Muj: mujahid or mujahideen, insurgent
RSO: Regional Security Officer
TCN: Third-Country National (non-American, non-Iraqi employee, e.g., from Jordan)
Terp: Interpreter

Expressions

Coordinating: hosting meetings referenced in "ramping up" or "looking into"
Interagency Discussions: attending meetings referenced in "ramping up," but in a different building
Looking into: see "ramping up"
Ramping up: "We haven't started doing anything concrete yet, but have had several meetings."
Your patience assists us in facilitating the process: "Please stop asking us for updates on your case."

Agencies/Bureaus/Programs/Groups

CMOC: Civil Military Operations Center
CPA: Coalition Provisional Authority
DHS: Department of Homeland Security
DOD: Department of Defense
DOS: Department of State
IOM: International Organization for Migration (the traditional OPE of the State Department)
IRMO: Iraq Reconstruction Management Office
ISI: Islamic State of Iraq
KBR: Kellogg, Brown & Root
MEK: Mujahideen-e Khalq
NDAA: National Defense Authorization Act
NSC: National Security Council
OPE: Overseas Processing Entity (organization contracted by the State Department to conduct refugee screening)
PCO: Project and Contracting Office
PRM: Bureau of Population, Refugees and Migration (at Department of State)
SIV: Special Immigrant Visa Program
UNHCR: UN High Commissioner for Refugees
USAID: US Agency for International Development
USCIS: US Citizenship and Immigration Service
USRAP: US Refugee Admissions Program

Miscellaneous

LZ: Landing Zone
MOAG: Mother of All Generators
MWR: Morale, Welfare, and Recreation tents on military bases

Further Reading

General History of Iraq

Al-Askari, Jafar Pasha. *A Soldier's Story: From Ottoman Rule to Independent Iraq.* Arabian Publishers, 2003.

Batatu, Hanna. *The Old Social Classes and the Revolutionary Movements of Iraq.* London: Saqi Books, 2004.

Davis, Eric. *Memories of State: Politics, History, and Collective Identity in Modern Iraq.* Berkeley, CA: University of California Press, 2005.

Khadduri, Majid. *Socialist Iraq: A Study in Iraqi Politics Since 1968.* Washington, DC: Middle East Institute, 1978.

Khadduri, Majid, and Edmund Ghareeb. *War in the Gulf 1990–91: The Iraq–Kuwait Conflict and its Implications.* New York: Oxford University Press, 1997.

Nakash, Yitzhak. *The Shi'is of Iraq.* Princeton, NJ: Princeton University Press, 2003.

Iraq War and the War on Terror

Baker, James A. III, et al. *The Iraq Study Group Report.* New York: Vintage Books, 2006.

Bobbitt, Philip. *Terror and Consent: The Wars for the Twenty-first Century.* New York: Alfred A. Knopf, 2008.

Chandrasekaran, Rajiv. *Imperial Life in the Emerald City: Inside Iraq's Green Zone.* New York: Alfred A. Knopf, 2006.

Chehab, Zaki. *Inside the Resistance: The Iraqi Insurgency and the Future of the Middle East.* New York: Nation Books, 2005.

Filkins, Dexter. *The Forever War.* New York: Alfred A. Knopf, 2008.

Finkel, David. *The Good Soldiers.* New York: Sarah Crichton Books/Farrar, Straus and Giroux, 2009.

Gordon, Michael R., and Bernard E. Trainor. *Cobra II: The Inside Story of the Invasion and Occupation of Iraq.* New York: Pantheon Books, 2006.

Hard Lessons: The Iraq Reconstruction Experience. Washington, DC: Special Inspector General for Iraq Reconstruction, 2009.

Hashim, Ahmed S. *Insurgency and Counter-insurgency in Iraq*. Ithaca, NY: Cornell University Press, 2006.

Mayer, Jane. *The Dark Side: The Inside Story of How the War on Terror Turned into a War on American Ideals*. New York: Doubleday, 2008.

Miller, T. Christian. *Blood Money: Wasted Billions, Lost Lives, and Corporate Greed in Iraq*. New York: Little, Brown and Company, 2006.

Packer, George. *The Assassins' Gate: America in Iraq*. New York: Farrar, Straus and Giroux, 2005.

Perry, Walter L., et al. *Withdrawing from Iraq: Alternative Schedules, Associated Risks, and Mitigating Strategies*. Santa Monica, CA: RAND/National Defense Research Institute, 2009.

Ricks, Thomas E. *The Gamble: General David Petraeus and the American Military Adventure in Iraq, 2006–2008*. New York: Penguin, 2009.

Rosen, Nir. *In the Belly of the Green Bird: The Triumph of the Martyrs in Iraq*. New York: Free Press, 2006.

Shadid, Anthony. *Night Draws Near: Iraq's People in the Shadow of America's War*. New York: Henry Holt, 2005.

Walzer, Michael, and Nicolaus Mills, eds. *Getting Out: Historical Perspectives on Leaving Iraq*. Philadelphia: University of Pennsylvania Press, 2009.

West, Bing. *No True Glory: A Frontline Account of the Battle For Fallujah*. New York: Bantam Books, 2005.

Iraqi Refugees

Amos, Deborah. *Eclipse of the Sunnis: Power, Exile, and Upheaval in the Middle East*. New York: PublicAffairs, 2010.

US Department of State and the Broadcasting Board of Governors, Office of Inspector General, Middle East Regional Office. "Status of U.S. Refugee Resettlement Processing for Iraqi Nationals." MERO-IQO-08-02, May 2008.

US Government Accountability Office. "Iraqi Refugees and Special Immigrant Visa Holders Face Challenges Resettling in the United States and Obtaining U.S. Government Employment." GAO-10-274, March 9, 2010.

Vietnam

Coleman, Bradley Lynn. *Foreign Relations of the United States, 1969–1976, Volume X: Vietnam, January 1973–July 1975*. DIANE Publishing, 2012.

Halberstam, David. *The Best and the Brightest*. New York: Modern Library, 2001.

Herr, Michael. *Dispatches*. New York: Alfred A. Knopf, 1977.

Logevall, Fredrik. *Embers of War: The Fall of an Empire and the Making of America's Vietnam*. New York: Random House, 2012.

Memoranda of Conversations, 1973–1977. Gerald R. Ford Presidential Library and Museum, Ann Arbor, MI. http://www.fordlibrarymuseum.gov/library/guides/findingaid/Memoranda_of_Conversations.asp#Ford.

Ninh, Bào. *The Sorrow of War: A Novel of North Vietnam.* New York: Pantheon Books, 1995.

Sheehan, Neil. *A Bright Shining Lie: John Paul Vann and America in Vietnam.* New York: Modern Library, 2009.

Snepp, Frank. *Decent Interval: An Insider's Account of Saigon's Indecent End.* New York: Random House, 1977.

World War II and Jewish Refugee Policy

Breitman, Richard, Barbara McDonald Stewart, and Severin Hochberg, eds. *Advocate for the Doomed: The Diaries and Papers of James G. McDonald, 1932–1935.* Bloomington, IN: Indiana University Press, 2007.

———. *Refugees and Rescue: The Diaries and Papers of James G. McDonald, 1935–1945.* Bloomington, IN: Indiana University Press, 2009.

Paldiel, Mordecai. *Diplomat Heroes of the Holocaust.* Jersey City, NJ: Ktav Publishers, 2007.

Other Wars

Crapanzano, Vincent. *The Harkis: The Wound That Never Heals.* Chicago: University of Chicago Press, 2011.

Horne, Alistair. *A Savage War of Peace: Algeria, 1954–1962.* New York: Viking Press, 1978.

Jasanoff, Maya. *Liberty's Exiles: American Loyalists in the Revolutionary World.* New York: Alfred A. Knopf, 2011.

To Help the List Project

To support and learn more about the List Project, a 501(c)(3) non-profit, please visit www.thelistproject.org. A portion of the proceeds from book sales will benefit the List Project.

Readers are also encouraged to join Netroots on thelistproject.org, where thousands of Americans have formed chapters in order to help newly resettled Iraqis transition to their new lives.

Contributions can be made online or mailed to:

The List Project
P.O. Box 66533
Washington, D.C. 20035

On Twitter: @TLPHQ
On Facebook: facebook.com/thelistproject

Index

Page numbers of photographs appear in italics.

ML   9-13